OVER
AND OUT

OVER
AND OUT

Albert Trott:
The Man Who Cleared the
Lord's Pavilion

Steve Neal

First published by Pitch Publishing, 2017

Pitch Publishing
A2 Yeoman Gate
Yeoman Way
Worthing
Sussex
BN13 3QZ

www.pitchpublishing.co.uk
info@pitchpublishing.co.uk

A CIP catalogue record is available for this book
from the British Library.

ISBN 978-1-78531-286-1

Typesetting and origination by Pitch Publishing

Printed in the UK by Bell & Bain, Glasgow, Scotland

Contents

For Julie

Acknowledgements

I T WAS David Frith's essay on Albert Trott in *Silence of the Heart*, a book that I've always enjoyed re-reading, that originally inspired my interest in Albert's life. I would also like to thank David Foot and David Luxton for their encouragement along the way. It was their support which convinced me that a biography of A.E. was worth pursuing. Sandy Brodine's research into the Antiguan ancestry of the Trott family was more than helpful, and her generosity in sharing it was appreciated.

I would like to thank those who courteously answered my queries and provided essential information, in particular the following: Margaret Sedlins and Gerard Hayes, State Library of Victoria; Clere Warsop of Warsop Cricket; Clifford Wadsworth of Willesden Local History; David Studham, Melbourne Cricket Club Library; Stawell Heard of the National Maritime Museum, Greenwich; Karen Cummings of Collingwood Historical Society. Staff at the British Library, Somerset libraries, London Metropolitan Archives and the National Archives were always helpful. My thanks to Christopher Saunders Cricket Books for supplying the photograph of the 1907 Middlesex team.

The generosity of Marylebone Cricket Club in allowing free and unfettered access to their archives was much appreciated. I would like to thank Neil Robinson, Library and Research Manager at MCC, and Robert Curphey, Archive Cataloguer, for their help in identifying and providing material. In particular, I would like to thank Marylebone Cricket Club Library for supplying the early photograph of the Pavilion at Lord's.

At Pitch Publishing, I would like to thank Jane Camillin and Paul Camillin for commissioning *Over and Out* and their support throughout the project. The team at Pitch responded to my endless requests with patience, courtesy and efficiency. Thanks to Graham Hughes for copy-editing the manuscript and Dean Rockett for proofreading; however, the mistakes still belong to me. Duncan Olner has designed a great cover and I would like to thank Graham Hales for the typography and, in particular, his work on the plates. Thanks to my wife, Julie, for reading the manuscript and providing comments. It's been a bit tricky having Alberto as a house guest for the last few years, so I'd like to thank Julie, Alice, Frank and Eddy for putting up with him and me. Finally, Eddy Neal – thanks for suggesting that particular visit to Lord's that day in August 2010. Chance is a fine thing.

1

Clearing the Great Pavilion –
31 July 1899

T HE LONDON weather is fine this late July day, and the
crowds turn out an hour before the start to secure their
favourite spots in the Lord's ground. At the toss, W.G. Grace
calls correctly in his high-pitched voice and decides that MCC
(Marylebone Cricket Club) will bat against Australia. Earlier in
the summer, the great man had shown his age, just turned 51, when
fielding in the first Test, finding it difficult to get his arms beneath
his great belly to gather the ball. The jeering Trent Bridge crowd
made him stand down from the England side, the selector dropping
himself, but he was not yet ready to give up the first-class game.
He strides out to bat from the great pavilion with Plum Warner.
Albert Trott and the four other professionals, playing for MCC, tuck
themselves away in the professionals' pavilion (sometimes referred
to as the 'bowlers' pavilion') and hope to stay there, playing cards
in peace and privacy, for as much of the day as possible. But the old
man is soon back, caught off Noble, and the pace of Ernie Jones
proves too much for a clean-bowled Plum Warner. MCC's score is
14/2, and the pros shuffle, look up and wonder what kind of day
they are going to have.

Here comes the amateur Charlie Townsend, who has played for
England this season, and with the great Ranjitsinhji he sets about
securing the innings and building it, waiting for Ernie Jones to tire.
It's lunch and time for a fortifier in the professionals' pavilion, a chance

to keep the legs rested after the hard work of bowling, the limbs tired after the first three months of the season. Play restarts and Townsend goes soon after, undone by Trumble's spin. Francis Ford, who has played with Stoddart's England team in Australia, comes in but he only makes nine before Ernie Jones knocks over his stumps. It's 123/4. It's better than it was, but MCC need to consolidate – it just needs someone to come in and hang around with Ranjitsinhji and allow him to really get going. However, the batting order has been decided, and there's no communication between the two MCC dressing rooms. 'You're in,' someone shouts, and Albert stacks his hand of cards and rubs his cigarette in the ashtray to put it out, barely feeling the singe on the tips of his great fingers.

Albert looks across from the balcony and checks that Mr Ford is back through the gate and taking the steps up to the great pavilion before he begins his walk out, the ground looking mellow on this sunny afternoon, the 10,000 heads in the crowd lapping it up. He pulls his cap down a little to shade his permanently narrowed eyes, as he doesn't like squinting in the sun. The crowd clap, more than Victorian good manners, because they know what he can do and they've turned up expecting something. He's one of the *Wisden* cricketers of the year after not even a full season in the county game. There's a cry of 'Good old Alberto,' or something like that, but he's shutting out everything as he makes his way at an angle to the wicket.

He's 26 years old, long arms and legs, with his trunk still reasonably slim, although he has put on weight since he came to England. At one time, when he first played Test cricket, you would have used the word 'rangy' to describe him, but that's gone. His face is older than his years – he's been told that more than once of late, and that's because of Australian sun and English coal fires. It's the skin that ages; his thick moustache gives him a false seniority, and his hair is thick as well, but it's rarely seen because he always wears a hat.

At the turn of the century, in *Annals of Lord's and History of the MCC*, Alfred D. Taylor described Lord's as 'an amphitheatre for gladiatorial contests with its massive and mighty circle of seats, stands, boxes and buildings.' And in 1899 it looks like that, with the pavilion higher than anything else and the stands stretched out low, like arms linking to enclose the space from the world outside. All Albert thinks about is that it's a contest between me and him, whoever they put up against me: it's a contest and one of us will win. Albert likes batting with Ranjitsinhji, the Indian prince, and thinks him the very best batsman in England, with his wristy strokes and the way in which he scores behind the wicket on the leg side. No one has done that before – a true innovator. Ranji is an entertainer, and with the two of them together at the wicket, the sense of expectation stirs around the corners of the ground as men grab their beers and hurry away from the bar. As Albert takes his long strides towards the wicket, he makes a skyward lunge or two with his bat, stretching his shoulders, getting them ready. His bat is from James Cobbett of Marylebone, a 'Jubilee' Patent No. 3386-87, Gutta Percha Driver. (Gutta Percha, the wonder patented stuff, similar to rubber, was used for bat grips and also to insulate the underwater cables that sent news of the cricket to Australia.) From the opposite crease, Ranjitsinhji shoots him a quick look and gives a little smile, but neither of them says a word: their minds on the game and what's coming next.

This season there's only been one plan for Albert when batting at Lord's and facing the pavilion. Have a quick look and then send the ball back over the head of the bowler, and make the beggar rick his neck as he catches sight of the dark ball inrushing the clouds. Against Yorkshire, he hit 137 in an hour and a half and twice struck the upper balcony of the main pavilion. But the top – he has to get to the very top, over the pavilion – that is his aim. MCC members know that, W.G. Grace and the amateurs know that, the pros know that and so do those who have paid cash at the gate. The Australians have to counter. Everyone watches to see what will happen.

Darling chooses Hugh Trumble to operate from the Pavilion End. Trumble has taken wickets throughout the tour with his off breaks and has never been easy to hit; it would later be said in *Wisden* that 'whenever the ground gave him least advantage he was deadly'. Albert has played with him in the Victorian team, so he knows about his well-disguised slower ball, which often results in a caught-and-bowled. Trumble runs in and Albert off-drives him high over the enclosure by the professionals' pavilion. That was one for the pros. One of them comes down and throws the ball back over the rope to the Australian fielder. Next, Trumble tries to surprise him with his quicker ball. He gets hold of this a treat and sends it into the top row of seats in the pavilion. That's one for the members. It's gone a long way. It was cruel luck too, though, for the ball was still rising when it struck the seats, and without that obstruction the ball would have cleared the pavilion. Albert grins under his thick moustache. He's enjoying this, but Joe Darling isn't. Enough. It's time for it to stop. He takes off Trumble and puts on Monty Noble, the thinking crafty cricketer.

Monty Noble – the man from Sydney the same age as Albert, the exact contemporary, the man you measure your own career against. When Albert broke into the Australian team, Monty was still playing for Sydney Juniors against A.E. Stoddart's XI. Both are all-rounders, and Noble bowls off breaks and medium pace like Albert, and he has a curve ball too – just like Albert, developed from playing baseball, where he used a special grip to fool the batter. Monty, the all-rounder, the man who occupies Albert's true place in the Australian team.

Darling and Noble confer and assess the field, adjusting the position of the men out on the boundary until they are in a better place. The man from Sydney frowns and pauses and makes Albert wait, but he just taps his bat twice on the ground and watches for the ball. His long arms stretch towards it and he hits. From the moment the ball leaves his bat, he has no fears for its future. He puts a hand on his hip and watches the ball rise until it is no more than a pea in the sky and it seems like it will go on forever, but it strikes one of the long chimneys of the pavilion and bounces over the other side. It's gone. He half bows, half nods to the applause of the crowd. Those in the crowd that day will remember two things: the ball going over and their own roar when it happened. The Australians fidget and give uncomfortable laughs. Someone fetches another ball.

Monty Noble's face has soured, and he fiddles with his field yet again; when he runs in to bowl, it's as if he doesn't ever want to reach the crease. All Albert wants is more of the same, but a higher, farther hit unsullied by seats or chimneys, a shot where the ball is only troubled by the clouds. He gets to the ball and has the power, but he doesn't middle his shot – the ball loops up high in the air, and Joe Darling catches him just inside the third man boundary. Out for 41. Monty is happy and smiles as if it's all been part of a plan.

And Albert walks back to the little pavilion next to the big one, and the crowd are pleased because they've come today and seen the hitting, but they're disappointed because he's out and they still expected more. He's irritated too, wanting more, but his regret gives way to a pleasure achieved. He's a man of his word, for he's done what he said he would do. He slows down, not milking it for himself, but for the crowd. He hears and sees that they want to applaud some more, but he's the only one who notices that he's walking slowly. The crowd know the hit over the pavilion is the biggest hit ever, because you've got something so big and grand and well known to measure it against at the greatest cricket ground in the world.

There are long beers waiting for him in the professionals' pavilion. There's never a shortage of those wanting to treat Albert Trott. The chat is about whether the hit will be credited with a six, as no one knows whether it dropped in or outside the ground. But, as the ball landed in the garden of a house where a dressing room attendant lives, still within the confines of the ground, it is only four runs.

The Times is complimentary of his 'wonderfully tall hitting', and *Cricket* says of his innings: 'Trott's batting was altogether interesting after he had steadily played himself in, for he set forth to make big hits with a determination which was very refreshing. With each hit he seemed to acquire greater strength, and presently he drove a ball which pitched on the seats in the top gallery of the pavilion —a very big hit.' MCC get up to 258 off 95.4 overs, with Ranjitsinhji out for 92. Around 5.20, Albert is out on the field again as the Australians begin their innings. He opens the bowling, and before a run has been scored he has Worrall caught at point by W.G. Grace. He gets Trumble lbw, which brings Victor Trumper to the crease. Victor Trumper, the greatest batsman of the Golden Age, has scored 300 not out this summer against Sussex, the highest score by an Australian in England. In June, W.G. Grace visited the Australian dressing room and presented Trumper with his own bat, declaring, 'From the present champion to the future champion.' Trumper, in his slatted pads, with his unique shot of a leg glance between the legs, the most natural and gifted of batsmen is the man to score the runs. Today, though, he makes only four of them, for Albert clean bowls him. The Australians are 18/3. Trumper returns to the dressing room. Perhaps this was the moment when he had the time to scrape his initials 'V.T.' and the year '99' into the soft terracotta of the balcony in the dressing room.

It's not been Trumper's day or Noble's or Ranjitsinhji's day but Albert Trott's day, 31 July 1899. He's cleared the Lord's pavilion, which has never been done before (and, at the time of writing, it hasn't been done since), and taken the wicket of the greatest batsman of the age. 'I'm glad I did it against them,' he says.

* * *

The first time Albert 'Alberto' Trott saw the pavilion, he eyed up the height at the very top. It was bigger than any pavilion he'd ever seen, and he tried to estimate the distance from the wicket and how it compared to the size of the grounds that he'd played on in Australia. He liked the feeling that came with a big hit. 'I'm going to smash some poor bowler clean over the top,' he said. That was three years earlier, when he'd first arrived in England from Australia, fresh off the boat, and MCC, his new employers, showed him around his place of work, Lord's cricket ground. His other aim was to break the clock face on the racquets court, but he hadn't done that yet.

The 1890s were the age of cricket pavilions, built by clubs and schools at home and throughout the Empire. Specialist prefabrication firms, such as Rowell's of London, sold everything from the simple wooden rustic model, harking back to the village origins of the game, to the grand design with ornate cast ironwork. But there was nothing prefabricated about the pavilion at Lord's commissioned by the private members' club, MCC. It was designed by the architect Thomas Verity, one of the most skilful planners of the day, who was noted for his work on theatres such as the Criterion at Piccadilly and the Comedy Theatre at Haymarket. The Queen Anne style, with its red brick and detailing, featured the motif of MCC and the decorative terracotta heads supporting the upper terrace, modelled on committee members. The tower at each end marked out the space it occupied, and there were hints of a defensive fortress, but the pitched roof with projecting canopies added a lighter touch, and the white painted balconies and plate glass softened the façade. The higher the pavilion stretched up the more fanciful it grew, with the final decorative squares of ironwork pointing up to the sky.

The pavilion spoke of power and pleasure in equal proportions, planned for the benefit of MCC members, so they had a good view of the cricket from the tiered viewing terraces and the Long Room, the best seats in the theatre. Inside there was a library, committee rooms, a writing room, so that the business of cricket could be conducted effectively and very close to where the game was being played. Its message to the world was clear. In 1890, *Baily's Magazine* described it as 'really magnificent ... the building is apparently meant to stand forever ... it is impossible to count the number of rooms, bathrooms, lavatories etc. ... a "grand Law court of cricket".' Built in an age of wealth and prosperity, the building not only said that MCC was in charge of the game of cricket but that it intended to be so for a long time.

Of course, another important function of a pavilion is to provide a dressing room for the players. The home-team dressing room was at one end of the pavilion on the second-floor level, the away-team dressing room was at the other, and the players could watch the progress of the game from the balconies with their terracotta balustrades. Or at least some of them could enjoy the benefit of this vantage point.

Born in Australia, Albert had played Test cricket against England in the final three matches of the 1895 series in the country of his birth, with considerable success. He achieved the best ever bowling debut in an Ashes series, taking 8-43 at Adelaide, and finished the series with a batting average of 102.5 on the basis of some hard-hitting knocks, including some big hits off the leading English fast bowler, Tom Richardson. However, when it came to the 1896 tour to England, he was not selected. Undeterred, he took up an offer to play for A.E. Stoddart's Middlesex. He spent two years qualifying for the county, playing for MCC at 30 shillings a week plus £5 for a first-class match and £3 for a second-class one. Middlesex, MCC, Lord's was his new allegiance and England his home. He enjoyed a mightily successful first-class season in 1898. Despite an early-season injury, which meant the loss of a month's cricket, he still took 130 wickets at 17.94, including ten wickets in a match five times. An impressed Lord Hawke invited Albert to tour South Africa, where he played for the England team against the colony and took 17 wickets in the two matches at 11.64. He'd renounced his cricketing birthright and gone over to the other side.

His reputation stood high. He was one of the in-form bowlers of the day, and, wanting to field the strongest possible team, MCC selected him for this match against the touring Australians. On the morning of 31 July, he'd taken the Metropolitan Railway to Lord's from his home in the new, growing suburb of Willesden Green, walking past the grand villas of St John's Wood and into the ground. But he didn't turn into the main pavilion and take the stairs to the dressing room to join his teammates, including those stars of the Golden Age of Cricket W.G. Grace, Plum Warner and Ranjitsinhji. Instead he took the entrance to the players' room. This had been built at the same time as the main pavilion, as a low extension abutting the north side. Visually it was different from the main design, more of a nudge on the side, and the style, as pointed out by *Baily's Magazine*, 'was very much of the same pattern externally as the well-remembered rustic Pavilion'. It was here where he changed and watched the game. He was not allowed in the dressing room of the main pavilion.

The irony of there being a separate dressing room for those who were paid to play was that some of the amateurs, such as Grace and

Ranjitsinhji, were making far more in expenses than the professionals were earning in match fees. The Australian tourists also straddled the amateur/pro divide in an odd way. They were housed in the away dressing room in the main pavilion and on their tours of England were always treated as amateurs. However, one of the purposes of the tours was to make money for the Australian players, who split their share of the gate money between them – cricket as a business proposition. The 1899 tour consisted of 34 matches including the five Test matches, a game against Midland Counties, one with Oxford University Past and Present and a match in Truro against what was billed as an 'England XI'. In some of these tour matches, when an early finish looked to be on the cards, games were sometimes extended to the third day as the home team made an unexpected fightback and the tourists secured an extra day's gate receipts. The pot of money was divided up before the boat journey back to Australia. Young Victor Trumper, on this, his first tour, was originally on a lower percentage than the more established players, until, on the strength of some excellent performances, he was promoted to a full share by a democratic vote of the team.

The Australian game was run on more egalitarian lines than the English one. When the England team toured Australia, the local press, anxious to highlight the hypocrisy of separate accommodation for amateurs and professionals on tour, turned up at the hotels to quiz and hound the team's management. James Phillips, an Australian who had umpired in Test matches in both countries, was well placed to comment on the way things were ordered in the two teams.

'In generalship the Australians are easily first. They play more in unison; they exchange views in the dressing room and thereby their captain is assisted materially in many of his plans.

'Off the field an Australian captain receives the benefit of the opinion of his comrades, as if he were chairman of a board of directors. The average English captain is more of an autocrat. He rarely seeks advice from his men. If a consultation be held it is invariably confined to the amateurs and the batsmen, not the professionals and the bowler. I can recall instances when I have been standing umpire when able and intelligent professional players on an England side have seen the fallacy of some plan of their captain, but nothing has been said by them, no suggestion made, to remedy the mistake.

'Another mistake is made in England which does not improve cricket as a science – that is, the system of isolating professionals off the field. Surely, if a man is good enough to play on the same side he is good enough to dress in the same dressing-room. It is there most useful hints and ideas are exchanged when a game is in progress, which cannot be done so well on the field.'

'Dimboola' Jim Phillips played with Albert in the Middlesex teams, and had watched him bowl from his umpire's position in the Tests in Australia. Always ready to scout talent, it was he who had steered Albert in the direction of Lord's after he was not selected for the 1896 tour of England. A fearless and respected umpire on the county and international scenes, Jim Phillips was one of Albert's continuing links with his old home after he moved to England, and Albert would have been well aware of his views on the English game.

Jim Phillips was not the only Australian to be critical of how the game was organised in England. Joe Darling, the captain of the Australian team, said that the English amateurs treated the professionals like dogs. The amateurs at Middlesex addressed the professionals at Middlesex by their given names when things were going well, but slipped back to surnames when there were problems on the field. As late as the 1920s, Lord Harris reprimanded the Middlesex amateur A.J. Webbe for addressing the professional Lee by his first name, 'Harry'. Albert Trott, though, shrugged this to one side because of his ability. He was the kind of man who attracted nicknames, from his teammates or from the crowds at the games, going by the names of Albatrott, Alberto or just plain Trottie.

Today he had been up against this new-style Australian team, with its strong leadership off the field and a disciplinary system that curbed the excesses of some of the earlier tours. Heavy drinking, fisticuffs and a general roughness of behaviour were no longer the way. It was a very different team in attitude from the one that Albert had played in some four years previously. Times had changed, and a gap had grown between him and his cricket roots, over 10,000 miles away. It wasn't just cricket and country – it was also family. One of the big changes that would have struck Albert was that his older brother Harry was no longer the Australian captain. He wasn't even in the Australian team, where he'd been a fixture for the last 11 years.

Harry's replacement as skipper, Joe Darling, was 28 years old, son of a grain merchant who disapproved of young men playing cricket. Darling was a well-educated Presbyterian from Adelaide, a man who was ready to lead the way on the muscular, orthodox Christian view of sport as being a moral and suitable activity for young men. His methods of managing the team had the support of the emerging star batsman Victor Trumper, who also preferred early nights and a restrained regime. On board the ship, Darling made the team exercise on deck and work down in the hold, shovelling coal to improve their fitness. On this day they had been up against hard-drinking Albert Trott, the man who had rejected Australia for England, the man who stole the scene with his big hits. And Captain Joe Darling had a 'plain man's aversion to foppish or showy players'.

The Australians didn't rate him, and they had let him know it throughout the tour. Albert always wanted to do well against them. On this July day, he had made his point after not being selected for the tour three years earlier.

2

How sweet it is to be free

BRISTOL, ENGLAND, October 1854. Adolphus Trott shivered on the dockside as the wind picked up, and he pulled the cuffs of his jacket over his wrists. He tried to make himself look that little bit smaller, less than his 17 years, as his ticket, booked for him by his uncle Edward, was for a 14-year-old child. This came with only half rations on board, but that was the price to be paid – economies had to be made. A voyage across the Atlantic was behind them and another, longer, voyage was yet to come. The ports of England were familiar with diverse groups of people travelling together as they hauled themselves around the Empire, trying to build new lives, but by any standards this was a slightly unusual one, cutting across three generations, that had set out together from Antigua some months earlier.

Antigua, part of the Leeward Islands, was transformed into a lucrative British colony in the seventeenth century when Sir Christopher Codrington imported the latest sugar technology from Barbados. In common with the other West Indian islands, the plantations relied on slaves, shipped from Africa, to carry out the back-breaking work of planting the cane, harvesting it and processing the crop into sugar with dangerous machinery, working in the heat. There were huge profits to be made as people in Britain developed an insatiable demand for the sweet taste in their drinks and tea, but the plantation was underpinned by violent coercion with the cudgel, the whip and more unusual punishments, ingenious in their brutality. When the slaves rebelled, as was the case with an uprising led by the slave Prince Klaas, the response of the authorities was severe and in public. Before a crowd at St John's, the island's capital, Prince Klaas and four others were strapped to a cartwheel and their bones were broken; six were put in chains and left to starve, 'put out to dry', and 58 were burned at the stake. The event lived on in the oral history of the island, and the field where the executions took place became the Antigua Recreation Ground, where Test cricket was played from 1981 until 2009.

The oldest in the party of nine on the Bristol dockside was Adolphus's grandmother, Elizabeth McGilvray, aged 67, daughter of an African woman slave and a white man from the plantation. Her name on the passenger list had been changed from her slave name, Betsey, to the more formal Elizabeth. In 1817 she appeared as Betsey McGilvray, coloured, in an inventory of 364 slaves owned by Samuel Byam Athill on one of his Antiguan estates. In this particular list, only the occasional slave was described as coloured – the large majority were black – and what was also unusual was that Betsey had her father's surname: for many of the slaves, a single name sufficed, or a nickname such as New Negro Jenny or Little Nelly. This acknowledgement of Betsey's parentage suggests that the relationship was established and publicly recognised.

Betsey's liaison with George Ick, a white Antiguan planter of some means, had followed a similar pattern, with the children taking the name of the father, even though there was no legal marriage ceremony. Three of the children from this relationship, which lasted for some years, survived into adulthood. Edward Edwin Ick was born in 1806, and Georgiana Augusta Ick in 1809. In 1813 their father, George Ick, returned home to England, where in December that year he married an English lady, the 18-year-old Frances Badcock, nine years his junior, in Tonbridge. He brought his new wife out to the West Indies, but he clearly did not end his relationship with his mixed-race mistress, Betsey, for he fathered a further child, Mary, with her in 1815.

This inventory of 1817 does not give the job or place of work of individual slaves. For the most part, the mixed-race slave with the lighter skin worked as a maid or servant in the house, rather than labouring in the fields cutting the sugar cane. In view of this established relationship, and although she was owned by Samuel Athill, it's extremely likely that Betsey worked in George Ick's house, where she would have seen the young wife, Frances, settle in and take control of the house, perhaps giving Betsey orders. George Ick and Frances went on to have three children in Antigua, and Betsey would certainly have known them. She may even have had to nurse or look after the children from the marriage. Did she feel jealous at being supplanted by an 18-year-old white woman? Or was she the hard-headed realist who took satisfaction from the benefits of being a long-standing mistress of a white man, with its accompanying material benefits, avoiding the back-breaking work in the cane fields? New wife Frances clearly knew about old mistress Betsey, and with the birth of Mary she must have realised that her husband's sexual interest in the slave had not been halted by his marriage. And how did that knowledge affect the everyday exchanges between the two women and the running of the household? Certainly, at this time in Antigua, a man running two marriages side by side, one with a white lady and one with a mixed-race woman, in full view of society, was not an uncommon occurrence. It would be many years before this kind of arrangement would be viewed as unacceptable.

After a few years, George and Frances Ick returned to England for good to enjoy their wealth created by sugar and slavery, the family anxious to erase their plantation life in Antigua. Their eldest son took orders at Cambridge, in time reclaiming the original family name to become the Reverend Brodick. But what of those who George had left behind? The important thing was that Betsey was there on the dockside, finally in England, the home of her old lover. While she had survived to the age of 67, George and Frances had succumbed to the effects of those years in the debilitating West Indies climate and had died at around 50 years of age.

The oldest male in the dockside group was Betsey's son, the 47-year-old Edward Edwin Ick. Accompanying him was his wife of the same age, Annie, and their children, Thomas aged eight, George aged six and Annie aged three, and Edward's younger sister Mary aged 39.

The remaining members of this unwieldly group were two teenage boys. Adolphus Trott had been an orphan for some time. His mother, Georgiana Ick, daughter of Betsey McGilvray, had married his father, John Alexander Trott, in St Peters, Parham, Antigua in 1835. John Alexander Trott was a schoolteacher of fairly modest means who owned just one slave, for whom he was paid compensation of £19 16s 3d in October 1835. Georgiana died shortly after Adolphus's birth, in 1838. His father quickly remarried another mixed-race woman, Eliza Nanton, and in 1843 she bore him a son, Julian, but both parents died soon after. Julian was an orphan like his half-brother, Adolphus, and at 12 years of age he was on the dockside beside him at Bristol. It seems likely that when the sons of John Alexander Trott were orphaned, Edward Ick and his wife, Annie, took in the boys. It was they who held this three-generation family group together, and it was probably their idea to leave Antigua for a better life in Australia, to test the power of fortune.

Betsey and her children by George Ick had all been born into slavery. In February 1823, they were manumitted, that is released from slavery, as part of a small group of six at the expense of Samuel Athill, who paid £300. The names on the manumission list bracketed together included Betsey, Georgiana, Edward and possibly Betsey's mother, Joanna. Samuel had probably paid for their release because of their faithful service. Manumission was still a relatively rare event, despite the lobbying of the anti-slavery movement in the United Kingdom, and a female slave of mixed race stood a far better chance of being freed than a black man. In many cases, the slave had to repeatedly beg and implore the owner, but freedom was rarely given, despite the banning of the slave trade in 1807 and the growing influence of the anti-slavery movement. For the plantation owners, slavery was economically essential to their business of producing sugar, so the majority were not going to give away their property until it was absolutely necessary. As Mary Prince, a slave in Antigua, remarked to her owner when she pleaded for her release, 'To be free is a very sweet thing.' And Betsey had achieved this significant and unusual thing for herself and for her children.

However, as a freed slave, it was difficult to make a living in a society built around slavery. A shortage of land meant that they were unable to strike out on their own and take up farming. The problem for mixed-race ex-slaves was that the white population regarded them as little better than the enslaved population. When Georgiana Ick married the white schoolteacher John Alexander Trott, even though he was not especially well-off by planter standards, she must have hoped that it would give her financial security. It goes without saying that there was no formal system of education for the ex-slave, but some did learn to read and write. It's likely that by the age of 17 Adolphus Trott had picked up more than the rudiments. His schoolteacher father had died before he could teach Adolphus, but the boy may have acquired some education through the influence of his uncle Edward Ick or the Wesleyan Church. In 1846, the British parliament passed the Sugar Duties Act, which gradually removed the tariff protections for sugar coming into Britain from its colonies. This spelled the beginning of the end for the West Indian sugar industry and made life even more difficult for the Ick and Trott families.

Edward Ick, realising that the economic prospects for himself and his family were grim, took the brave decision to take his ageing mother, his young children, his orphaned nephews, his wife and his sister on not one but two dangerous sea journeys. They were carrying out the slave trade journey in reverse, travelling two legs of the triangular slave system, but instead of going to Africa they were going to Victoria in Australia. The family had heard stories about the discovery of gold in Victoria, how you could pick up large nuggets straight from the ground without even digging. Gold made sense of leaving home, a chance to test their power of fortune.

So, at Bristol, they boarded the *Seringapatam* with many others who shared the same dream of the wealth that could be made on the other side of the world. The majority of the 112 passengers were young men emigrating alone or young families, and Elizabeth McGilvray stood out – not only because of her skin colour, for she was by far the oldest at 67.

On board the ship, Adolphus would have been excited about the prospects ahead of him, which would have taken his mind off the cramped conditions in steerage, the smells from the jakes, the creaks from the ship's timbers as it was rocked by the waves. As he looked forward to his life that stretched out ahead in a new country, there was something of his old home that he remembered. Whenever the Empire had stretched its tentacles into foreign lands and taken a grip, cricket had soon followed. Cricket had been played in the West Indies for almost 50 years, brought out by new colonists, played by soldiers in the barracks and by sailors when the ships were docked, and then taken up by the population at large. The first first-class fixture in Antigua would not take place until 1895, when a team from the island played the touring R.S. Lucas's XI from England at the St John's Recreation Ground. But, for the match to take place then, the game would have had to be fairly well established, and Adolphus Trott would certainly have watched matches and played a knockabout version of the game as a boy. Throughout Adolphus's life he would be a great enthusiast for the game, and this would have immense consequences for both Australian and English cricket – but the seeds from which his love of cricket grew were sown early in his birthplace, a place to which he would never return.

As soon as the family boarded the *Seringapatam*, they were building a new identity away from Antigua, where the white population would never accept them socially. After a voyage of around 12 weeks, they arrived in Melbourne on 6 January 1855. The wharves at Melbourne port were full of migrants disembarking, cargo being unloaded and new arrivals searching for the quickest routes to the goldfields and their fortunes. The Ick and Trott family would also have encountered the exorbitant prices of Melbourne, which would have taken their toll on their small amount of resources as too many people chased too few goods. During the Gold Rush, between 1851 and 1861, the population of Victoria grew from 97,489 to 538,628. As the Victorian Gold Discovery Committee wrote in 1854:

'The discovery of the Victorian Goldfields has converted a remote dependency into a country of world-wide fame ... it has done for this colony the work of an age, and made its impulses felt in the most distant regions of the earth.'

Hopeful people from different parts of the world had arrived at Bendigo, Ballarat and Mount Alexander in search of gold. And, although not a digger or prospector, Adolphus Trott tried to make a living on the back of gold mining. As he made his way in a new country, we gain the occasional fleeting glimpse of him in the coming years.

In November 1855, after surviving slavery and bravely making the two long sea voyages at the age of 67, his grandmother Elizabeth McGilvray died in Melbourne.

In 1859, at the age of 21, Adolphus married Mary Ann Stephens in his own home at East Collingwood. Mary was the same age as Adolphus and had been born in Brighton, Sussex, arriving in Melbourne in 1855. In September in the same year of his marriage, his son Gustavus Adolphus was born. Children followed regularly, with seven of the eight surviving into adulthood: Mary Georgiana Trott in 1862, William Alexander in 1864, George Henry Stephens – known as Harry Trott – in 1866, Anna Trott in 1869, Albert Edwin in 1873, Frederick in 1875 and Walter in 1878.

It's impossible to know what Adolphus, over the years, told his wife and his children about his past life in Antigua, their mixed-race ancestry and his mother born into slavery. If the subject ever did come up, it was probably dealt with briefly, with Adolphus, in common with many other parents, giving an edited version of his past life, relying on a series of often-told stories. A family secret may not have come about through deliberate suppression, but because the opportunity for a full discussion or explanation of the facts never arose. Besides, he was too busy with making a living for his growing family.

Adolphus had a facility with figures, and he found work as a clerk. In 1865, when Adolphus was working as a bookkeeper for Toohey and Co., his name appeared in *The Argus* in a report of a hearing at the city court. He verified that a case of gin out of a consignment of 20 had gone missing, and that two men had been seen carrying it out of the warehouse.

Living on Park Street in Melbourne and working for other people, Adolphus was able to save money, and in 1867 he was in a position to buy 175 shares at £5 each in the New Alhambra gold-mining company at Matlock. It was a considerable outlay for a man in his position, and he may have had to borrow the money, but a year later the company collapsed when the manager, George Warlow, was found dead next to his bed. The medical evidence showed the cause of death to be dislocation of the neck by falling from the bed. There may have been a gold rush, but economic life could still be precarious. In 1871 his uncle, Edward Ick, was declared insolvent as the Keeper of the Wesleyan Home in Melbourne, which provided accommodation for new immigrants with nowhere else to stay.

Later, Albert was to describe his father and mother as staunch Wesleyans. It may have been the church's long-standing support for the anti-slavery movement that made it the natural place of worship for the Trott and Ick families.

Adolphus aspired to be of public service, and in 1873 he put his name forward for election to the school board in East Collingwood. He was successful, coming fifth of 12 candidates. In 1876, he was visiting schools under the board's control and also involved in the setting up of new ones for the growing population. He reported back to the board that there would soon be ample schools for the whole city. His enthusiasm apparently didn't last, though, for by 1878, in a report on the school board's activities, 'Mr. Trott's seat was declared vacant through non-attendance.' Of the 16 meetings of the board held during the year, Adolphus had managed to attend only two. Perhaps by now, with his older children growing up, there were other things on his mind.

In 1874, he was appointed auditor for the municipal elections in Collingwood, a part-time position, working of an evening, which confirmed his position as a respected member of the community. Yet by December of 1875 he, along with the other auditor, F.A. Holland, was in dispute with the council, demanding £26 5s for his services while they were only willing to offer him £11 11s. Adolphus instructed his solicitor to serve a summons on the council for the full amount, with costs of a guinea. An appeal went to the Supreme Court, and eventually, in August 1876, Adolphus and Holland received the full amount of their claim after a ruling by the Chief Secretary. Although he may have won, there was a feeling in the press that the claim may have been inflated, and the council had been at fault through not fixing the rate before he had carried out the work.

Even though Adolphus had clashed with the council, a semblance of good relations was preserved, at least on the cricket field. In front of a decent crowd, in an affair intended for afternoon amusement, a match between the councillors of Collingwood and Fitzroy took place. Collingwood fell nine runs short of Fitzroy's 80, with the mayor top-scoring and Adolphus following closely behind him.

By 1884 Adolphus had stashed away enough capital to strike out on his own account, and he set up as a grocer and wine and spirit merchant. It was not a success, though. A year later he had conveyed all his 'estate, property and effects, whatsoever and wherever' to an accountant so that tenders could be made for what was left. His attempt to set up his own business had not paid off, and, unsurprisingly, there was no cash left but only the assets of £324 stock in trade, good debts of £180 and bad debts of £42. By 1887 Adolphus was back working for another wine and spirit merchant, serving a distress warrant on a customer. He was never afraid to try new things, whether it was sailing across the world or searching for new opportunities at home – traits that he was to pass on to his fourth son, Albert Edwin.

His pursuit of the gold sovereign never sailed smoothly, often touching on the precarious whenever he tried a new venture, yet he always had the compensation of cricket. The South Melbourne Cricket Club (SMCC) was founded in 1862, and Adolphus became an umpire and a scorer for the club, skills that he taught to his children. Cricket was growing and becoming more formalised, as the game shifted from the recreational to a grand spectator sport. And the voyage across the world would produce something that he could never have anticipated when he left Antigua and boarded the *Seringapatam* at Bristol.

3

'He is an Australian and must therefore have a sport'

IN 1873, the growing Trott family were living in a wooden house on Hoddle Street in Abbotsford, part of the municipality of Collingwood bordered on the east by Merri Creek and the Yarra River, just outside the city boundaries of Melbourne. It was here, in the family home, that Albert Edwin was born on 6 February, the sixth child of Adolphus and Mary. The naturally healthy children thrived, not succumbing to disease, and it took an accident to strike them down. Tragedy dropped on the family in 1871 when their son William, seven years old, drowned one Saturday afternoon while on a fishing expedition on the Yarra River in the company of his older brother, Gus, and another boy. He'd climbed on a stump, accidentally fallen backwards and been taken by the river before help could reach him.

Twenty years earlier, Collingwood had barely existed, with relatively little European settlement, the area largely rural in nature since it had been taken in trade from the Wurundjerri tribe, who had lived on the falls near the Yarra. But the influx of migrants in search of their fortunes brought a swift transformation, for the land was auctioned off in lots, cleared and fenced, then sub-divided some more and sold off to developers after the last of the Wurundjerri were resettled, forcibly pushed further away from the growing town. The lack of building controls encouraged quick growth, and the developers sketched out some rudimentary streets that often suffered from flooding during the winter after heavy thunderstorms. By 1875, the population of Collingwood had shot up to 21,000, and it continued to rise in the next 15 years. Most of the residents were employed in local factories churning out large quantities of boots, hats and clothes, or worked in the brickyards or tanneries.

The wealth of the inhabitants varied, with the poor living in the Collingwood Flat tenements built on the swampy plain and the more affluent few enjoying life in the grander homes on the banks of the Yarra. We can see where Adolphus aspired to be, with his involvement in municipal life and his attempts at improving the financial lot of the family. The Collingwood Flat was the poorest district of Melbourne, and throughout the 1860s and into the 1870s there were outbreaks of typhoid, diphtheria and measles, bred in the murk of an inadequate sewerage system where householders were responsible for the construction and maintenance of their own drains. In 1861, 10 per cent of all Collingwood children under five died.

Dr John Singleton, a Dublin-born physician and philanthropist, and a driven advocate of abstinence from drink, who worked in and around Melbourne, wrote in his autobiography *A Narrative of Incidents in the Eventful Life of a Physician*: 'I found that a great number of the poorer classes, artisans with large families, labourers, aged people, widows and deserted women, often with many children to provide for, with others of the same classes had gone to Collingwood, where the rentals were then very moderate, and the cost of food, vegetables etc., equally so.'

Many in Collingwood were too poor to pay for medical attention, and the only place available was the Melbourne Hospital. In January 1869, Dr Singleton opened the Collingwood Free Medical Dispensary in Wellington Street, and in the first year 3,000 patients applied for medical aid. The Collingwood Municipal Council had agreed to pay the rent for the building, but when they found out that Dr Singleton's waiting room provided periodicals such as *The Cottager's Friend* and the *Band of Hope Review*, which were directed at the Wesleyan spiritual needs of the patients, the council withdrew their offer. One of the unremitting messages of these magazines was, of course, abstinence, and the temperance movement was not short of support in the growing city. Drink versus temperance was an ongoing fixture in late-nineteenth-century life, both in Victoria and back home in Great Britain. The temperance movement in the 1870s tried hard to offer a sober alternative to the attractions of drink by building two substantial coffee palaces in Collingwood. These provided hotel rooms, ballrooms and a range of other accommodation to encourage their use by the population. However, there were vested interests in brewing, not least because substantial sums of money could be made from the manufacture and sale of drink. The Gambrinus Brewery and Foster's Brewery began to brew lager in Collingwood in the 1880s, the latter using machinery imported from America. Adolphus Trott, with his work for the wine and spirit merchant and his attempts to set up his own wine and spirits business, stood in the drinks lobby, despite his Wesleyan background.

Still, while poverty always lurked within the confines of the new town, for those with money Collingwood was a pleasant place to live, offering a free public library of nearly 4,000 volumes, strolling players and local concerts. During the 1880s boom, the city continued to grow with its imposing town hall, while in Smith Street there was a range of large stores. The town also boasted the 16-acre Darling Gardens, a large state school and a cable tramway connection to Melbourne. And then there was cricket, a game that had quickly been taken up in the new colony, a 'manly' activity in the fresh air.

Dight's Paddock, on the banks of the Yarra River, was within walking distance of the Trott houses, both in Vere Street and in the bluestone house in Nicholson Street, where they moved later. It had been used for cricket for some time, for as far back as 1857 the boys from Scotch College, who all lived locally at Abbotsford, had used it for practice. The boys, when they left school, had gone on to form the Abbotsford Cricket Club, which played at Dight's Paddock, and this then became the East Melbourne Cricket Club when they took over Captain Lonsdale's cow paddock, adjoining the Melbourne Cricket Ground. Abbotsford Cricket Club was very much a colts' cricket team, led and organised by former pupils of the Presbyterian college, which exemplified the old Scottish ideal of education, in which church and school were inextricably connected. There is no record of Adolphus Trott and his sons being involved with the Abbotsford club, despite its proximity to where they lived. Dight's Paddock had a significant effect on the development of cricket in Melbourne. As well as the Scotch College boys, there were other teams who played there, including Yarra Yarra and the Capulets, who were formed in September 1874 at the Lancashire Arms Hotel. The secretary of the Capulets' newly formed committee was F.A. Holland, Adolphus's fellow auditor, and the two men were close associates. Together they would take their dispute with the council over their auditors' fees to court. Through personal connections in the town, the Capulets became Adolphus's club and, more significantly, the club of his older sons. Adolphus had found a place with people he knew, where he could pursue his interest in the game.

The eldest son of Adolphus, Gustavus, latched on to his father's cricketing enthusiasm and started to play the game; and, after some good batting performances for the Venus team, he signed up for the Capulets. His first significant cricketing mark came in January 1878 at the age of 19, when he opened the batting for the Capulets and bowled in their nine-wicket win over Yarra Yarra in the Collingwood Challenge Cup. Some controversy hung over the game, for that season he had already played for another club, Venus, in a Junior Challenge Cup match. Gus and the Capulets' committee shrugged it off, and he carried on playing for his new club, where he also kept wicket when needed. In a Boyle and Scott's Cup match played between Capulet and Queensberry in 1883, the *Mercury and Weekly Courier* reported that wicketkeeper Trott was in 'splendid form, stumping four of the Queensberry.' There were 4,000 spectators at the ground to witness it. It wasn't long before his younger brother, George Henry Stevens Trott, known to one and all as Harry, joined him in the team. By day, both of them worked for the Victorian Post Office delivering letters, and at weekends they played cricket.

There were, however, significant differences between the two elder Trott boys. From early on it was apparent that Harry was a much better batsman than his older brother, and in addition he was more than a useful bowler of slow leg spin. For their prowess at the game, cricketers were naturally rewarded with the prime metal of the colony – if you were good you were given gold. At the 1884 end-of-season Capulet Cricket Club social, Gus was awarded a gold locket for his bowling average in all matches, while his 18-year-old brother, Harry, won a gold medal for batting in cup matches. This was junior club cricket, yet both of them were good enough to go on and play senior club cricket for South Melbourne, Harry more frequently and with greater success than Gus. It's worth pausing for a moment to consider junior cup cricket, and in particular the attendances at some of the matches in which the older two of the Trott brothers played for the Capulets. The junior cup match against North Fitzroy in 1884 pulled in over 2,000 spectators, while in the 1887 match against Ormond, 4,000 turned out to watch, the figures a clear indication of the interest and status of cricket in a predominantly working-class community that had barely existed 30 years before. Cricket in Collingwood was far more than a way of passing the time.

Albert Trott grew up in a cricket-mad household where, with his father, he watched his elder brothers Gus and Harry, respectively 14 and seven years his senior, play the game. Cricket was there on his doorstep at Dight's Paddock: the matches, a place to practise where he could develop his natural talent, with the continual chat about the game at home, discussing the last match, anticipating the next and pondering the prospects of a new season during the winter months. Cricket was Albert's life from an early age. At school, he wasn't a great success, with little opportunity for formal academic learning beyond reading, writing and arithmetic. His classroom-based education, although free and compulsory, was also very likely incomplete, for the attendance of the pupils at state schools was patchy. At the newly opened school of Abbotsford, enrolment reached 1,509 in 1877, but the average attendance was only 765. As for the classrooms, each of the large gallery rooms accommodated more than 100 pupils, with instruction often carried out by pupil teachers. On a Sunday, Adolphus insisted that Albert attended the Wesleyan Sunday School.

Albert maintained that he received little formal coaching as a boy, and that he was a natural cricketer. 'If we wished to be cricketers it was a matter for us alone, and the only school was that of self-reliance amid very crude and rough surroundings.' By the age of seven or eight, he had found three or four other boys who were keen on cricket, but they didn't have bats or balls. So, for a wicket they used a trunk of a gum tree, for a bat they fashioned a piece of wood, and they used fir cones for a ball, later replaced by composition balls. Other times they would use a stack of empty salmon tins filled with stones for wickets, and on one occasion Albert cut his left knee on a tin, a scar that never disappeared.

He was so keen on the game, he forgot about his books at school: 'I was one of the rowdy boys and always in trouble even though I was not more than eight or nine.' One day, his young lady teacher came up to him in class and said that there was a message from his mother asking him to return home urgently. When he went outside, though, it was to find a group of boys who wanted him to play cricket because he was the brother of Harry Trott. In the game, he wasn't much use, as he didn't take a wicket, didn't score a run and dropped a catch. When he returned home, he was given a smacking for coming out of school without permission, and at school he was given a smacking for playing cricket. 'But chastisement or no chastisement I stuck to cricket. I played anywhere and everywhere.'

While Albert was completing what remained of his education, his brother Harry was playing regularly for South Melbourne. In March 1885 against Carlton, he made 101 out of 204, the result of 'first class batting'. The next month, against St Kilda, it was the turn of his bowling to come to the fore, making good use of a day that offered 'a cloudy sky, bad light and a sticky wicket'. Harry took 5-18 with his slow leg breaks. It was a delivery that Albert was to utilise later on. With Adolphus scoring, it's natural that Albert would have gone along and watched his 18-year-old brother play in these games. A wider audience than the family noted Harry's progress as an all-rounder. He was picked for a match against the Australian XI at Melbourne in January 1886. A wicket didn't come his way, but he made 18 not out, batting at nine in the second innings. Playing against a hardened Test match team was a significant step up from senior club cricket, but he must have shown something. 'Old Cricketer', in January 1886, commenting on the first part of the season in his column in the *Weekly Times*, wrote with considerable prescience of Harry: 'Among all-round cricketers who have gained ground during the period under review, perhaps the most prominent is young Trott, of South Melbourne, who has performed consistently with both bat and ball, particularly the latter. His style of play is taking, and he should yet develop into a first class man.'

Mr Major, the Victorian selector, agreed with 'Old Cricketer', for he picked Harry for the intercolonial match against South Australia in Adelaide in a timeless game. He took 4-26 in the first innings, and went into bat at six, where he made 54 not out against an attack that included 'Adelaide's undisputed champion', George Giffen, who had match figures of 18-20. This was the first time Harry came up against the great Australian all-rounder, and George Giffen was a man who would loom large and have a significant effect on the careers of the Trott brothers. In the second innings, Harry picked up a further three wickets from 59.2 four-ball overs to complete his all-round performance. The irony was that he wouldn't have played if other Victorian players had been available. But Harry had taken his chance.

The next season, he established himself in the Victorian team and also played for Melbourne Cricket Club's Australian XI versus the English touring team, A. Shaw's XI. He was in demand. The following season, he was selected for an Australian XI against both of the rival English touring teams: A. Shrewsbury's XI and G.F. Vernon's XI. Against the latter at the Melbourne Cricket Ground, he opened the bowling, as reported in the *Weekly Times*: 'The wonderful start made by Trott, was really sensational. Rarely indeed is it that on a good wicket, four grand batsmen are settled at a cost to the bowler for only 10 runs.'

At the age of 21, he was picked for the 1888 Australian tour of England, where he played in all three Tests; and in 1890 he toured England again, playing in all of the Tests. He had quickly established himself as a valued and popular member of the team. Over the course of a season there were relatively few matches designated as first-class in Australia – Harry played seven in 1887/88 – but he continued to play for South Melbourne to a high standard, alongside Test and colony players.

It was at South Melbourne where younger brother Albert made his start at the age of 16. In the earliest available photograph of Albert, the lineaments of the younger man can still be traced. He's slim, rangy and loose of limb with his long legs stretched out, and at the end of his long arms his large hands make the cricket ball look surprisingly small as it rests between his fingers. It's the physique of a bowler. Five years on at the age of 21, he will have grown to 5ft 9in, around 3in taller than the average Australian male of this time, and will weigh 12st 9lb. As a boy and as a young man he's an adjunct, another Trott on the production line, the little brother of Gus and Harry, as he tries to push on and find his own light in the game. The model, in the form of brother Harry, was there before him, pointing in which direction to go. 'I was immensely proud of my brother. He never showed me anything. I was not a success. But I persevered.'

Albert's first real nudge into the game came from Jack Barrett, another South Melbourne player. Jack had played two Test matches for Australia, with some success. In the 1890 Test at Lord's, he opened and carried his bat for 67. Albert's first experience of organised cricket had been with the South Melbourne third XI, where, as a fast bowler, he topped the team's averages. One day in 1890, he was bowling fast in the nets to a member, 'sending wild and fast balls'. Club captain Jack Barrett wandered in and suggested he should have a go at breaking the ball, on the grounds that he may have inherited some of his brother's talent. Barrett taught him how to break the ball and encouraged him, but his first attempt at a leg break went over the top of the net and he couldn't get it right. Then Barrett, a left-hander, picked up the bat. This time Albert changed his grip, fixing the ball between his first and second finger, and tried a leg break to the left-hander. He pitched it outside his leg stump and it came back a little and bowled him.

'There was not a prouder man in Australia that day than myself; fancy bowling an Australian XI man! Well I stuck to it after that and find it is my best ball.'

Jack Barrett was an educated man, a doctor, and he took the young man under his wing. Soon Albert was bowling three or four hours at a stretch and he could break the ball both ways. For his off break, all the twist came from his forefinger, and before long it grew stronger and thicker than the corresponding one on his left hand.

In January 1892, at the age of 18, Albert played for South Melbourne, in a team that included Dr Jack Barrett and brother Harry, against Lord Sheffield's touring team from England. He bowled John Read, a Test batsman, and came up against W.G. Grace for the first time. In the same month he played his first game in the newly formed Victorian Cricket Association Premiership, for South Melbourne. At this point he was not an established first-team player, and it took some good performances bowling for the second team to win selection for the first team. It was the next season, in November, that he made his first decisive impact at this level, against East Melbourne in a three-day game spread over three weekends. He began with a smart run-out of the East Melbourne opener Jack Harry. Next he cleaned up the tail with a spell of 3-14. For the first wicket, Harry Trott, fielding at his usual position of point, took a rasping low-down catch off his brother's bowling. There was more to come from the brotherly double act when South Melbourne batted, with Albert hitting 63 going at in at seven, supporting brother Harry as he made 196. Adolphus no doubt watched on proudly, noting every run in the scorebook as his two sons piled on the runs together. Albert was out a couple of runs after Harry, clean bowled trying to glance a ball to leg.

It was this combination of smart fielding, destructive bowling and hard hitting in the same game that became the mark of the young all-rounder. He was a player in his own right, not just Harry's kid brother. He continued to impress, and in the same season he opened the bowling and took 4-89 against Fitzroy.

At the next level up, the structure of the game was changing. The previous year, the Earl of Sheffield had made a profit on the tour, and before he left for England he presented a £130 shield to the cricket associations of New South Wales, Victoria and South Australia. The crowds came and showed that there was a public appetite for the new competition between the colonies, with over £2,000 taken in gate money at two of the matches. Victorian cricket was strong, and the Victoria side dominated the inaugural season, winning all of their games. Representing Victoria in the Sheffield Shield must have been the next thought on Albert's mind – but he had to wait.

On 1 April 1893, at the end of the Sheffield Shield competition, there was a fixture between Victoria and Western Australia at the Melbourne Cricket Ground. The Western Australian association announced that they came not with the intention of beating Victoria but of learning more about the game. Albert must have thought he was in with a chance. His brother and a few of the other Victorian players had boarded the mail steamer the *Orizaba*, with the Eighth Australian Eleven on the 1893 tour of England, with the help of assorted speeches, a little fizz and the waving of handkerchiefs. There were places available in the Victorian team. At first he was named as an 'emergency' for the game, but at the last minute Frank Laver pulled out to give Albert his first-class debut. He batted at ten, and didn't get a bowl in the first innings as the Western Australians were rattled out for 38. In the second innings, he took the wickets of both openers but never got back on, as the Western Australians collapsed again and lost by an innings and 243 runs.

There is no record of how Albert earned his living after he had left school. A trade, training or occupation seems to have passed him by. There was only cricket. He surely must have contributed to the family expenses, for Adolphus wasn't a rich man, and in Collingwood every fit member of the household was expected to earn his or her keep. There were also two younger brothers at the table, Fred and Walter, who were respectively two and five years younger than Albert. There had also been a major shift on the economic front, with the land boom that ran on the back of the Gold Rush, when Australians enjoyed an unusually high per capita income, which finally came to an end around 1890. Banks had lent a little too freely, and in 1891, 16 small banks and building societies went under in Melbourne. In 1893, the Federal bank collapsed and the government of Victoria implemented a five-day bank holiday to quell the effects of a rising tide of panic. The slowdown in the economy and unemployment in Melbourne may have affected Albert's financial prospects. He probably earned some money at South Melbourne bowling in the nets to the better-off members, but East

Melbourne made him a better offer. By September of 1893, he was a member of the ground staff at Jolimont. In the morning he helped prepare the wicket and outfield, and in the afternoon he bowled to members in the nets. He was also going to play for East Melbourne at the Jolimont ground, and there was newspaper talk of brother Harry joining the East at the end of the year, and of Harry Graham, another Test player, also joining them. The latter two never arrived, but the attempt signalled East Melbourne's intention to buy the strongest team to win the Pennant competition. It may have been that Harry never seriously contemplated the move, and the talk of East Melbourne may have been a stop-off point in his negotiations for a better deal with South Melbourne, who had 'always treated him well'. However, Albert signed up, and his profession was that of cricketer.

In the winter of 1893, there had been another significant development in Albert's sporting career. Cricket had been his only sport, but now baseball came into his life. The game had been growing in popularity in Adelaide and Melbourne over the previous few years and played to a high standard. There was even speculation that it was time to welcome an American baseball touring team to the colonies. The introduction of the sport had been marked by a debate about whether it should be a summer or winter game in Melbourne and Adelaide. In May 1892, the new Victorian Baseball League decided to play in the winter, in order to encourage cricketers, with their similar set of skills, to take up the game. A special sign-up session was held at the Exchange Hotel for cricketers who wanted to play baseball. The organisers took the names of the cricket clubs to which they were affiliated, and, in a clever piece of promotion, the baseball matches were played between one o'clock and three on the cricket grounds before the start of the Australian Rules football games. The plan in Melbourne was for future Australian cricket teams to cut short their visit to England and then go to America for a six-week baseball tour. The team would be strengthened by a couple of pitchers and catchers who would join the cricket team in New York. In 1893, South Melbourne entered a team in the Victorian Baseball League for the first time, and Albert Trott signed up.

While an obvious attraction of baseball for Albert was that it kept him fit in the winter, you get a sense that he enjoyed playing with those he knew from cricket. The leading cricketers, such as Bruce, Harry, Kemp, Laver, Over and Boyle, had all taken to the new fielding, striking game. With its winter slot now secured, baseball became an extension of cricket, not a rival. Albert adapted quickly to its demands. In April, he hit a home run in a game between East and South Melbourne, and he must have enjoyed himself, for he carried on playing in all of the games, even turning out in a friendly for St Kilda. The quality of his pitching also attracted the attention of observers, including a reporter from *The Age*: 'The pitching of A.E. Trott, for South, and of J. Harry, for East, was good, the former player giving promise of developing into a first rate exponent of that branch of the game.'

An athletic fielder at cricket, he also excelled in this area in baseball, so in both games of hardball he was a true all-rounder. Pitching on the baseball field also made an impact on his play at cricket. It was here that he must have experimented with the baseball pitcher's curve ball, with that grip and snap of the wrist that gives the ball forward spin and sends it downward as it approaches the batter. Another addition to his bowling armoury was the quick one from his fast arm that he would suddenly unleash on the unsuspecting batsman. Variations in delivery and speed were the hallmarks of his bowling from an early age. Baseball also developed his taste for the big hit in cricket.

This was shown in his first season for East Melbourne. In November 1893, in his second game for the club, he hit 63 coming in at number nine, the news of his success passed on by telephone to Adolphus in the South Melbourne scoring box. 'Felix' (the pen name of Tom Horan, a former Test cricketer who wrote a weekly column for the *Australasian* newspaper) praised him for his clean and sound batting and the vigour of his driving, but did offer some advice: 'He has, however, a tendency to let go rather recklessly at times, and his batting, as good as it is, will be improved by the exercise of judgment in timing his stroke to suit the particular class of ball sent down. The defect mentioned caused him to make two or three sky-scraping strokes, which must be regarded as blots upon an otherwise most commendable essay.' His hard-hitting batting style was there for all to see at the age of 20, and the crowd gave him a warm reception as he made his way to the pavilion, his face flushed with exertion and pride. He was not yet finished. When his turn came to bowl, he took 8-16 as Fitzroy keeled over, all out for 29.

In the previous game against Melbourne he had taken 8-51 in 24 overs; seven of his wickets were clean bowled. *The Argus* said they had already discovered the bowler of the season, 'unless he is overworked as a ground bowler'. At first it seemed a mystery how he could beat such good batsmen on a good wicket, but from behind the bowler's arm all became clear. He was bowling big off breaks on a good length, and when the batsmen tried to score they were getting out, a couple of them playing on. At the presentation after the game, he was given a couple of guineas by the East Melbourne club for his performance. Runs and wickets led to financial reward – the link was there to see. At East Melbourne his cricket had reached a higher level, and it may well be that the stimulation that came from a change of clubs, as well as playing baseball in the winter, had sharpened his batting and bowling skills.

For his club, he continued with some steady form, and although he was not picked for Victoria in the early Sheffield Shield matches, he did play in the intercolonial game against Tasmania. His contributions with the bat were modest, and there were complaints that he had been sent in too late at ten in the first innings. With the ball, though, he took 4-53 and 7-85, and could have taken more if it had not been for dropped catches. The Tasmanians, troubled by his variations in pace, regarded him as 'a really good man'. In the second Tasmanian innings, Albert bowled Gatehouse for a duck. Tasmanian captain Kenny Burn said to new batsman John Watt as he walked in, 'Don't let them bustle you.'

Watt took his guard at the crease and said, 'They never bustle me, Kenny.'

Albert bowled and Watt made his way to the pavilion for a duck. 'They never bustle me, Kenny,' observed Albert.

The next month, playing for East against South Melbourne, one of the opposing batsmen proved to be of a much higher calibre. Albert certainly didn't expect any favours from brother Harry, which was a good thing because none were given. Harry made a perfect 71, and Albert seemed to have lost his bowling form as his elder brother despatched him several times over the boundary chains. One of the spectators was their father, Adolphus, who tried to retain a sense of balance. 'Never mind,' he said. 'That only goes to prove what a splendid batsman Harry is.'

When Harry was lbw to Laver, Albert brightened up considerably and took four of the remaining six wickets, rescuing his figures from the earlier mauling to a respectable 4-51.

Brother Harry apart, Albert had done enough to impress and he was now selected for his first Sheffield Shield match against South Australia. He travelled with his brother and the rest of the Victorian players, a 20-hour journey by express train to Adelaide, his first real trip outside of Melbourne. The indomitable George Giffen, the leading all-rounder of the day, led the South Australians. Going in under a cloudy sky, Albert batted with a degree of circumspection and played out a maiden from the quickie Ernie 'Jonah' Jones, the man who bowled a ball through W.G. Grace's beard. In the next over, though, he faced George Giffen and fell into the wily bowler's trap for young players, a drooping ball that Albert sent back to Giffen for a caught-and-bowled.

At the Adelaide Oval, Albert was given very few opportunities to bowl by his captain, his brother. In the first innings he sent down a meagre nine overs out of 128, and in the second he took his solitary wicket, when he caught and bowled Reedman, but he bowled just eight overs out of 114. The South Australians were a strong team and won the game by 58 runs, so it may have been that his brother, on this occasion, wanted to give him only a taste of bowling at the higher level. He can't have been in the team for his batting, as he went in at ten for his first-innings duck and failed to score in the second, when he was not out batting at 11. He would have learned much, though, watching Giffen square-cut brother Harry so proficiently as the South Australian made a match-winning 89 not out.

Back in Melbourne, he soon found himself back on the field again with his brother Harry, but this time they were on opposing sides, although not in a club match. At the Melbourne Cricket Ground, an Amateurs versus Professionals game was organised by John Worrall, an Australian Rules footballer and Victorian cricketer of Irish descent. The game's purpose was to establish a 'fund for the relief of cricketers who through misfortune, may become indigent'. The aim was to hold it before the intercolonial matches, serving as an aid to selection, and the hope was that it would be similar to the Gentlemen versus Players match in England, one of the main events of the cricket season. All those present at the lunch interval greeted Worrall's ambitious proposal with hearty applause.

The fixture had the necessary names from Victorian cricket to make a success of the event. Harry Trott led the amateur team, which included Dr E. Barrett, and Albert Trott played for the professionals alongside such men as Jack Harry and Ambrose Tarrant. All of the professionals turned up as arranged, but several last-minute substitutions had to be made to the amateur team. The event was not a great success. The players, umpires and officials gave their services free of charge, but the meagre attendance meant that the fund was unable to benefit many indigent cricketers.

Albert had made a promising start to his career at East Melbourne, and they had finished runners-up to North Melbourne in the Pennant competition. In all matches, he had bowled 3,026 balls for 102 wickets, averaging 11.09 a wicket. With the cricket season at an end, Albert began to play baseball for East Melbourne. He was reported to be an excellent pitcher with a 'full command of the curves and drop'. While he played baseball, he knew that the next season would bring another England cricket team to Australia, to be led by Mr Andrew Stoddart. If he kept fit and played well, he knew that he might just have a chance of selection.

Meanwhile, the East Melbourne club had other diversions during the winter months – a skittles team. The writer of the history of the East Melbourne club took great pains to point out that it was not of the 'beer and skittles variety' but keenly contested premiership matches requiring a great amount of skill. Along with Jack Harry and the other cricketers, Albert was a keen player. As *The Bulletin* was to put it a year later, 'He is an Australian and must therefore have a sport.'

4

A box called George Giffen, some warm moments and the arrival of Mr Stoddart's XI

GEORGE GIFFEN had a favourite story about Albert Trott that he liked to tell. It concerned what followed after Albert's return home from his Sheffield Shield debut for Victoria against South Australia in Adelaide, where he'd taken the solitary wicket. In his book *With Bat and Ball*, George said of Albert:

'When he first came to Adelaide he did not take a wicket, and I made a fair score against the Victorians. Soon after his return to Melbourne he erected three stumps, with a stout box in front of them, where a bat would be if a match were being played. Then he started to bowl, and, with an occasional break back beat the box and hit the wicket. His brother Harry came along and asked what the box was for.

'"Oh, that's George Giffen."

'"Easier to get past that than George's bat, isn't it?" Harry suggested.

'"That's just it, Harry. I found at Adelaide that straight stuff would never get him, so I am learning to bowl breaks."'

George Giffen liked the story and often told it. After all it showed him in a good light – the batsman that you can't get out. As for Albert, the story is used to show that he had an appetite for practice but perhaps not in the smartest way. The story is one that has stuck and been re-told with variations. Sometimes it's an empty orange crate he is bowling at, and sometimes it's an empty kerosene can. It's the essential chunk of Albert Trott folklore that travels around with him. But Albert could already break the ball: there are plenty of recorded instances of him doing that before 1894. And why would you bowl at a box when you could bowl at the East Melbourne members? Maybe he was just messing around in the nets one afternoon while waiting for someone to turn up for a session. Perhaps he was making a point to Harry about his lack of bowling opportunities at Adelaide. Maybe it was just a joke, something that just came into his head at that moment, a box called George Giffen. As Albert pointed out at a later date:

'It is stated that I used to stick up an old box and say, "Now, you're George Giffen," and try and bowl round the box. It is a very pretty story, that is if it only happened to be true, but it ain't true. I never stuck up any graven image or wooden box. I am not that sort of man. I want something alive to bowl at.'

Stout box or not, the story does contain one significant truth about George Giffen. At this point the South Australian was a large immovable object, a significant presence in Australian cricket, and you had to work your way around him. It didn't matter whether you were playing against him or in the same team, whether you were a selector or a fellow Test player: George Giffen was one who was never reluctant to ride roughshod and he had ways of getting what he wanted.

George Giffen, born in 1859, was Australia's best player. As an all-rounder his presence in the team meant the difference between a side winning and losing, such was his ability to make an individual impact on matches. For many years, the weight of his runs and wickets carried the South Australian team in intercolonial games. In 1891 against Victoria, he scored 237 and took 12 wickets for 192. The following year in the same fixture, he made 271, in an age when the condition of the pitches made double centuries a rare event, and then he took 16-166 with the ball. For ten years against Victoria, he averaged 138 with the bat and 11 wickets a match. These performances ensured that his was the first name on the Australian team sheet, and by 1894 he had already made tours of England in 1882, 1884, 1886 and 1893, turning down the invitation to tour in 1888 and 1890. The conditions in England didn't suit him so well, but at home they called him the Australian W.G. Grace.

His batting was built around the most solid of defences and strong driving, a batsman who never gave his wicket away. He bowled right-hand at slower than medium pace – it was the age of medium-pacers – with well-concealed flight and an extremely effective slower ball. This was tossed high and seemed to be coming up to the batsman before it pitched short, resulting in yet another caught-and-bowled victim.

His cricket, and in particular his bowling, had an attritional quality about it. When he captained the team, his Plan A was always to bowl himself. If it worked, he kept himself on; if not, his Plan B was to bowl himself some more. Never did it vary. In December 1888, on a perfect Melbourne wicket, South Australia's champion opened and bowled 28.4 overs unchanged in the Victorian first innings. In the second innings he did the same, although this time his unchanged spell ran to 53.4 overs. Against New South Wales in 1890, he bowled 83.3 overs out of an innings that lasted 185.3 overs. He could only have bowled another nine overs in the innings. Taking a rest, trying a change, even for the odd over, were avenues rarely explored by George Giffen. His reputation shielded him from outright criticism, and the press frequently referred to him as the Adelaide crack or champion. While he was captain, no one seemed able to challenge him. It was expected that Giffen would have charge of the Australian team that toured England in 1886, but as *Wisden* pointed out, 'his merits as a leader were not commensurate with his merits as a player'. *Wisden* might also have pointed out that Giffen's merits as a member of a team were not commensurate with his merits as a player. He liked to have his own way.

In 1890, he refused to tour England as a member of the Australian team, despite being the best player in the colonies. In December of the previous year, in South Australia's match against Victoria, he had been involved in an acrimonious on-field dispute in Adelaide with the umpires and Jack Blackham, the Victorian wicketkeeper-captain and Australian Test player. While batting, Giffen had played at the ball and fallen. A few moments later, one of the fielders noticed that he had dislodged a bail and appealed for a hit-wicket decision. This was given by the visiting Victorian umpire Tom Flynn, but Giffen wasn't leaving the crease – not content with disputing the decision but also questioning the power of the umpire to give him out. There was a long delay while Giffen refused to budge, and Blackham wanted to take his players off the field in protest at Giffen's behaviour but was deterred from doing so by the presence of a large crowd who had paid their money to watch Giffen bat. The game was resumed and Giffen, his determination fortified, went on to make 85. The Victorians had to be content with firing off a letter of protest to the Marylebone Cricket Club in London. The correspondent for Adelaide's *Express and Telegraph* intimated that a gust of wind had been responsible for the fallen bail and not George. Such was Giffen's standing that the South Australian Cricket Association backed him to the hilt and beyond, and informed the Victorians that intercolonial matches would be suspended unless an agreement could be reached regarding umpires.

When Giffen announced his decision not to tour, he denied that this had anything to do with the dispute in the game against Victoria. 'I would never dream of allowing such a thing to influence me.' Was it difficult for him to get time off work? He could, of course, get leave from the Post Office, but he didn't seem to have the inclination to go to England again. 'I would not like to risk my permanent health by having to do the amount of work I did the last trip I made.' The more the press and the selectors tried to persuade him, the more he dug his heels in. As *The Leader* commented, 'At various times Giffen has displayed some eccentricities of manner and temper which have jeopardised his popularity, but the Australian public are generously ready to excuse mistakes made in the heat of a moment.'

Giffen would not and did not tour. Later in the year, though, when his display of petulance had run its course, he backed down from his hard-line position regarding the umpiring dispute against Victoria. The South Australians withdrew their previous letters, and matches between the colonies were resumed; for the moment, it was the end of this particular phase of Giffen's cussed awkwardness.

Three years later in 1893, Giffen did go on the eighth Australian tour of England. However, it was openly said that he only agreed to do so if the selectors also picked his younger brother, Walter. The press enjoyed this, including *The Bulletin* of Sydney:

> Pray what's the use of being great,
> An indispensable big brother,
> If Walter may not share the gate
> And get his whack like any other.

Walter apart, the eighth Australian team were strong and included most of the players who had won the rubber against Lord Sheffield's team in the Australian season of 1891/92. As well as the dashing young South Melbourne batsman Harry Graham, they included more experienced men such as Hugh Trumble, William Bruce, Jack Lyons and Harry Trott. Yet the tour was a disaster, rowdy and unsuccessful both on and off the field. After losing the opening game at Sheffield Park, they lost a further nine matches, relinquished the Ashes and failed to win a single Test of the three-match series. The leadership of the captain, Jack Blackham, although a highly competent keeper, teetered between the superstitious and downright nervy, either unable to sit still and watch or hiding away in the dressing room. He grew even less popular with Giffen, for he did not bring him on to bowl until late in an innings and did not allow him to bowl for long spells. One mid-match argument on the field of play between Giffen and Blackham reached the point of blows until Trumble stepped between them. Discontent and odd behaviour seeped throughout the team. This was the tour where at Blackpool, the man reputed to be 'addicted to monkey tricks peculiar to Brisbane', a cold and bored Arthur Coningham, lit a fire made from twigs in order to keep warm while fielding on the outfield.

Great Australian hopes rested on the shoulders of George Giffen, but he did not have a good tour by his standards, making only a couple of centuries against the counties. For *Wisden*, 'there were many occasions on which he conspicuously failed'. In the representative matches, he averaged 12 with the bat. In ten of the 12 innings in which he played against Tom Richardson, the Surrey and England fast bowler got him out. *Wisden* thought that Giffen's batting suffered from playing too often on the true and easy wickets of the Adelaide Oval.

It wasn't just George who was unhappy. Tour manager Victor Cohen had a poor relationship with the players throughout. His failure to provide a proper statement of the finances, along with his high-handed attitude, irked them. He reported that some players broke into his room to steal his account books, while others were drunk all of the time. For their part, the players were concerned that Cohen was holding back their full share of their taking on this profit-sharing tour. As the *Sporting Life* put it: 'Fines as penalties for ill-natured behaviour lost effect because they were not enforced. Manager Cohen complained of disrespectful language and said he had to defend himself from assault by "some drunken brute". Members of factions within the team lost their tempers on a railway journey into Sussex. When the train reached Brighton, porters saw one of the Australians' compartments "spattered with blood".'

As soon as the players set foot on Australian soil again, the reporters were ready with questions. One of the few to emerge with any credit both on the field of play and in the aftermath was Harry

Trott. As reported in the *Weekly Times*, when it was put to him that the poor form of the team had been put down to quarrelling among the players, he replied:

'Well, I don't know about quarrelling. I didn't notice much of it; not more than in any other teams. There were warm moments now and again between certain members of the team, but this was only the result of their keenness in the game. Look here, I'd rather not say much about it, if you don't mind.'

But the reporter wouldn't let Harry go and asked, 'What was that little affair at Scarborough between Bruce and Blackham?'

'It was trivial compared to published accounts,' Harry replied. 'Some hot words passed between Billy and Jack, and there was, I believe, some pushing about by the shoulder but it was all over in no time. Why, there they go! (pointing towards the side-walk). Bruce and Blackham together, so you can see it could not have been so very dreadful.'

The affable diplomat Harry Trott would have made a far better captain than the nervy Blackham or the stubborn Giffen. He had taken over the captaincy for the last few games of the American leg of the tour, beginning with the game against New York and District at Central Park. If he had captained in England, things may have been of a different order. Albert, of course, would have learned all about what happened first hand on his brother's return to Melbourne, and he would have been aware of the divisions within the team.

It had been a troubling few months for Harry. While on tour he had been cited as a co-respondent in a divorce case back in Australia. John O'Reilly, a driver of South Melbourne, had sought a divorce from his wife, Elizabeth, on the grounds of her adultery at Smith Street, Collingwood and Victoria Street, South Melbourne. In 1889 he had returned home to find his wife sitting on the couch next to Harry Trott and 'one or two others'. When he asked his wife if she had been familiar with Harry, she replied that Harry was a better man than her husband and if he didn't like it he could go. Harry described himself to O'Reilly as his wife's 'fancy man'. After this incident, Elizabeth had gone to live with a man named Millership and had been 'liberal with her favours'. Still, despite the presence of other co-respondents, it was Harry who paid the price for his pleasure. Costs of £78 were awarded against him, a not inconsiderable sum. No wonder he was concerned about his share of the profits from the tour. 'Would you believe it,' he added, 'but the dividend was only £50 or £60 until we took hold of the books and pushed it up to £190.' Another worrying consequence for Harry was that, as an employee of the Post Office, he was classified as a civil servant, and one report announced that he had been sacked from his job. Luckily, the Post Office seemed content with an enquiry into his conduct, and this he survived. No doubt things had cooled down between the divorce proceedings in May and his return to Melbourne in November. Articulate Harry would have found the right words and the right way of expressing them to explain away his lapses to his employer. Nevertheless, it must have been an unsettling few months for Adolphus and Mary and the extended Trott family, and particularly Harry's wife, Violet. They had married in 1890 when Violet, a daughter of a bricklayer, was six months pregnant with their son, Francis Henry. This was an age where personal morality was a legitimate subject of public scrutiny and concern.

The disconcerting clouds were not confined to tours abroad and the personal life. While the team were away in 1893, the crisis in banking had spread to cricket. The City of Melbourne Bank had closed, and the Melbourne Cricket Club's balance sheet showed debts to the tune of £2,336. A breathing space was found when Frank Grey, the club's president, saved both the day and the club by arranging a £500 overdraft. This solution, though, was only temporary. Money had to be found. The club and the Victorian Cricket Association moved quickly, and in January 1894 they invited Andrew Stoddart to bring out an English touring team of amateurs and professionals, representative of the best talent in England, for the next Australian season. The tour would include five Test matches and matches against the colonies. The Melbourne CC would take a half-share of the profits.

When A.E. Stoddart arrived in Adelaide with his team on 30 October 1894, interest in cricket had reached a new height. This was only the second five-match Test series, ten years after the first. Although the English team lacked W.G. Grace, Arthur Shrewsbury and Stanley Jackson, they did have Albert Ward, Jack Brown and Archie MacLaren, all of them more than adequate replacements. In addition the professional bowling attack was strong with the fast men Tom Richardson and Bill Lockwood, and the spinners Bobby Peel and Johnny Briggs.

The series was eagerly anticipated – sport as an antidote to hard economic times. The *Bird O'Freedom* wrote warmly of the team: the 'encouraging manner of Captain Stoddart, which contrasts distinctly with the bombastic way in which old W.G. used to swagger about.

Stoddie moves among the crowd most unpretentiously as if he were walking upon velvet.' And as for the three Surrey professionals, Lockwood, Brockwell and Richardson, they are 'quite comely-looking fellows, evidently owning a fair share of animal spirits. Each takes pride in a beautiful flowing moustache, and in this respect they quite outpoint the amateurs.' However, the division within the English team was picked up by a local observer in Adelaide, who noted that the pros and amateurs stayed in separate hotels in 'the old, obnoxious English tradition'.

After a match against the 18 of Gawler, the tourists' next fixture was against South Australia, led by George Giffen. Johnny Briggs had described him as 'the finest cricketer that the world has ever seen'. And the Englishman might have added that he was also one of the prickliest. In September of that year, Giffen had managed to fall out with Norwood Cricket Club, where he had been a member for 18 years. 'Piqued' (as reported in *The Tasmanian*) at being opposed by fellow South Australian Harry Blinman for the captaincy, he had resigned and joined the Adelaide club. At times, it seems, Giffen's need for disagreement with his fellow players was so deeply rooted that he needed the spice of confrontation to perform well on the field. Against England he turned in yet another complete all-round performance, 64 and 50 not out with the bat: 5-175 off 53 overs in the first innings, and 6-49 unchanged in the second innings as the English batting collapsed. Joe Darling's maiden first-class century also put the essential runs on the board. How good were these English tourists?

A week later in Melbourne, Albert and the Victorian team found out. Albert had enjoyed a good start to the season in the couple of Victorian Premier League matches he had played for East Melbourne. He took six wickets for 16 against Fitzroy and scored 63 batting at number nine. At this level, and at this stage of his career, he was judged to be primarily a bowler. The match against A.E. Stoddart's England XI was only his fourth first-class game and the chance to see how good he was at this higher level. Opening the batting for England was Archie MacLaren, the Lancashire amateur, making his Australian debut. In England he had been regarded as solid rather than sensational, but on this day he hit 228 runs. 'Nothing could be better than his hard skimming shots along the turf,' reported *The Argus*. This was the first time that Albert Trott and Archie MacLaren had come across each other, the Englishman two years older than the Australian. Albert should have had MacLaren caught at mid-off by

Mitchell when he had made 168, but the fielder misjudged the flight. Nevertheless, he bowled well and took 6-103 off 42 overs, surprising the opener Ward with a fast one. Blackham had put Albert down for the number 11 batting slot, and he made a useful 25. His first ball from the quickie Richardson was hit to the fence on the off side, and he saved the follow-on with a four off Humphreys. In the second innings, he kept himself in the game with couple of wickets and three catches. Victoria lost by 145 runs, but Albert had made an impression. *The Leader* in Melbourne had plenty to say about his work with the ball: 'A better bowling achievement than that of A.E. Trott on Saturday on such a perfect batsman's wicket has seldom been accomplished in a match of equal importance. The judgment he displayed in mixing his pace was worthy of a veteran, and at the present time there is certainly no bowler in the colony who can make the ball do so much on a true wicket.'

Down in Adelaide, they saw things rather differently, with 'Point' of the *South Australian Register* saying that Trott's 6-103 read well but 'I doubt if he is up to representative form.' Nonetheless, the Englishman Bobby Peel was impressed and spent some time talking to Albert after the game, one pro to another. Peel pointed out that when Albert bowled an off break his upper thumb stood up prominently and offered the plainest signal to a batsman of the ball that was coming before it had left his hand. But, as a self-taught bowler, Albert couldn't bowl it any other way. It was too late to change. Besides, as Albert was to point out later, it was often the ball that didn't break which brought the wicket.

After the game against Victoria, with less than a month to the first Test, the Englishmen showed exactly how good a team they were. They beat New South Wales by a comfortable eight-wicket margin and then disposed of Queensland by an innings and 274 runs. Stoddart (149) and Ward (107) were among the runs, and Richardson was at his best with 8-52 in the first innings and a spell of 3-11 to finish off the match in the second innings.

It would need a strong Combined Australian team to beat Stoddart's XI. The selectors for the Test series were George Giffen, Jack Blackham and Charlie Turner. They had a difficult task, not only because the initial communication between them was by means of the telegraph, but also because they were trying to appease the representations from the different cricket associations on behalf of their own players. Indeed, there was disquiet about the method of selection even before the panel had arrived at their final choice of team.

Giffen and Blackham had been able to meet when Victoria travelled to South Australia at the beginning of December for the Sheffield Shield match. Turner, though, had been excluded from the preliminary discussion, which drew up a list of ten players. Inter-colony wrangling also played a part. A letter to Adelaide's *Evening Journal* questioned the place of Blackham on the selection panel. Writing in reply 'An Australian Native' born in New South Wales pointed out that 'the cream of Australian cricketers always elect him as their skipper'. He went on to say: 'The author of the letter evidently belongs to those prejudiced South Australians referred to by Mr. G.M. Evan (Chairman of the S.A.C.A.) who were pleased when the Englishmen beat Victoria and New South Wales.'

Albert's name was mentioned in many newspapers as a possibility for the 11th player in the team, including *The Telegraph* of Brisbane: 'Certainly A.E. Trott has proved himself a better bowler than H. Trott.' But this wasn't his time. What may have counted against him was his failure to take any wickets for Victoria in the Sheffield Shield match against Giffen's South Australia. In the same game Giffen, in the form of his life, took 12 wickets and hit 94 not out.

The first Test, which began in Sydney on 14 December, never palled in interest throughout its six days. Blackham, once more elected as captain, won the toss and batted in favourable weather conditions. However, it was England who made the better start, with Richardson clean bowling the first three batsmen for 21 runs. After that, though, the game shifted Australia's way, with Giffen hitting 161 and Syd Gregory 201, including a partnership of 154 with Blackham, the record ninth-wicket stand for Australia. Gregory's fine innings prompted the crowd to hold a spontaneous whip-round for him, which drummed up £103. Blackham's score of 74, made at 40 years of age, was his highest in Test matches. Australia's 586 all out put them in a powerful position in this timeless Test.

England were bowled out for 325 and made to follow on. A solid 117 from Albert Ward formed the backbone of the Englishmen's 437. On a hard pitch, Blackham tried out eight bowlers, and this was one occasion when he didn't under-bowl Giffen, who sent down 75 overs. However, Blackham under-bowled the South Australian fast man Ernie Jones on a pitch suited to his bowling. Australia had to make 177 to win, a straightforward target with the fine weather and all the time they needed, and by close of play they were 113/2. The game was as good as over. The Englishmen relaxed in their usual way.

Blackham was woken early by the sound of the rain, and he rose from his bed to watch it fall from the Baden Baden hotel balcony. At breakfast, the sun was shining, and Giffen, who had slept soundly, walked into the dining room to find Blackham with 'his face as long as a coffee pot'. Strong sun after rain: the worst combination for batting on a wicket left uncovered.

The English spinner Bobby Peel had overslept, and when he got to the ground he thought the dark stains on the pitch had meant that someone had watered it. 'Give me the ball, Mr Stoddart,' he is supposed to have said, 'and I'll get t'boogers out before lunch.' For a moment Peel had forgotten about the five teeth he had had extracted before the game, as Stoddart ordered him under the cold shower to freshen up.

Only a few hundred had turned up to watch the first-ever sixth day of a Test match – the ground eerily quiet, 'silent as a cemetery', as the sun dried the overnight rain to provide the perfect sticky wicket surface for the English left-arm spinners. The game was over ten minutes before lunch, with Australia ten runs short. Peel had taken six wickets. Last man out was Jack Blackham, batting in pain, the top joint of his thumb badly injured and the flesh cut. As the Englishmen celebrated, Blackham strode back and forth along the balcony muttering, 'Cruel luck, cruel luck.' This time everyone agreed with Jack Blackham, even Stoddart in his post-dinner speech. It was to be Blackham's final Test – the man who had played in the very first one back in 1877. But this close game with changing fortunes, great performances from players in both teams, chance and weather turning the game, was the perfect appetiser for the greatest-ever Test series. Albert Trott waited for his chance to take part in it.

The fixtures came thick and fast, with little time for many of the players to recover. The day after the Test, Harry Trott and the other Victoria and New South Wales players caught the express train to Melbourne, as they had a Sheffield Shield fixture the following day. The Englishmen remained in Sydney because they were to play in a two-day game against a Sydney Juniors 18 the next day. The game was a portent of an Australian cricket team yet to come. Monty Noble, 21 years old, the same age as Albert, made 152 not out – but it was the 17-year-old Victor Trumper who caught the eye, displaying a greater range of strokes with his 67 in 85 minutes.

Albert was fresh and ready to play against New South Wales. The game began on 22 December and was completed after Christmas. He knew he was close to selection for the Australian team, and this was an opportunity to make an impression before the next Test team was selected. Brother Harry had taken over the Victorian captaincy duties from Blackham, but Albert had to be content with batting at number 11. Here he made 24 out of a total of 175. When New South Wales batted, Harry opened with the medium-paced McLeod brothers, Charlie and Bob. It was Bob who did the damage, bowling unchanged and taking 6-20. Albert didn't get a bowl. In the second innings he was promoted to number eight in the batting order, but was bowled by the selector Charlie Turner for nine.

He had had a quiet game. It was the fourth innings before Albert was to make a real impact, as New South Wales chased a target of 355. He opened the bowling, but Harry switched him. As *The Argus* put it: 'A.E. Trott was much more awkward on the change of ends and he got up a good deal at the railway pitch.' He took five wickets, three of them with the same quick delivery, which took out the batsman's leg stump. Off his brother's bowling, he took two catches at short slip, one very low on the ground and another catch off Charlie McLeod to get rid of Syd Gregory. He topped this by running out Callaway from slip, snatching up the ball and throwing the wicket down. He had been involved in nine of the ten wickets to fall, as Victoria won by 161 runs. 'The Trott Trap', proclaimed the *Argus* headline. However, his efforts had come too late in the game. The team for the second Test had already been chosen, as four new players came in, including the Queenslander Arthur Coningham. *The Argus* said: 'By this time it had become a question of whether a mistake had not been made in leaving A.E. Trott out of the combined team – for he has shown his undoubted capacity to bat, bowl and field. He will, I fancy, develop into one of the best all round men Australia has yet turned out.' For now, though, Albert had to be content with watching the Test at the Melbourne Cricket Ground.

Before the second Test could begin, the delicate question of the Australian captaincy had to be resolved. There was some mention of Harry Trott or Bruce taking on the job, but in the event neither of them would stand for election against Giffen. Iredale proposed and Trott seconded Giffen, who was elected without opposition. A large thunderstorm had soaked the wicket the previous day. Giffen won the toss, but didn't look any happier; he conferred with his senior players, and finally asked England to bat. His indecision was understandable, as this was the first time in a Test that a captain had chosen to field after winning the toss. It looked the right decision. By 3pm the tourists were all out for 77 thanks to Turner's 5-32 and Trumble's 3-15, and Coningham getting MacLaren with the first ball of the innings. It was over so quickly that Giffen couldn't even get himself on to bowl. The Englishmen, though, had hit out and got out in the latter part of their innings in order to get at Australia while the wicket was still giving help to the bowlers. Giffen was out there facing a fired-up Richardson keeping a fine length, far sooner than he would have liked, and at the close of the first day the Australians were all out for 123.

The pitch was rolled on the Saturday night to remove the rough spots, and rolled again on the Sunday, when there was no play. This was against the laws of the game, but there was a need to ensure that the match would last into the Monday and Tuesday, which were New Year holidays. On the third day, a crowd of 20,000 paid their money at the gate and the tour moved into a profit – all expenses met – but the game got away from Australia. As the wicket eased, the Englishmen went about posting their then record score of 475 in Australia, built around a careful innings of 173 from Stoddart. To win, Australia had to make 428, an almost impossible target, but the wicket was holding up well. Harry Trott, opening the innings, started off brightly and made 95; but Australia were all out for 333, 94 runs short. After two Tests, there had been moments when they could have taken the games, but they had nothing to show for their efforts. Luck had run against them with regard to the weather and the rolling of the wickets.

The third Test was the following week at Adelaide. Blackham had seen Albert's bowling and fielding against New South Wales from the pavilion. Giffen, however, was of a different frame of mind. And while Blackham was pressing the claims of the young Victorian, Giffen's last sight of Albert had been at Adelaide, where he had failed to take a wicket. As the *Barrier Miner* put it: 'George is naturally conservative, and does not hastily jump at new men who burst suddenly into prominence in this world of cricket.' Besides, George was tired of picking teams. '"You get no thanks, you know, and you can't please everybody," is his way of explaining it,' said the *Barrier Miner*.

Albert, though, had support from a different quarter. He had already impressed the English team when he had played against them, particularly Andrew Stoddart and Archie MacLaren, who had said, 'Albert Trott was the best bowler of the lot, from my point of view.' Major Ben Wardill, secretary of the Melbourne Cricket Club, the organisers of the tour, accompanied the England team for many of the matches and took breakfast with them. It was at one of these that Archie MacLaren spoke up on Albert's behalf.

'After we had won the first two Tests, however, I remarked to him that Albert Trott was a much better bowler than I imagined and we were convinced that he ought to be in the team against us in the next Test. We got him to realise that we were serious and that we gave it as our honest opinion. I don't know to this day if we helped Albert Trott's selection, but I rather feel that we did, for he was chosen for the Test at Adelaide.' Albert had finally made the team.

5

Enter the outsider

COUNTRY RESIDENTS flocked into Adelaide, keen to see the much talked about match, while sporting types from the other colonies travelled to the city by express train. It had been a long time since an event in Adelaide had excited such general interest, as the hotels and lodging-houses rapidly filled up. On train and tram, in club and pub, in the restaurant and in the street, the talk was of nothing but the upcoming cricket match. A half-day's holiday had been declared for the Monday because of the interest in the game and the expectation that normal business would have been paralysed anyway. The wider world was not ignored. Special provision had been made by the telegraph department 'to facilitate the transmission of messages to the other colonies, and if necessary to England'.

A five-match Test series was a novelty, and far from feeling that they were out of it after losing the first two games, the Australian public looked forward to a revival of their team. They had not lost faith, and regarded the team as strong in batting and bowling and, in the words of the *Express and Telegraph*, 'unsurpassed in fielding'. The weather was hot, too hot for prolonged practice for both teams, the glass nudging 101°F (38°C) in the shade. Albert had never achieved much in the way of batting or bowling on this ground, but, at the age of 21, it was unlikely to have troubled him, for all he could see was time and opportunity stretching before him.

Albert's first contribution to the game was unexpected. Giffen won the toss and Australia batted. Peel sprained his ankle and had to leave the field, and it was Albert who came on as a substitute, fielding for England, until Gay could get changed into his flannels. No one could stay with Giffen, and at 124/6, Richardson, the quickest of the bowlers, had taken four wickets in the heat. After the tea interval, Albert's moment arrived: batting at number ten, he walked out with Giffen. Almost immediately Giffen was out for 58, caught by Lockwood off Brockwell. At 157/9, the Australian innings was as good as over. The crowd had been expecting a better start than this by the home team. There was some talk of the wicket not playing well, but in truth it was the magnificent effort from Richardson that had done the damage.

Albert opened by hitting Lockwood over the chains, the first 'fiver' of the match, with the ball landing in a buggy, 'but the crowd were too depressed to indulge in more than a feeble cheer'. However, their mood soon lifted. Callaway hit a couple of fours, and then a fine drive from Albert was heartily cheered by the crowd. The last-wicket pair were frustrating the English players, the visitors ragged from a hot day in the field. Albert made a couple of excellent drives and Callaway cut one to the chains, but this was no tail-ender slogging. At one point they were patient enough to allow Brockwell to bowl six successive maidens. Albert's only false stroke was a miscue on the leg side that Richardson failed to reach. At five o'clock, the killing pace was too much for the fielders and they took an unauthorised drinks break. According to the *Barrier Miner*, 'Half a dozen of them gathered round one of the waterplugs on the ground and wetted their whistles, while an active commissionaire carried out "something" diluted in a glass to one or two more dainty ones.' When play resumed, Albert sent a huge carpet drive to the far end of the oval and the pair of them ran five. Albert was hitting hard but not taking any undue liberties. The stand was finally over when Richardson clean bowled Callaway. They had put on 81 for the last wicket in an hour and ten minutes, with Albert 38 not out and Callaway making 41. They returned to the pavilion to a perfect storm of applause, the grandstand on their feet, the pair of them having more than made amends for the failures of the leading batsmen in the team.

A hot night followed on the heels of the hot day. The English team couldn't sleep after their day in the field with their soaked sheets and throbbing heads, some of them resorting unwisely to successive showers to cool down. Stoddart was spotted in the corridor at 3am heading for his fourth cold bath of the night. The Australians used different remedies when taking the field the next day. On the advice of a local police constable, each of them wore a lettuce leaf under his cap, and Blackham brewed them his special hot-day drink of oatmeal and lemon.

Giffen had to give up his usual end because it was against the wind. Albert opened the bowling, and in his first over he forced Briggs to send a sharp chance to Jack Harry in the slips – it touched the fingers but could not be held. When Briggs cut Albert for a couple of fours, Giffen decided enough was enough and put himself on in the next over. But it was Callaway at the other end who was the most dangerous with his medium-fast bowling, taking the first two wickets for one run while 20 were scored off Giffen. The disturbed night had drained the English, and their efforts were disappointing because there were no demons in the wicket. Callaway and Giffen were aided by some fine Australian fielding, with one-handed catches from Harry and Worrall. Giffen bowled Stoddart for one with a straight one, after five balls that had broken back. Albert never got back on, as the English were bowled out for 124, with Callaway and Giffen taking five wickets each.

Australia started their second innings with a useful lead of 114, but Harry Trott was out without scoring. When Giffen went for 24, caught by Ford off Peel at slip, a silence fell over the crowd, their champion back in the pavilion. Bruce took up the attack, hitting a run four and snicking Richardson to the boundary, the batsmen taking 13 off the over. In all Bruce made 80, putting on 98 with Iredale.

The third day was cool, the sky cloudy, the weather fine for cricket, with Iredale batting well yet looking for support. His partners never remained for long, though. When Lockwood temporarily went off with a split finger, it was Albert, the perennial substitute fielder, who replaced him. He dived to make a sensational stop with his left hand, followed up by an excellent throw. It didn't matter which team he played for, he was determined to make an impact on the game. When Affie Jarvis was out, Australia were 283/8 and Albert came to the crease. Now playing for his own team, he supported Iredale, running well between the wickets. He also took a liking to the right-arm fast bowling of Lockwood and drove him grandly, batting with the same confidence and finish as in the first innings. Iredale had made 140 when he hit a full toss from Peel high in the air, and the bowler got hands, chest and legs under it to make sure of the catch.

Callaway, the last man, came to the wicket, the scoreboard showing 347, with no one in the crowd expecting to see a repeat of the first innings. Callaway blocked at his end, drawing in the field, and scoring where he could, leaving the bulk of the stroke play to Albert. With the score at 370, enough was enough for the English captain, and Stoddart brought back his premier bowler, Richardson, in an effort to curtail this last-wicket nonsense. Even on the longest of the days, Richardson never dropped his pace. The batsmen, though, scored off nearly every ball, and the cheers rang out again as Albert reached fifty, his next stroke for four being one of the finest off drives of the match. Briggs almost bowled him with one that shot along the ground, and Albert's smile at his survival from misfortune could be seen from the pavilion. His drives, which rivalled those of Iredale, had been the feature of his innings, but one of his more unorthodox strokes – described by *The Argus* as his 'poorest stroke' – was a cut over the head of cover that brought up the four hundred.

It was Richardson who brought an end to the stand when he bowled Callaway. The crowd cheered Albert all the way in and Giffen, Iredale and Lyons formed a queue to congratulate him. 'Even his own comrades were astounded at the perfection of his batting,' reported *The Argus*. He had taken 90 minutes in making his 72 not out, with 11 clean, well-timed fours.

England had to chase 526 to win in this timeless game. Callaway and Giffen opened the bowling for Australia, but neither could make the breakthrough, and Albert took over from Callaway. He slowed the scoring rate down, his opening six overs going for eight runs. Archie MacLaren, determined not to be tied down, smashed the ball to point but Harry Trott couldn't hold it. It didn't make much difference, for in Albert's next over he had MacLaren caught at long on, striking out. With the third ball of the next over, he clean bowled the other opener, Ward, smashing his stump. Harry Budd, the East Melbourne secretary, claimed it for the wall of his club, as a memento of the feat by one of their players. Albert's final act on that day came from his quicker delivery, when he hit Brown with a severe blow that stretched the England pro out on the ground.

It had been a day when everything had gone right for Albert – a hard-hitting not-out score and a couple of important wickets, carried off with more than a touch of panache. 'By Jove he's fit for any team in the world,' said a follower of the England team, while Frank Iredale observed, 'Playing fast bowling is to that fellow like drinking water.' *The Age* tried to offer a more balanced view of what lay ahead, its words a cocktail of hope mixed with caution. 'He is apparently one of those sensible young fellows who will not be easily spoiled by the attentions which too many followers of cricketers heap on rising players, under the delusion that they are showing them kindness.'

It had been one of those days. The match was not yet won, but Phil Sheridan, the father of the Sydney Cricket Ground, was already anxious that they would not be able to accommodate the thousands of spectators who would want to watch the next game. Meanwhile, Major Wardill said that if the Australians could win the next one, the fifth and final game at Melbourne would break the world attendance record. Half of what came from Sheridan and Wardill was the showmen within them, talking up the series, half of it pleasure at their unexpected turn of good fortune. The series was saved; the Melbourne Cricket Club's finances were restored. The match, though, wasn't yet over.

At the start of the day's play, Andrew Stoddart was still at the crease, after his watchful performance of the previous evening where he had made a single run in 30 minutes. He briefly opted for the counter-attack and jumped down the pitch to Albert and drove him for four, but he soon retreated, back to his crabby defence. Brown was driven back on to his stumps by one from Albert and was bowled off his pads.

Stoddart had made eight when he played Albert sharply into the slips, where it came straight to Giffen who dropped it. The escape seemed to rally the English, and, though the chase was difficult, they weren't giving up. Giffen persisted with himself and Albert, as Brockwell began to score a little more freely, quickly bringing up the hundred. It was Albert who broke the partnership. At 102, Brockwell stepped down the wicket and got plenty of force behind the drive, but Albert leapt in the air, stopped it with his right hand and caught it with both hands as it dropped. Peel came in and spooned it back to Albert for a first-ball caught-and-bowled, the easiest of chances. Stoddart tried to get him away over the chains, but he got too much under the ball and, though it went in the air, it fell safely. He didn't have to wait long for his next wicket. Ford lunged forward, the ball looped in the air to point, and brother Harry took it.

Next man in was Briggs, who faced three balls and was in trouble from all of them. For the third delivery he was expecting a quick one, but it wasn't the quick one and he was clean bowled. Eight wickets down, the end now in sight, and in came Lockwood, determined to have a swing. He hit Albert high to long on, and a magnificent running catch by Iredale, perhaps the very best in a match of magnificent catches, gave Albert his eighth wicket. Last man: Richardson. Never one to hang around, he hit Giffen for 11 runs in an over. But, at the start of Giffen's next over, Richardson tried to swipe one time too many and the ball curved high into the air. Underneath it at slip was Albert, who caught the ball and slipped it in his pocket. It belonged to him. His analysis read 27-10-43-8. The English were all out for 143, with Stoddart 34 not out, and Australia had won by 382 runs. With his 110 runs without losing his wicket, Albert's all-round performance was the most sensational debut in Test cricket. Moreover, 120 years later he still holds the record for the best bowling figures in an innings on a Test match debut. Luck had not come into it. *Lika Joko*, the London satirical magazine written by Harry Furniss, commented on the win in 'The Kangaroo to Mr Stoddart':

> You didn't expect it, my sonny?
> Yet truly complain you must not;
> For you wanted a run for your money,
> And complying I gave you A. Trott.

Small boys rushed to pat him on the back as he left the field. In the absence of anything more suitable, one of his own team presented him with a loaf of bread. On the morning of the match, unbeknown to Albert, the president of the East Melbourne Cricket Club had telegrammed with the promise of a guinea for Albert for every wicket he took. It proved no incentive, though: he had taken them all before the news of the offer reached him. Other gifts of money came his way. In the post-luncheon speech, Stoddart, who had watched his bowling performance from the other end, put aside his pipe and said,

'I can't help congratulating our young friend Trott, and I rather take credit on myself, for having, on the first occasion that I saw him play, said he would be one of the finest cricketers Australia has ever seen.'

The Bulletin introduced their readers to the colt 'who had eclipsed all records', not quoting Albert directly but providing a paraphrase of his words, saying how no one was more surprised than the colt himself at his achievements. He had never been 'in better trim', and he was as cool as if it was a club match – the hard wicket suited him perfectly. 'This fine young athlete ... He is moved by the cricket spirit; he would rather field for the opposition than sit still and look on.' In the age of the anxious, this perfect physical specimen had no nerves and had never visited a doctor in his life. As regards his personal habits, he was a teetotaller, but he did have one vice. He was a habitual smoker of cigarettes, continually lighting one after the other.

Meanwhile, several Australian newspapers reported that Walter Humphreys, the slow underarm bowler in the English party, had offered Albert a contract to play for Sussex. It was said that Albert would not give an answer until he had returned to Melbourne. The public eye was on him; attention now came thick and fast.

* * *

Back in his home city, more money came Albert's way when East Melbourne set up a subscription for him. In the first instance the club had set aside a sum of money for him, and then members of the club and the public were invited to make a contribution. His next game was for the East Melbourne club in a Pennant match against Melbourne. Those in the crowd who had come along just to see the new great Australian bowler would have gone home disappointed. Graham and Bruce proved to be of sterner stuff than the English batsmen, and he went for 63 runs without taking a wicket. The small size of the East Melbourne ground made it safe for the batsmen to hit out. East Melbourne, however, were anxious to retain their young professional and to ward off any interest from English counties. Harry Budd announced that 'East will take good care that Trott doesn't go'. Shortly after, it was announced that Albert had signed a five-year contract with the club for a salary of £200 a year. In some quarters he was lauded for being a 'true Australian' in turning down the offer from Sussex. And why should he go, others asked, when he was already a certainty for the next tour of England?

Albert travelled with the rest of the Victorian team to Sydney for the New South Wales intercolonial match. Rain had been falling for the previous week, and there were concerns about the quality of the wicket. After his performances with the bat at Adelaide, Blackham had promoted him to number five in the order. The first ball he received he hit high to cover, where he was caught.

The next day, lowering clouds and a southerly wind brought drizzly rain, and the umpires were reluctant to start play in a fine mist. The Sydney crowd had paid their shillings to get in and they blamed the Victorians for the failure to start, showing their displeasure by beating on the railings and booing. It was close to three o'clock before play resumed. The English players had already arrived to practise, and they watched the proceedings from the side as the McLeod brothers made best use of the conditions, picking up the bulk of the New South Wales wickets.

On the third day, the wicket rolled out hard and true, the wind doing the work of drying it out rather than the sun. In Victoria's second innings, Albert, promoted to number three, quickly went after the bowling, hitting a quick 24 before being out to a ball that just touched the bail. It was the batting of Frank Laver (65) and Harry Graham (61) that enabled Victoria to set a target of 155, well within the reach of New South Wales on a wicket that had become relatively tame.

With Blackham off the field, Harry Trott took over the captaincy, and he and his brother bowled in tandem for most of the innings. Harry picked up five wickets, the crosswind aiding his leg spin, and Albert four, with Albert also involved in the other wicket, a run-out. The final wicket to fall was that of Monty Noble, making his debut as New South Wales were all out for 99. The last six wickets had fallen for 30 runs. At the post-match reception, all were agreed that it was the bowling of the Trotts that had been decisive in bringing an end to the game. The Victorians enjoyed their win and Albert walked around the pavilion, hand in hand with his four-year-old nephew, Francis Henry, the boy repeatedly saying 'Victoria'.

In the pavilion, the selection panel of Turner, Giffen and Blackham met to pick the team for the fourth Test, which was due to start the next day. There was no question about Albert's place in the team, but there were questions about others – no dictum about not changing a winning team. After an hour of fractured discussion, a team emerged. Turner, Moses and Graham replaced Callaway, Harry and Worrall. Callaway was certainly unlucky after his excellent bowling in the first innings at Adelaide and the part he had played in the last-wicket stands with Albert. Giffen wanted Callaway in the team rather than Turner. Blackham would have preferred Charlie McLeod to Turner. However, Turner was on the selection panel, and despite the strong opposition of the others he wouldn't back down. Turner was aided by the fact that the other two couldn't agree on who would replace him, so Turner gave himself the nod and his name was on the team sheet. Giffen also wanted Lyons in the team, but Blackham stood firm, stating that Richardson would get him out quickly as he had done before. 'Giffen left the room rather hastily towards the end of the meeting,' said the *Sydney Morning Herald*. The correspondent was being diplomatic, as Giffen would have stormed out of the room. The idea of having current players as selectors, one from each colony, was bound to end in disagreement, particularly when men of such singular personalities as Giffen and Blackham were involved. The *Sydney Morning Herald* tried to be optimistic: 'It is to be hoped that all will work together as one man and with the one end in view.'

Showers fell overnight and in the morning, and there was a sharper downfall before midday. The toss was going to be of paramount importance. In the Australian dressing room, Bruce proposed Giffen for captain and Iredale seconded it. When Giffen passed through the gate with Stoddart, a spectator handed him a two-shilling piece, supposedly with magical properties that always ensured a winning toss. This time the coin's magic worked for Stoddart, who called correctly. Giffen flipped the coin back to the spectator on the way back. 'I don't want it,' he said.

Stoddart did not immediately say whether he would bat or bowl. Instead he kept Giffen and the crowd waiting, and returned to the dressing room to fetch his slow left-arm orthodox men, Peel and Briggs. Watched over by their captain, the two English pros perused the wicket like a pair of rag-pickers in search of a bargain, while the crowd rumbled with impatience. The bright and bubbly Peel must have enjoyed the conversation, with their faces screwing up at what the wicket was potentially going to do. 'You will have to go in,' said Stoddart to Giffen. The South Australian nodded, for he would have chosen to bat, expecting the wicket to improve after lunch.

For the Australians, it was a case of surviving the initial onslaught. As Albert waited in the pavilion, watching the game and smoking cigarette after cigarette, he knew it wouldn't be too long before he would be batting out there. His brother Harry and Bruce opened. On the fifth ball of the first over, Harry hit Peel to point, where Brown took a low catch. Harry looked doubtful. Giffen joined Bruce. Peel was turning the ball sharply, and at the other end Richardson was making it rise to chest height. His lithe frame was built for fast bowling, and he banged it in short and then slipped in a yorker. Richardson had found a bumpy spot, and between deliveries the two batsmen hammered away at it with their bats, trying to flatten it out. Richardson whacked Giffen with one in the middle of the back, as he attempted to get out the way, but Giffen renounced a rub in favour of a leg bye. It was a case of taking the runs where you could. Bruce was the next to go, hitting out at Peel, with Brockwell taking it in the deep. A few runs later, Peel bowled Giffen, tricking him with one that didn't turn, and before long Australia were 26/4. A silence had fallen over the ground, as people seemed afraid to speak. Cheap railway fares had brought them in from across New South Wales, from as far west as Bourke, where the game was played on concrete-like pitches, to Albury in the south, where they played on pretty park turf pitches, and from Tenterfield in the north. There was a large contingent from Victoria, but the crowd was voiceless as Australia limped to 51/6. The wicket had yet to show signs of improvement, and there was a case for giving up the ghost and getting the Englishmen in as soon as possible.

Harry Graham had arrived at the crease, with the plan to go down the wicket to Richardson. If he missed, the ball would bounce over the stumps, and wicketkeeper Punch Philipson was too far back to stump him – but if he swung hard and connected, there were runs. He hit Richardson high over the field for four. Richardson sent down the next one short at his uncovered head, and Graham, the Little Dasher, dropped to his knees at the last moment. The next one Richardson pitched further up, but still at his head, the ball narrowly missing his temple.

These small moments shifted the momentum of the game. Stoddart gave Richardson a breather. Left-hander Joe Darling came in and took advantage of Peel and Briggs, as the sun baked the moisture out of the wicket and turned it into a rock-solid batting strip. He hit Briggs into the tennis courts, and that sparked up the Little Dasher, who gave a horizontal pull to anything short of a length.

The sun combined with the hitting and the chasing seemed to agitate the Englishmen, and they started to make mistakes. The crowd laughed when Philipson messed up an easy run-out and Darling survived. The Little Dasher dolloped one up high in the sky, and some knockabout fun followed when Briggs got in the way of Peel and dropped it. Briggs started to complain, saying the Australians didn't know how to play cricket, and Stoddart had to caution restraint.

Stoddart called Richardson over. It was time to bring him back. The field was spread wide and deep as Richardson sprinted in to bowl. It was short. Joe Darling pulled him long and hard and high in the direction of Archie MacLaren on the boundary. The ball bounced into his cupped palms and then popped straight out of them over his shoulder. He didn't even try a second clutch at it. A full roar of delight came from the crowd.

Richardson wasn't having this. Next ball he ran in even harder, but the ball slipped from his hand and ended up as an awkward high full toss. Darling somehow managed to get some bat on it, but only to divert the ball on to his wicket. They were 119/7, and next in was Albert, promoted to number nine in the order, cheered on by the crowd.

Richardson was less welcoming than the spectators, and before Albert could score the Englishman hit him hard on the leg with a short one, which laid him out on the pitch. It took several minutes for him to come round, with the aid of vigorous massages from the England players. While the blow had hurt, it hadn't softened him up, and he cut Peel for four. The pair of them started to pressurise the field, running four at the expense of Ford's leisurely fielding and throwing. Albert lifted Richardson back above his head and MacLaren got near it, but it was barely a chance. The pitch easing and the counter-attack made the English jittery, and the reluctance of some to bend, including Stoddart and Richardson, allowed the ball to go through legs and the batsmen to enjoy some free runs. The vigour of the driving forced Richardson to post a couple of men on the fence for the first time. When Brockwell came on, Albert took a liking and played him both sides of the wicket with relative ease. Ford was tried as a bowler, but Graham hit him to the fence, with Albert taking a more secondary role. In an hour, the two of them had put on 86 runs. The crowd's earlier gloom had evaporated, and the impetus was firmly with the Australians. At four o'clock, they went in for tea with the score on 192, with Albert having made 40 of them.

After the break, Richardson switched ends and came in with the wind behind, bowling at a terrific pace. Albert went hard at him, scoring 12 with three late snicked fours. Graham raced through the nineties and brought up his hundred with a pulled four, while two beautiful drives from Albert demonstrated to brother Harry and the crack bats in the pavilion that he was an authentic batsman. When he had scored 105, Graham came down the pitch to Briggs and Philipson stumped him. The pair of them had put on 112 for the eighth wicket.

Affie Jarvis didn't hang around long, but Charlie Turner, the selector, coming in last, rose to the occasion, batting for over 50 minutes, 'agreeably surprising his friends and upsetting his detractors' according to *The Age*, matching Albert run for run. The pair ran well between the wickets, but when they had put on 45, Turner hit out to midwicket and Richardson took a catch. Albert hadn't given a chance, and his century had beckoned, with his batting free but never reckless. His not-out score of 85 joined his other not-out scores of 38 and 72 from the previous Test. The English players, as well as the crowd and his own team, applauded him, his return to the pavilion creating a furore. It was almost as if people now expected this kind of performance from him.

On the Saturday, the weather before noon was fine, but half an hour before the start of play a gale came up from the south-west, and at three o'clock there the umpires went through the pale formality of abandoning the day's play. The English team were delighted, reckoning that their best chance of avoiding defeat lay with the weather. In the afternoon, the Australian team went out to Coogee to look at the breakers coming in over the cliffs.

The Sunday brought fine weather, but, with no play scheduled, Stoddart drove out to Coogee on the evening to visit the Australian team. As soon as he left, the rain splattered down on the pavements and it continued to drizzle all night.

On the Monday morning, the sun turned the pitch from sloppy to sticky, offering a decent foothold to the bowlers and fielders with only a sprinkle of sawdust required. It revealed its nature straight away when Harry Trott's leg breaks rose high and turned. Stoddart, a quarter of an hour at the crease before scoring, chanced his arm, came down the wicket to him, missed the ball and was stumped. 'It's the worst wicket I've ever seen,' he said, and soon they were five wickets down for 40.

Harry had taken 2-15 that morning, when Giffen took him off and replaced him with himself. *The Age* diplomatically said 'some surprise was expressed' at this action but added later, 'The action of the Australian captain was generally approved by his team.' Well who wouldn't want to bowl on this wicket? Albert could only watch as Giffen cleaned up, 'the wicket playing terrible pranks'. England made 65. Lockwood remained in the pavilion, his arm in a sling. With his hand having been injured by an exploding soda water bottle before the start of the game, he should never have played.

Brown, the not-out batsman, didn't take off his pads but went back out there as England followed on. This time Giffen took the ball from the very start and he bowled Brown with his fourth delivery. With their stalwart of the first innings gone, this was the cue for some extravagant English hitting, the state of the wicket inducing a gung-ho frame of mind. They scored 72, the innings lasting 90 minutes. The series was two apiece.

Albert had watched all of this from slip, trying to catch George Giffen's eye, but once the ball began to fizz and the wickets started falling, he knew that, barring a miracle, he was never going to be brought on. Turner and Giffen bowled unchanged, and his 8-43 in the previous Test had been forgotten. When a side bowls out the other twice in a day and wins by an innings, no one asks whether it could have been done more quickly by changing the bowling. Besides, it wasn't as if he had done nothing in the game, for his 85 not out had contributed greatly to the eventual result. And there was another game to play, and that would no doubt bring the chance to show what he could do with the ball.

For the moment, there was a win to enjoy, and a large crowd, many of them boys, gathered at the pavilion, remaining there for some time, to see if the Australian players were different to other men. 'It is a demonstrative, ribald crowd,' said Bill Brockwell, the English pro, eyeing the gathering suspiciously. 'It has so much to say in a way that is personal that a big man like Lyons won't face it alone.'

Albert did eventually get a bowl that day. Bill Brockwell had a camera, and some of the Australian players posed for him on the bowling green. This involved holding a position so that an action shot could be taken. There was some difficulty with Albert, who was so keen on bowling at Iredale that at the moment when he should have been half over the line, with arm uplifted and first finger crooked around the ball, he was actually letting it go.

Meanwhile, the Australian selectors wasted no time, even though the final Test was still a month away. They immediately telegrammed Charles Eady of Tasmania and asked him to join the team in Melbourne. After a century in each innings against Victoria, the selectors wanted a closer view of the 15st, 6ft 3in all-rounder who bowled fast. They did not want to miss the chance of strengthening their winning team.

6

Decisive encounter

ALBERT, WHO had turned 22 on 6 February, returned to Melbourne with his place in the Australian team secure. With a month to go to the next Test, he could spend it at home, enjoying his newly minted acclaim and the attention that came with it. Stoddart and the English team rated him, with his three good scores with the bat, and they hadn't even got him out yet. What would he have done at Sydney on that wicket if he had got hold of the ball? Not bowling at Sydney had increased his stock. By now there were rumours of an Australian tour of England in 1896, to cash in on the interest created by the series, and the newspapers saw him as a certainty for selection. England wanted to see this new Australian star in the flesh, after hearing via cablegram of his performances on the field.

Back at his work at the East Melbourne club, Albert found there was money to be made, with everyone wanting to be coached by the new star. The talk of offers from English counties wouldn't go away, and Adolphus spoke to Felix of *The Australasian*, who wrote: 'In a chat with Mr. Trott I said, "I hope A.E. will not be prevailed upon to go to England."

'"He can't very well go," rejoined Mr. Trott, "seeing that he has entered into a three years' agreement with the East Melbourne Cricket Club, to date from the close of this season."'

Aware of the interest in Albert's services from the home country, East Melbourne had moved quickly – and, they hoped, pre-emptively – and extended his contract. Adolphus went on to emphasise the legal nature of the agreement between Albert and the East Melbourne club, and the fact that he would be in the service of the club during the football as well as the cricket season. It was all-year-round work with a steady income: no wonder Adolphus was in favour of it. Mr Manning of East Melbourne told Felix that the testimonial fund for Albert had now reached the sum of £50. Everyone was looking after the boy. Adolphus added that it was his and Mary Ann's wish that their son should remain an 'Australian'. One day, Albert received a registered letter, done up in a great style. When he opened it, he found a single sixpence towards his testimonial fund.

Another opportunity that came Albert's way was a women's cricket match at East Melbourne, its purpose to raise money for charities, scheduled for 18 March. One of the teams was to be captained by Violet Trott, Harry's wife, and Anna Trott, sister of Harry and Albert, was also to play. Many of the other players were wives or sisters of cricketers, and Albert's job was to coach the two teams. Another recruit was the author Millie Finkelstein. Later that year, she was to publish her novel *The Newest Woman: The Destined Monarch of the World*, an anti-feminist dystopian vision of a Melbourne in faraway 1950. The novel had the message that a woman's true place was in the home, as well as containing a 'strong vein of sport and sensationalism in the work'.

In the middle of February, George Giffen arrived in Melbourne with the rest of the South Australia team to play Victoria in the Sheffield Shield. Although the Test series had gripped the public's interest, the intercolonial matches had lost none of their spice, and this one was no exception. Victoria needed to win to retain their title chances, as they had lost to South Australia at Adelaide. It was also an opportunity for Albert to show Giffen what he could do before the next Test match, as the Adelaide crack was always supremely competitive, particularly in games against Victoria, which he had dominated for many years.

Harry won the toss, for which his team thanked him. The day was so hot that only 3,000 enthusiasts had ventured out to watch, and they headed for the shade, leaving the ground looking eerily deserted. Giffen made frequent changes of bowling at the railway end, but once he had come on at the pavilion end he kept himself on, his arm never dropping for one moment. When Laver was caught and bowled by Giffen for 78, in came Albert, promoted to number five in the order, joining his brother Harry. This was the highest he had ever batted at this level, for in his last appearance for Victoria he had gone in at number 11 in the first innings. Now, though, bigger things were expected of him on his own ground. His appearance at the crease gave the innings more impetus, and one of his first scoring shots was to hit Alf Jarvis for three, somewhat uppishly but safe. He then pulled Giffen nicely for four, and his brother matched him with an almost similar stroke for the same result. However, soon after, Harry, going after Giffen, was caught at mid-off. The elder Trott had batted flawlessly for 152 in three-and-a-quarter hours.

Albert scored freely, bold enough to leave his crease to drive Alf Jarvis for four and welcoming the return of paceman Ernie Jones by cutting him neatly across the chains. It looked good, but didn't last. Jones bowled him with a perfectly pitched delivery. The verdict was that Albert had played a good, sound innings for 41, although it was not up to the standards of his batting in the Test matches.

The following day, Victoria were all out for 348. Ernie Jones had taken 5-71 and Giffen a painstaking 5-147 off his 47 overs. The wicket still looked good and the score well within the reach of the South Australians. Giffen, coming in at three, was cheered to the wicket by the Melbourne crowd. At first he went after Harry and hit him for four, but then a cordon of well-placed fielders hampered his scoring. When the score had reached 24, Harry gave way to his younger brother. First of all, Albert sent one past Giffen that seemed to go right through the wicket but without hitting it; then, just before lunch, he had Darling caught behind. After the break, Affie Jarvis lunged at Albert's first delivery, knocking it up to mid-on, while the second ball clean bowled him. Albert then sent down a beauty to Giffen, which drew him out, but the ball broke over the shoulder of the bat and trimmed the bails with some force. It was a wicket to remember, and not just because the ball broke the bail, which Albert kept as a souvenir of this episode in his battle with Giffen. This was the riposte to Giffen's claim that Albert had been unable to get past him. He had taken three top-order wickets for two runs. He took the final wicket, bowling Ernie Jones, to finish with 4-24 off 13.1 overs. Charlie McLeod and Harry had also bowled well, taking three wickets apiece, and the strong South Australians had been bowled out for 118 on a good wicket. Although the Victorians bowled well, it should never have happened – 'inexplicable' and a 'fiasco' was the verdict of Felix.

With rain in the forecast, the Victorians would have liked to have batted again, and a couple of sessions at the crease would have extended their lead and put the game beyond the reach of the South Australians. However, the Victorians didn't have a choice. In 1895, the rules of the game said it was compulsory to follow on after a deficit of 120 runs. This time around, Lyons found his old form and hit a splendid hundred, said to be the best innings he ever played, as he hit the ball strongly along the ground. 'I really thought the Major's handsome iron fence would be damaged,' said Felix.

The next morning, though, the promised rain arrived and play was called off for the day. When play began at noon on Tuesday, the wicket had changed, the ball rising nastily at times, and 80 minutes later South Australia were all out for 245. The Victorians quickly knocked off the 16 runs to win. The low attendances, particularly on the last day, meant that the Victorian Cricket Association had lost £500 on the season, but they felt confident of recouping it the following year, without the attraction of an English touring team. After the match, Albert and Frank Laver, another baseball player, gave an exhibition of throwing, matching one another for distance in an impressive fashion, until Albert, in taking the ball, put his finger out and had to get it pulled back into place.

For their part, Giffen and the South Australians were anxious to get away to Sydney, where they were to play the final Sheffield Shield match of the season, which they needed to win in order to secure the trophy. However, they lost to New South Wales, meaning that the Sheffield Shield went to Victoria. The match was significant in Australian cricketing history for several reasons. Giffen's performance with bat and ball – 65 out of a score of 160, and ten match wickets – meant that any talk of the champion growing stale in his 36th year could be discounted. Finally, and perhaps most significantly, Tom McKibbin, the New South Wales off-spinner, found form at the right time with his 6-123 in the first innings and then 8-66, bowling the selector Giffen and then having him stumped. Before the match had finished, it was announced that McKibbin would travel to Melbourne with the other Australian players. 'McKibbin is in this team for a certainty,' said George Giffen as he left Sydney on the southern express, and this was before the selection panel had met. Giffen was a man used to having his own way.

When McKibbin arrived in Melbourne, a thousand people trailed after him to watch him bowl in the nets, the crowd anxious to see the man who had wreaked havoc on the strong South Australian batting line-up. An unknown at the start of the season, McKibbin's appearance against South Australia was only the second Sheffield Shield game for the 24-year-old. His repertoire included a leg break mixed in with his off spin. McKibbin also seemed to be able to 'puzzle the vision' of batsmen by his use of his arms and legs when delivering the ball. 'Puzzle the vision' might just be a euphemism for chucking it, and there were plenty who thought McKibbin's action was not entirely fair. However, Jim Phillips, the experienced Australian umpire attached to Stoddart's party, judged his action to be legitimate. Before the game, it seemed to be the common assumption that he was going to play in the Test, all on the evidence of Giffen's support. Doubtless the inevitability of McKibbin's selection was discussed at South Melbourne Cricket Club's continental ladies' night at the town hall, where the English and Australian elevens joined members and their lady friends.

The other possibility for selection, Charles Eady – who had been brought over from Tasmania so that the selectors could look at him more closely – was not optimistic about his chances of playing. 'To be candid I have no show of being chosen, but all the same I regard it as a distinct compliment to be asked to come across.' Eady was given the chance to show what he could do in a competitive match when he was selected for Melbourne to play an East Melbourne team that included Albert. The Tasmanian's appearance pulled in a good crowd, but he was soon out, clean bowled for a dozen, thus ending his already remote chance of selection. Albert bowled Bruce with a quicker ball that broke from the off, and he picked up another couple of wickets. But he had been expensive, conceding 101 runs off 192 balls, and Felix commented that his bowling 'wasn't up to the mark'. This was the first hint of criticism of Albert since his appearance on the international scene.

With the series at two games apiece, everyone wanted to know who would be in the team. The selection committee met on the afternoon before the game and agreed to make the final decision on the night. In order to minimise the friction between them, they decided to write down their choice of teams on separate sheets of paper and then compare the results. Luckily, in the first instance, the system appeared to work in that a team quickly emerged. Blackham and Giffen selected the same XI, with McKibbin and Lyons in and Turner as twelfth man. Turner too had gone for McKibbin – he knew him well, as they both came from the same town, Bathurst – but Turner judged him to be a chucker. Turner had gone for himself instead of Lyons. The discussion between the three selectors was brief, and Charlie Turner didn't take his omission lightly. He immediately announced that he wouldn't play for Australia again – a sad end to a distinguished career as a Test cricketer. Although never especially quick, his medium-fast bowling had proved valuable to Australia, as was shown in 1888 when he took 283 wickets on the tour of England, and he had been a *Wisden* cricketer of the year. The English were surprised that he had been left out, for MacLaren and many of the English players still rated him.

In selecting McKibbin over Turner, the Australians were short of a pace bowler, and Giffen and Blackham had failed to consider the balance of the attack in their insistent need to get the latest form bowler into the team. Although the convention of opening with a couple of quickish bowlers and then bringing on a spinner or medium-pacer had yet to be established, it was customary to have a range of bowling options in the attack. The English, for their part, with only 13 players in the touring party, went for an unchanged team, once they had satisfied themselves that Lockwood's hand had healed. With so few players at their disposal, they enjoyed the advantage of continuity of selection.

In the days before the game, the Melbourne Cricket Ground had an unfinished look about it as Major Wardill arranged for extra accommodation to be built, including a four-tier standing gallery and a new ladies' pavilion for 500, while elsewhere in the ground there were new seats. It was like the Melbourne Cup week as spectators poured in by express train from the other colonies – £3 from Sydney – and Major Wardill had the additional problem of finding room for the great and the good with a new-found interest in cricket. With the latter, perhaps the Major was too liberal in his generosity, for while 11,682 paid for a seat on the first day, the crowded reserves contained at least a further 6,000 with complimentary tickets. For many, though, you couldn't get a seat for love nor money – and, if you were fortunate enough to have one, you didn't dare leave it. It was a Niagara of a crowd. 'The people were literally banked up round the rink, the great trees appearing to grow out of a vast bed of straw hats,' said the *Bendigo Advertiser*.

The Australians wore the dark blue caps and sashes of Victoria, but the word from the dressing room was that this was to be the last time the team would play in the colours of the host colony. In the future, the team said, they would wear green and gold, the colours of a national team. The team had responded to the excitement and the weight of expectation from the nation. The weather was set fair, perfect for this grand finale of the game, when the Major walked out to the middle with a captain on either arm as they prepared to toss. Giffen smiled, but his hands trembled as he sent his latest lucky shilling into the air, while Stoddart's grave expression didn't shift, as he made 'no pretence at being easy in his mind'. Giffen gave a little jig and kept the shilling, which a South Australian friend had given to him, while Stoddart shook his head at losing his fourth toss out of five.

The Australians made the most of batting first, with a useful 42 from Harry Trott and 57 from George Giffen. At the end of the first day, however, it was Darling and Gregory who were in control, with both of them not out in the seventies and Australia on 282/4. Albert had managed to find his way on to the field as a replacement fielder for Lockwood. His contribution was overly keen for a substitute, nearly running out Syd Gregory with a fantastic stop and throw, which left Syd galloping fast to get home. A voice was heard to call out from near the elms, 'Here, don't do that again, Albert Trott; can't you see it's Syd Gregory?'

Darling and Gregory fell quickly at the start of the next day, and it was left to Lyons to steady the innings. The team was over-packed with batsmen, with Harry Graham down at eight and Albert coming in at nine when the score was 304. As he came to the wicket, he didn't show any sign of uncertainty and set about the bowling of Richardson, scoring a two and a three on the leg side. He put one from Peel over cover point's head that was almost a catch, but it curved away from the fielder. Next ball, he repeated the stroke, but this time it went straight to Lockwood, who caught it. *The Argus* decided he must have picked up the stroke from coaching lady cricketers, because he had certainly never used it at Adelaide or Sydney. Still, his dismissal finally gave him an average – of 205. This time the tail duly did its work without him, and Australia made 414, an encouraging start.

At the start of the England innings, Giffen opened with Harry Trott, who picked up Brockwell when the English opener came down the wicket, fell and was stumped. Stoddart came in, to warm applause – the English captain always popular with the Melbourne crowd – and quickly got on top of Giffen, who wasn't at his very best, often pitching on leg. He later blamed this on an injury sustained while fielding. Albert came on with McKibbin at the other end, with many in the crowd convinced that the debutant would clean up the Englishmen as he came in, bowling off a long run that began with a 'short, shuffling, mincing step'. But Stoddart scored freely off him, hitting him to leg. It took the return of Harry Trott to get Stoddart out for 68, stumped when he missed one. Soon after, McKibbin picked up his first Test wicket when he bowled Ward.

Albert came back and plugged away, and took his first wicket with a quicker delivery that surprised Brown, and England were 166/4. However, through the rest of that day and into the next, MacLaren and Peel rebuilt the England innings, with Peel cutting at Albert's off breaks and MacLaren forcing away balls on a good length. MacLaren's 120 enabled England to reach 385, the teams neck and neck with England only 29 in arrears. Albert had taken a solitary wicket and Giffen an attritional 4-130 from his 45 overs. By the close, Australia were stretching away and had made 69/1 with Harry Trott and Giffen at the crease.

The fourth day brought a stern wind gusting across the ground, driving away the spectators, sending road dust into their eyes as it took away their hats. The Major's new awnings suffered, with the savage blasts renting the fabric. Richardson, though, worked the wind to his advantage and bowled with it behind him, of course, and the story of the innings was his ability to remain fast over the course of a day. Illustrated newspapers skittered about the field, as the play went on.

The Argus reported: 'One broad sheet flapped weirdly in the top branches of an historic elm, and a short-sighted veteran asked, "What's that white in the trees?", "The ghost of the man who planted it – come back to see Richardson bowl," was the strange reply.'

The Surrey man took 6-104 from his 45 overs, returning renewed for each new spell. Four of his victims were clean bowled, including Albert for a duck, when after successfully keeping the first ball out he completely missed the next. His average halved to 102.5, he returned to the pavilion with his head held disconsolately – 'The glory of those unfinished innings in Adelaide and Sydney was gone,' according to *The Argus*. It was a reminder of how quickly fortunes shift in the game.

Giffen and Darling made fifties in Australia's total of 267. England had to make 297 to win on a pitch that was still holding up, in this timeless game. At the end of the fourth day, they had made 28 for the loss of Brockwell. Nine wickets for Australia or 269 runs for England were the two teams' targets at the start of the fifth day. The five-match series had come down to this simple equation. As David Frith put it in *My Dear Victorious Stod*: 'All Melbourne, all Australia, all the Empire, was agog.'

When Harry Trott's first ball rapped Stoddart on the pad and Jim Phillips' finger was raised, the crowd roared as much in surprise as in pleasure. Stoddart out first ball! Giffen and the Australians felt they were in with a good chance of winning the match. But Jack Brown came in, under an overcast sky. His first touch on the ball was a snick through the slips that came within a foot of Giffen's hand, a rare ghost of a chance. Undeterred, Brown took control. From Giffen's first ball, he set about him, and every time he scored someone in the crowd responded with 'Rule Britannia' on a tin whistle.

After lunch, the sky cleared. Giffen continually switched the bowling, conferring with the two Trott brothers and with Bruce. In the absence of McLeod and Turner, Albert, most likely under the instructions of Giffen, bowled only his fast stuff for a long period, and Giffen tried him from the Richmond End. After a while, he seemed to find his length. Brown played a quick delivery into the slips, where Giffen and Iredale were standing close together, but Giffen only got his fingertips to it.

Another hope gleamed faintly when Ward had made 54 and the total was less than 200, as he played forward to a delivery from Albert and there was a loud appeal from the Australian fieldsmen for a catch behind. Umpire Phillips said 'not out'. It was a difficult call, but the feeling was that, for once, Phillips had made a mistake. Brown and Ward were rarely troubled. As *The Argus* reported: 'Everywhere one heard the vaunting of the men who were neither consistently British nor Australian, but who invariably shout for the top dog.'

Ward drove Giffen clean over the fence, the stroke of the match, and proof that Giffen had been pitching it up too far. It was no great surprise that yet again he had bowled too much. After the match, Giffen was to claim that Harry Trott had told him he was the best bowler available and said, 'Better stay on, Giff.'

Brown's innings was of such high quality that the question was asked as to why he had not shown this form earlier in the series. He was finally out for 140, Giffen catching him off McKibbin. They had put on 210 in 145 minutes. Forty runs later, Ward missed a Harry Trott yorker and was out for 93, but by then only a further 29 runs were needed. It was the two northern pros who steered England home in this, the greatest of series – with a third one, Peel, applying the final blow when he cut a Harry Trott full toss for the winning runs.

In this, his 11th first-class match, Albert hadn't batted or bowled as well as in his first two Test matches. Nevertheless, his contribution with bat and ball in Adelaide, and with bat in Sydney, had been instrumental in keeping Australia in the series after they had seemed to be out of it at 2–0 down, and his part in this comeback was recognised far and wide. The series had rekindled Australian interest in Test match cricket. When the programme of matches was arranged, it was widely predicted that Australia would not be able to put out a representative team for the five matches. Since England's loss at the Oval in 1882, Australia had won only one of the ten series played. Too-frequent tours and below-strength sides had bedevilled the contests between the two teams, and at this point, in the press, the series was not even referred to as the 'Ashes'. It would be another decade before that became common. The quality of the cricket and the success of the tour had lifted the morale of the country, as it left behind the banking crisis and recession, and moved towards federation, with its cricket team in its promised national colours – a symbol of a new unity.

At the post-match dinner, Stoddart was complimentary about his side's reception from the Australian teams and people. 'To have defeated such a side as Australia put in the field was a victory of which the finest eleven in England would have been proud.' The night before the game, Giffen had assumed that Australia would win and had prepared a speech in that vein, so when it came to his turn he spoke a little off the cuff. At the age of 36, his hair ash-grey, his all-round performance as a player in the series stood out – a bedrock of consistency with 475 runs and 34 wickets. He responded by saying there was no one in the Australian team who begrudged England their victory. And, in the spirit of Empire he went on to say that 'although his team were not Englishmen, they were just sprouts from the same old trunk'.

Still, pleasantries and an unprepared speech aside, George Giffen, as a selector and captain, had to try to explain the defeat. Sheridan, one of the tour's promoters, had said the omission of Turner had been a folly. The team had been unbalanced, rammed with batting and with only four full-time bowlers, with Albert Trott expected to take on the part-time role of the paceman. Others had criticised Giffen's field placement. George defended himself by deflecting attention away from himself and shifting the blame on to others. He reckoned that there was too much of a sameness about the Australian bowling, and that the side would have been strengthened by the inclusion of McLeod or Eady. 'Eady's a fast bowler you know, and believe me he's a jolly good cricketer,' said George.

George did not want to take anything away from Brown's innings, but he blamed the defeat on his bowlers – they had not been up to the mark. 'Our fellows did not bowl as well as they have done: not even Albert Trott. He was not at all in his best form, and a fast bowler makes a lot of difference to a side.' Then, for a moment, it looked as though George was going to take some of the blame himself for the defeat. He stated that even he had not been in his best form, 'But look,' he said, and he held up his puffed-up forefinger, the one he had injured in the game.

7

The Prince of Jolimont and the reasons why

FTER 19 matches, the 1894/95 tour had entered its fifth month. With the Test series concluded, it might be thought that this was the time for Stoddart and the other 12 tired members of the touring party to make their way back home to England. However, after the Test, the tour was to run for several more weeks, beginning with a visit to Tasmania. A view bordering on the uncharitable would be that the Major and Mr Phil Sheridan were making the most of this last chance to milk the profits, and that Stoddart and his men were happy to take their share. In those pre-television days, though, many people would have followed the matches in their newspapers, without the benefit of photos. The only way to really see what the players were like was in the flesh in a match. As well as the visit to Tasmania, further games in Victoria and South Australia were to take place.

As for Albert, after his disappointing performance in the fifth Test, he had ample opportunity to regain his form, playing for East versus North Melbourne. This Victorian Premiership club game, in a prolonged feat of scheduling, ran for six days from 9 March to 2 April. Albert scored 44 and 52, also taking 8-60 in the first innings, so his confidence had not been damaged.

The ladies' cricket match had finally arrived. Miss May McDonnell was the star player in front of a crowd of 2,000, cutting and hitting to leg. Albert, who umpired in the match as well as coaching the team, gave his protégé a few practice deliveries between the fall of each wicket, and she dealt with these effectively.

Before this tour finished, there was talk of the next tour to England that would take place the following year. It had all been agreed in Melbourne. Many newspapers reported on prospective players for the tour, and Albert's was always one of the first names to be mentioned. Stoddart had said that the English cricketing public looked forward to the visit of Albert Trott to the country. He could look forward with confidence to his cricketing future.

The penultimate match of the tour was between a Victorian team and England, played to raise funds for the Victorian Cricket Association. This time it was brother Harry's turn to pick up eight English wickets, while Albert, going in at number five, his place as a batsman now assured, hit an aggressive 46, the second top score – a flawless innings until he was bowled by Richardson. In the second innings, he took two wickets and hit 44 as the Victorians cruised home, winning by seven wickets. The fifth Test had been a blip, and he was clearly back to his best form.

Albert's next competitive club match was closely watched by Adolphus Trott from the score box, as Albert's East Melbourne took on Harry's South Melbourne. Adolphus was also there in the pavilion when Albert was presented with a cheque, the proceeds of the testimonial fund set up by the club after his performance in the third Test. Mr Clarke of the East Melbourne club hoped that Albert would continue to be a credit to the Trott family, the club and Australia. In reply, Albert began his speech brilliantly: 'I come from a family of great speech makers.' He then dried up and blurted out a couple of words. Fortunately, Adolphus stepped in and replied on behalf of his son, thanking the club for the many kindnesses they had shown the boy. His words were admirable – the proud father, protective of his son, anxious to say and do the right thing. Albert was always unsure when asked to speak in public, always happier when giving an account of himself on the field. He went on to hit 135, with Adolphus and the crowd lapping up Harry's attempts to bowl his brother with slow ones. East Melbourne won easily by an innings, and Albert had put one over on his brother. Now there were only a couple of local friendly games, and out at Hamilton he made 99 and tucked into the local oyster patties. Now, in April, the season that had changed his life, thrusting him into the public arena, was finally over for 'the well-known Prince of Jolimont'.

At the same time in Adelaide, George Giffen was still going strong, making the most of his very last opportunity to bowl at the Englishmen on the tour. In the first innings, his analysis read a gargantuan 87 overs, 12 maidens, 5-309. It's hard to credit that someone could bowl so many overs in one innings at the end of a long, hard season, but George Giffen did. This may have been the game where one of his team eventually plucked up the courage to suggest that it was time to stop and try something else. He nodded in agreement. 'You're right,' he said, 'I'll have a go from the other end.'

When the English returned home, they duly reported to the English press on the Australian team, and Albert was named as the promising all-rounder. There was an article about him, with a photograph, in the English magazine *Cricket*, and a piece by Giffen in the *Pall Mall Gazette* that praised him for his free batting. However, without naming Albert directly, Giffen went on to say that there were concerns about the Australian bowling, and his words were in the same tenor as his post-match comments. Meanwhile, the tour of England was set to go ahead the next year, and Albert was certain for selection – everybody said so. There was just the small matter of another Australian cricket season to come first.

As part of his contract with East Melbourne, Albert played baseball for the club over the winter months. Here his strength was his pitching, where his one that dipped and dropped did for many an opponent and his great pace was also destructive. East Melbourne won the Pennant competition, but the game was not catching on as a prelude to football matches. There was little press coverage of the matches, and it was clearly a diversion, a winter time-filler, rather than an alternative to cricket. But his success with the quicker deliveries was something he wanted to carry over into his bowling. He had bowled fast under instruction in the final Test. He may also have been prompted to continue with it by Giffen's complaint about the sameness of the Australian bowling, with its excess of medium-pace breaking from the off. Newspaper columnists also recalled the great days of Australian bowling, when Ferris, Spofforth and Palmer had been at their peak. The stuff they sent down today just didn't compare. All of this may have encouraged Albert to develop more as a quick bowler, although in truth, when you find you can bowl fast you usually do.

When East Melbourne visited Camberwell for a pre-season practice match in opposition to 15 of Camberwell on a matting wicket, Albert was in experimental mode. He put seven men behind the wicket, with the wicketkeeper standing back at short stop, and bowled 'wind jammers', presumably bouncers. It was not popular with 'Mid-On' of the Melbourne *Leader*, who said it was an unnecessary and injudicious procedure against juniors in a pre-season practice match. The young crowd were not impressed by the actions of their favourite either, and for the first time the young hero came in for some satirical barracking.

Further criticism came from Mid-On in his pre-season column. He felt that this was the right time to give a friendly warning, saying that towards the end of the previous season Albert had shown weak judgement in his selection of deliveries and that he shouldn't discount his value as a bowler by sacrificing everything to pace.

In the first Pennant match of the season, he took 3-71 off 30 overs against South Melbourne. However, fielding in the slips, he dropped a couple of catches, one of them sparing his brother Harry. He had to wait until the following week to show what he could do with the bat, when he came in at number three and woke up the bored spectators with an aggressive 98, his driving hard and clean. In the papers, more than one commentator said that in the long run he would primarily become a batsman. On 98, he signalled up to the scorer's box, as was his custom when approaching a century, to check how many runs he needed. It was his father, Adolphus, scoring for South Melbourne, who gave him the answer. It may have disturbed his concentration, because he touched the next delivery down the leg side and was caught behind.

In the St Kilda fixture, he was bowled by Fenton with a beauty, but then had to travel to Adelaide for the Sheffield Shield game against South Australia. He came in at four and cut Giffen for a couple, but Ernie Jones' quick one then proved too much for him, and he was clean bowled for three, with the Victorians all out for 220. He took a couple of good catches at mid-on to get rid of the hard-hitting Lyons and Reedman. When he came on to bowl, Harry gave him three men in the slips with the wicketkeeper standing back. It was clear that he was going to bowl fast, and he almost had Giffen, but the ball dropped just short. Joe Darling found it difficult to score off him, with the light fading, and he bowled him off the last ball of the day with a delivery that rose from a length. The next day, Albert returned to his off break style, and he lured Affie Jarvis down the pitch and had him stumped.

It was in this game that another player came to the fore and turned in a performance. Jack Harry polished off the tail with his off breaks and then opened the batting for Victoria. This rough diamond of a man was nearing 40 and always game. A man of many trades: miner, baseball player, ambidextrous bowler, sometimes a wicketkeeper, and an umpire in the Victorian Premier League, where he also played for East Melbourne. His whiskers were impressive too, seriously coating his upper lip in an era of top-heavy moustaches. It would be nearly a century before any Australian player came close to challenging them in size. He had appeared in the Test series against England at Adelaide but made little impact, twice clean bowled by Richardson. Now, he set about Giffen early on, scoring freely on the off side. Giffen was forced to take himself off. Jack Harry was set, and first with Harry Graham and then with Harry Trott he put Victoria on top. Giffen came back and almost had him a couple of times but he had made 107 before Giffen finally got him out. Jack Harry had shown himself to be a good all-round man at the right time and in the right place.

Victoria won the match by 66 runs. In the second innings, Albert had been told to take his time and play himself in, as befitted a top-order batsman, and it was 20 minutes before his first scoring stroke. Warming up, he pulled Giffen for four, but he then jumped out to the champion's hanging delivery, which he missed first time around and then desperately tried to play with a second attempt. When he bowled, he picked up Darling again, but a couple of his overs had been expensive. He hadn't had a disastrous game – it was not as if anyone had really got hold of him when he was bowling and, although his fast stuff hadn't been successful at times, he'd made a nicely judged catch off brother Harry. It was just that now, after his previous appearance on the ground, people expected more in the way of big scores and bags of wickets. But, at the post-match social at the Theatre Royal Hotel among the other players and officials, drinking the toasts and singing the songs, he had time to forget about the game.

Back in Melbourne, Albert found his old form with the bat, making 121 at the expense of Fitzroy. The next Australian tour of England was to be under the auspices of the Australian Cricket Council. Anticipation was building up as new fixtures were added by the day and a three-match Test programme was set up. The post of team manager was advertised and there were 33 applications from across the colonies, but the successful candidate was Melbourne's Harry Musgrove. The fact that he was a former cricketer was helpful, but what swayed it was his experience in managing theatrical tours. The selection committee, no doubt with the previous tour of England in mind, clearly felt that someone experienced in dealing with the temperamental stars of comic opera and wayward behaviour was the best person for the job. Musgrove was rumoured to possess a large stock of tact. Besides, he was popular with the players, as he had always been free with tickets for the Princess Theatre in Melbourne. The selectors for the tour were Bruce of Victoria, Garrett of New South Wales and Giffen of South Australia. They had to pick a team by 8 February.

There were a couple of intercolonial games against New South Wales before then, giving Albert a chance to impress. He was sixth-change bowler in the first innings, but still ended up with match figures of 9-171 on a batsman's wicket. The feeling was, though, that he was out of form with the ball, and, in trying to emulate the pace of the Englishman Richardson, he no longer mixed then up and had been slamming them down without regard to length. 'His friends persuaded him out of slamming,' reported the *Kalgoorlie Miner*, 'and now he bowls a slow break ball which has only to be watched to be smothered.' With the bat, he failed to impress, ending as one of McKibbin's eight victims in the second innings as Victoria lost.

In the return fixture a few weeks later, there were two selectors on the field of play, while the third one, Giffen, watched. If you had ambitions to tour, runs or wickets would be helpful at this juncture. In a rain-affected match, Albert made a start in each innings – 18 and 24 – but couldn't press on. With the ball, he took two wickets, accounting for number 11 McKibbin in both innings. The match still fresh in their minds, the three selectors adjourned to Garrett's house to pick the touring team. The 13 names they selected were George Giffen, Joe Darling, Ernie Jones, Harry Trott, Hugh Trumble, Harry Graham, Jack Harry, Alfred Johns, Syd Gregory, Frank Iredale, Harry Donnan, Charles Eady and Tom McKibbin.

No Albert Trott. There was no Lyons the hard hitter either, or Kelly the wicketkeeper or Charlie Turner. As 'Point' in the *Evening Journal* put it, 'Probably the most abused men in Australia to-day are Messrs. Giffen, Garrett, and Bruce, who last night completed the selection of the Ninth Australian Eleven.' Every colony had something to complain about.

Harry Trott said he was disappointed at his brother's omission, but it was left to Tom Horan, writing as Felix, to put the case, commenting on Albert's batting average. 'This splendid average was obtained against the flower of English fast and slow bowling, and in contests which required batsmen to stiffen their sinews and summon up their blood. A colt, mind you, does this, a colt named A.E. Trott. He wins the highest praise from every man in Mr. Stoddart's team. His fame is trumpet tongued to the world not only as a batsman but as a bowler and field, and now the famous selection committee, or, I should say, two of them, give him the cold shoulder and proclaim him unfit to represent Australia on the cricket fields of England. I have seen some queer things done by selection committees in my time, but this caps all.'

Others pointed out that England had expressed great interest in seeing the wonder player Albert Trott, and the financial success of the tour could be compromised if he was left out.

Some were, perhaps, less surprised or outraged by Albert not making the cut. It was pointed out that he had not played well that season, and perhaps his achievements in the Tests were something of a one-season wonder. Even at the time of his heroic feats a year earlier, there had been those who sought to downplay his achievements. E.J. Briscoe, the New South Wales umpire, who, earlier in his career, had refused to take the field when W.G. Grace impugned his integrity as an umpire, felt that Albert was a grand batsman and a great field, 'But as for his bowling I think that his eight for 43 against the Englishmen is no criterion of his real merit: it only shows that it was his day out. Give me Giffen, who got two for 57, far in preference to Trott.'

It seems that, when the selectors were discussing bowlers, they resolved to discuss his name at the end under the category of an 'all-round man'. It was Bruce, the Victorian selector, who favoured including him in this category. However, by the time they came to discuss him, the fast bowlers Eady and Jones had already been selected and they had a full complement of 13 players. Giffen thought they should be able to select 14 players, but the extra man Giffen wanted was not Albert Trott but the popular Lyons, his old South Australian comrade. The selectors wrote to the Australian Cricket Council, and to Lyons, informing them of this plan.

His non-selection can be put down to several things. His form in the two Sheffield Shield games in January had been ordinary rather than good and, as had been shown in the Test series, short-term form could send you in and out of the team pretty quickly. There was also the question of Albert's style of bowling. When he had bowled consistently fast, it hadn't come off: his mission to break away from 'sameness', to create a new version of himself, had been unsuccessful. The selectors, though, wanted two fast men in the team. Giffen had said as such, after the fifth Test, and Billy Murdoch had written to Sydney from England saying that the English batting was strong and Australia would need fast bowlers. Such was the selectors' faith in short-term form, they went for giant Charles Eady although he had never played a Test, on the basis of his fast bowling performances for Tasmania. Eady was also a useful batsman, capable of opening. With Giffen and McKibbin in the team, and the recalled Trumble, who had been discarded after the second-Test defeat in the 1894/95 series, Australia were well covered in the off break, right-arm medium-pace department. There was enough 'sameness' in the team without adding more. At the back of George Giffen's mind, there may have also been a recollection of his own failure to reproduce his Australian form in England, where in the past other Australian bowlers in the team had overshadowed him.

Events now came quickly. Within a week of the announcement of the selection, reports appeared that if Albert didn't secure the extra place, as the 14th man, he would move to England as a professional. Jim Phillips was the man who advised him to do this. Phillips was a remarkable man, who secured the maximum financial return from his cricketing ability in an age when the game of cricket was developing and spreading across England and Australia. He had the knack of making himself useful. In the Australian winter, he had found himself a contract with Middlesex, where he played in the English County Championship. In the English winter, he returned to Australia, announcing his impending arrival in the Melbourne papers, with a stock of English cricketing goods for sale. He had witnessed Albert's cricketing exploits at first hand – he had played for Melbourne encountering him in club cricket, played alongside him for Victoria, and watched as an umpire when Albert played in the Tests. He had seen almost all of Albert's first-class career. Mid-On, in *The Leader*, felt that Albert could not find a 'better guide, philosopher and friend' than Jim Phillips. The advice of Phillips was clear. Migrate, as there was not sufficient scope for Albert's talents in the colonies. Albert made up his mind to qualify for Middlesex, and he was almost certain to be offered an engagement by Marylebone Cricket Club.

The controversy over the tour rumbled on day by day. Jack Harry was removed from the team as deputy wicketkeeper when the selectors changed their minds. They replaced the Bendigo miner with James Kelly of New South Wales. The claim was that Harry had injured his knee, and with fitness concerns about the other wicketkeeper, Alfred

Johns, they didn't want to run the risk of having two injured keepers. Harry denied that there was any problem with his knee, and said that a spot of liniment, well rubbed in, would soon put it right. After all, the doctor had said to Jack Harry and Musgrove, 'Certainly why, he'll dance a hornpipe with anyone within a week.' Harry successfully claimed compensation of £160 from the Australian Cricket Council, on the grounds that he had given up his job and already spent £40 on equipping himself for the tour. Felix commented, 'Was there ever such bungling, blundering and botchwork since the game of cricket first started in the world?'

The East Melbourne club supported Jack Harry too, with E.B. Manning, the secretary, initiating a public subscription to pay for his fare to England, so that he could seek engagement as a professional or be available for the Australian team if needed. His friends and admirers, including the *Bendigo Advertiser*, stumped up the money.

Although the team had been announced, there was the sense that the final composition of the touring party could still be altered after the initial selection, either by form, lobbying or circumstance. The 19-year-old Clem Hill was added to the party after he made some runs in the remaining Sheffield Shield games, including a 206 not out against New South Wales. It was he who became the 14th man in the touring party, on special terms of £200 for the tour plus expenses, while the rest were on an equal share of the profits. Albert had done nothing to press his own case for late inclusion in the two remaining first-class games of the season, the South Australia match and then for the Rest of Australia in a practice match for the touring party. By now, he had dropped back down the batting order to eight or nine.

In one sense, though, it didn't matter – for he was on the boat to England, with his brother and the rest of the Australian team, with a point to prove, to show the selectors they had been wrong to omit him and to prove to himself that he was a player of quality. So, with Jack Harry, he boarded the *Cuzco* at Melbourne. There had been late moves to add Charlie Turner to the touring party, but this fell through when the Sydney man said it was too late to change his business arrangements. In Adelaide, waiting to board the *Cuzco*, an executive committee meeting of Giffen, Iredale and Trumble proposed to Musgrove that Albert Trott should be 'obtained when required' if the team needed him. Effectively he would be a reserve, but the vagueness of the arrangement probably suited Albert because he had already committed himself to playing for MCC.

Ten miles out from Australia, under the jurisdiction of British courts, the team signed contracts for the tour. This was followed by a significant moment for the tour. Tipped as captain in the weeks preceding departure, Harry Trott was now formally elected to the position by the other members of the team. Perhaps it was Harry Musgrove who had persuaded his fellow Victorian to put aside his long-standing aversion to standing against Giffen. The latter retained his place as a member of the selection committee alongside Harry Trott and Syd Gregory. With his brother in charge, Albert must have thought his chances of joining the tour had improved. He trained with the rest of the team, and in a tug-of-war match, Jim Phillips and he, representing the second saloon, defeated the Australian team. They would use Albert on the tour, if needs be – that was the cover-all decision for now, but there was no formal contract with the Australian team.

At Colombo, the *Cuzco* docked, and in an odds match the Australians selected a team of 12 to play 18 men of Ceylon. It was a means of stretching the sea legs and enjoying some colonial hospitality, rather than a serious game against a team largely made up of English army officers. As *The Referee* of Sydney reported, 'Although the blacks play cricket with much glee and apparently with the most gratifying results to themselves, they can scarcely be called first-class exponents of the game, as we in Australia understand it.' Always anxious to oblige, Albert turned out for Australia in this one-day game, picking up four wickets and making 26. The lunch was lavish, bordering on the princely, and not conducive to afternoon cricket. Eady didn't play because he was suffering from the effects of his first vaccination, and others may have been seasick, for Gray and Hetherington, crew members on the *Cuzco*, also made up the numbers in the Australian team.

Albert's position on the tour was still open to clarification, and it was resolved to leave the final decision to when the ship docked at Naples, so that he could write to his contacts in England, telling them what he was going to do.

His first sight of London, capital of the Empire, was not wide streets and tall buildings, carriages with fine ladies and the grandness that Harry had always talked about. As they docked, all he could see were steam tugs with their dirty smoke and warehouses, under a grey sky that met flat fields in the distance. There were men in smaller boats crossing the Thames, unloading goods and ferrying passengers across, who brought a knowing busyness to their work, used to the arrival of a big ship in their waters, as they edged their way around the multitude of vessels. The Australian team went on to a dinner at Surrey County Cricket Club and then on to a practice at the Mitcham ground.

This was the point at which Albert was without brother Harry, but there waiting for him dockside was his old, friendly adversary A.E. Stoddart, who had come to greet the Australian team. He no doubt directed him on the best route to Lord's and to the secretary of MCC. The contract was for five years. He was to receive 30 shillings a week, with £5 for every first-class match, and £3 for a second-class match if his team won or £2 if they lost. For a fifty in a first-class match, he was to be paid £1, and he would get the same amount for a hat-trick. He could supplement this with payment he received providing coaching to members. Out of this, he had to meet his own living and travelling expenses. It would be two years' residence in England before he was qualified to play for Middlesex. It was a job as a professional: different people, different place, but in essence the same as his job in East Melbourne. Jack Harry, the other disappointed Victorian tourist, was in the same role, qualifying to play for Middlesex, so Albert was not without Melbourne company. He could even play for Australia if they asked him. MCC at Lord's had said they would not put any obstacles in his way should his services be required by Australia. It had turned out well.

At Lord's, he saw the great pavilion and said what he was going to do. Then, he may have gone on to Queen's Park, Brighton, staying with a friend of the family, and playing for the Sussex club Lindfield under an assumed name.

A photograph taken a few months before he left Australia, with the rest of the Victorian team, gives a good indication of what Albert looked like on his arrival in England. Around 5ft 9in in height, he appears taller, slim, loose-limbed towards the rangy, with the moustache incipient, no more than a rime of beer. He could pass for less than his 23 years.

8

'Oh yes, I am satisfied'

T
HE ARRIVAL of Albert on the English cricket scene was generally welcomed, although there were some who were less happy. 'Vanderdecken' in *The Graphic,* while acknowledging Albert's ability, deplored the amalgamation of an Australian cricketer into an English county, as it meant one less opportunity for native talent. Albert was not the first Australian cricketer to be taken on by an English county. J.J. Ferris, the left-arm quick, had qualified for Gloucestershire via the MCC route. His stint at Gloucestershire had not worked out well, and Vanderdecken had hoped this would deter other English counties from importing players. However, with MCC offering the qualification opportunity, the arrangement was effectively endorsed by the body in control of the game and with an eye on its overall welfare.

Rejected by his country, the Prince of Jolimont now had to adjust to the selection practices of his new employers. Many expected him to be selected for MCC's game against Nottinghamshire at Lord's, but instead he had to make way for three amateurs who rarely had the opportunity to play first-class cricket.

Instead, Albert's debut in England was for C.I. Thornton's XI, away to Cambridge University at Fenner's. In the early part of the season, the universities of Oxford and Cambridge played a series of trial matches against MCC and other teams, with the matches classified as first-class fixtures. C.I. Thornton's XI had a mix of amateurs and professionals, for in addition to Albert there was the great opener Arthur Shrewsbury, and Walter Mead, the bowler. When the former was out for a duck, the innings of C.I. Thornton's XI never really recovered, and they were all out for 219 with Albert batting at ten, making 15. There had been some interest in how the students would cope facing the Australian demon, but as it turned out they did surprisingly well. Albert took just the one wicket from 19 overs that went for an expensive 76. In the second innings, he did better, scoring 58 and taking a couple of wickets, but the fact that he had failed to destroy the opposition was eagerly noted back in Australia.

The *Inquirer and Commercial News* reported: 'During his first match in England Albert Trott did nothing to maintain the great reputation he made when the Englishmen were out here, or to justify the extravagant eulogies of Victorians, who thought that he should have been in the Australian Eleven. It is to be hoped for his own sake that he will be more successful by the time he has qualified to play for Middlesex.'

A few days later, he played his first game at Lord's for MCC, against Lancashire in a team captained by Stoddart. In the first innings, he was expensive – 8-2-39-0 – bowling from the Pavilion End, and in the second innings he didn't take a wicket. The pitch was certainly suited to his style of medium-pace bowling, as the wickets were shared between Bill Attewell, Fred Martin and Jack Hearne. The latter, who played for Middlesex, found the right spot in the second innings and picked up five wickets. These experienced professionals had all played for England, and he needed to learn from them to find the best way of adapting to English conditions. With the bat, he started well but failed to make a decent score. The one bright spot was his outfielding, in which he looked sharp.

In his next game, for A.J. Webbe's XI, he was back at Fenner's for another university match, missing out on playing for MCC at Lord's against Leicestershire. It must have been a slightly lonely experience in Cambridge, for as the sole professional in the team he would not have had any company in the professionals' pavilion or at his lodgings. Here he found some form with the ball, his bowling and that of Bromley-Davenport demoralising the students, as they bowled unchanged and dismissed them for 126. Over the next couple of months, his first-class cricket was largely confined to university matches – playing against Oxford three times and Cambridge five. The fixtures had been on the calendar for over 60 years, and MCC supported the university teams with a payment of £300 to each of them. As well as providing practice for the teams before the Varsity match, there was clearly a social element, with graduates of the universities revisiting their old haunts.

With his bowling, he started to take wickets, but in these early matches he needed to show what he could do with the bat. He would later say he had grown quite despondent at his failure to time the ball, and he reckoned that in his first eight innings he was out six times through playing either too late or too early. In the Derbyshire game at Lord's, he opened the batting and made a 'sound and clever' 39, looking well set until he was unluckily run out by Board, one of the professionals in the team. Against Oxford University, he hit a vigorous 21 after Jack Harry had made 56 in an hour opening the innings. Although he hadn't played a major innings, he could console himself with the fact that he was getting more than a start.

But would Australia call him up? The tour marched on. Every day, he read the newspapers to see how his old teammates were doing without him. The answer was quite well, and this was down to some excellent bowling by Jones and Giffen, although they had yet to play a Test match.

It was nearly the end of May when an Australian reporter caught up with Albert in the nets, while he was practising his batting at the expense of the gentle lob bowling of the Irish amateur Sir Timothy O'Brien. Albert said he had not been asked to play by the Australians and that he was not particularly anxious for it to happen.

'I am very well content here. I like Lord's and I like England. I shall never leave it. I shall make my home here.' He said he would play for Australia if they asked him, as long as he could gain the permission of MCC. 'But to tell you the truth I don't want to, for if they ask me to play that will mean they are not doing well and I want them to win all of their matches without me.'

His answer was a touch ingenuous, saying he was happy with his lot, categorically stating his intentions, yet still being open to selection if needed and patriotically wishing the team well. No doubt the reporter had tidied up his words a little, but it was also a good answer, a diplomatic one. Neither MCC nor Australia could quibble with what he had said, but at the same time it was clear where he saw his future.

One of the fixtures arranged for the Australians by MCC was against Wembley Park Cricket Club in early June, close to Lord's, where MCC selected the team, bolstering it with their own members. Fred 'The Demon' Spofforth, veteran of the first-ever Test series, turned out for Wembley Park at the age of 42. Albert was selected for this game, but at the very last moment Mr Henry Perkins, secretary of MCC, left him out of the team and selected him to play against Kent because MCC were short of first-class batsmen for this game, which began the next day. He was disappointed, but had no choice in the matter.

Spofforth rolled back the years to take 11 of his countrymen's wickets, but to no avail. The Australians crushed Wembley Park in the club's sole first-class fixture; the ground on which they played now lies buried beneath Wembley Retail Park. As for Albert, he contributed little in the Kent game, where he opened the batting in both innings, made a total of three runs and was not called upon to bowl.

The next stop for the unbeaten Australian team was at his new home ground of Lord's, for an MCC fixture. While he could have been selected to play, he never seriously came into consideration. The aim of the hosts was to give the Australians a solid working over by a strong MCC team, with the leading amateurs taking the batting slots and the seasoned pros, who knew the Lord's wicket well, entrusted with the bowling. Besides, selecting Albert against his own country in this prestige fixture would have been a story in itself, and MCC wanted to win it without unnecessary distractions. On a wicket that was soft and slow from heavy rain, MCC put together 219. When Australia batted, Jack Hearne and Dick Pougher bowled them out in just over an hour for 18 runs in total, with the latter taking five wickets for no runs. Giffen had bowled earlier in the day, but didn't bat. He was reported variously as suffering from sciatica or a cold in the eyes. *The Argus* speculated that Giffen had left the ground, expecting to bat later, and had gone to Swiss Cottage for a recuperative glass of milk. The Australian score on a drying wicket was their lowest ever in England. Harry Trott, who had brought a new spirit to the team, did his best to make light of the disaster, saying to Fred Spofforth, who played club cricket for Hampstead and who had come along to commiserate, 'But tell me Spoff, are there any decent leg shows on in town?'

Albert must have had a strange mixture of feelings as he watched his former teammates, led by his brother, skittled by his new employers. Not exactly *Schadenfreude*, because he was still an Australian, and his father, Adolphus, as well as his brother, would have felt the defeat. However, part of Albert would have sensed an opportunity arising for himself through the failure of certain members of the team. Giffen yet again failed to appear, absent ill, denying Middlesex's Jack Hearne, one of Albert's new teammates, his tenth wicket in the second innings. Albert must have really wanted to have a go on this wicket.

But the tour continued without the Australians calling on Albert, and on they went to Yorkshire with a recovered Giffen. MCC decided to persevere with him as a batsman despite his failure to score runs against Kent. Within a week, he was playing alongside two of England's leading players at Fenner's for MCC, opening the innings with his captain, W.G. Grace. When Grace was out, in came Ranjitsinhji. The Indian prince was a year older than Albert and had been privately coached in batting while at Cambridge University. The two of them put on a partnership of 99, with Albert scoring 58 of the runs, with eight fours, before he was out for 62. Ranjitsinhji's keen eye and quick hands enabled him to play the late cut and the leg glance so well. Albert regarded the Indian as the best batsman he had come across in England, and he had a close-up view from the other end of the wicket when he batted with him. Ranjitsinhji went on to make 146, and the next month he played his first Test. 'He's a wonder. He's fearless as any man I ever saw. He'll face any bowler on any wicket and make all sorts of wonderful strokes,' said Albert. And if he came out to Australia? 'I don't think they will ever get him out on our wickets.' Ranjitsinhji's character impressed Albert in the nets too. When the professionals bowled at him, the Indian always put sovereigns on top of the stumps as an incentive.

The first Test of the three-match series was a three-day fixture at Lord's. After the drama of the previous series, it seems surprising that MCC did not retain the five-day, five-match series format, especially on such a long tour. However, a crowded fixture list, with a large number of social and other matches as well as county games, proved restrictive. There were just too many to fit them all in. Fortunately, what had carried over from the previous series was the public's appetite for Test cricket. As the *Pall Mall Gazette* put it, 'London is not out of town today: it has gone up to Lord's.' There were 15,000 passengers through Baker Street underground station before noon, and 30,000 in the ground, with many spread out on the grass. There was rowdyism too, as spectators threw missiles at those blocking their view, and there were encroachments on the field of play as boundaries were shortened.

Harry Trott won the toss, and Australia batted. The spectators who craned their necks saw Richardson tear in from the Pavilion End and clean bowl six Australian batsmen. They were all out for 53 in 22.2 overs. It's likely that Albert was in the Australian dressing room in the pavilion watching the game, enjoying the high vantage point, rather than watching from his usual place in the professionals' pavilion. When England batted, Donnan hurt his hand in fielding the ball and had to leave the field. Albert hurried through the Long Room, down the steps and on to the field of play. He was back on the field with the team, perhaps not in the way he had expected. It is unlikely that he had been named as substitute fielder, for the role was more of an ad hoc arrangement – as can be seen from the 1895 series, when Albert more than once fielded for England. How did it come about? Brother Harry was on the field, and it is unlikely that he would have called for his brother. Albert volunteered to go out there and was on the field before anyone had thought very much about it. Whether Musgrove, the manager, was around to object to the arrangement is not known. However, when the players returned to the field of play after lunch, it was Iredale, not Albert, who fielded in place of Donnan. Someone must have said something about Albert's appearance on the field, possibly Harry.

Fewer turned up on the second day, and the company was 'much more gentlemanly', to the relief of *The Times*. When England were dismissed for 292 and Australia were two wickets down for three runs, it looked as though there would be a repeat of the collapse in the first innings. But Harry Trott, watched by his younger brother, led from the front. Supported first by Giffen in a stand of 59, and then Syd Gregory, where they put on 221, he rebuilt the innings, and an element of contest was back. There had been chances in Harry's innings of 143 – he was caught at slip when he had made 61, but was given the benefit of the doubt, and there was another chance when he had made 99. Irrespective of these moments, it was a great fighting innings. However, it was not enough and the batsmen who followed collapsed to Jack Hearne; England went on to make the 109 needed for the loss of four wickets.

The day after the Test finished, Albert was playing Cambridge University, this time for a weaker MCC team, in the last of the trial games at Lord's before the Varsity match. While batting at three, without much success, Albert watched when the university bowlers made the ball rise awkwardly from bowling short. Not to be outshone, and after watching the success of Richardson in the Test, he decided that pace brought dividends on this ground. In the university's first innings, bowling much faster than normal, he took 6-59. A commentator noted that the pitch appeared to quicken. MCC set the university 507 to win. Albert continued with his fast style. He bowled W.G. Grace Jnr for a duck, then struck Marriott in the face – the 21-year-old student fell to the ground and was forced to retire hurt.

He had gone too far. This delivery brought not only Frank Mitchell, the Cambridge captain, from the pavilion and on to the field, but also Mr Perkins, secretary of MCC. Perkins, a clever yet unconventional man, was described by Lord Hawke as 'Perkino, short of stature, with the ugliest and scraggiest of beards'. He now asked for Albert to be taken off immediately. Later, Albert was to claim that he was just slipping in an occasional 'warm' delivery and that Marriott had snicked a ball that bumped on to his face, instead of throwing his head back out of the way. At the end of the season he looked back on this game and said, 'I am quite a fast bowler now. There were not many bowlers in England who were reckoned to bowl faster than I did at times.' It was to be his preferred style in the matches that followed.

With the moratorium on quick bowling now safely in operation, Marriott returned to the crease after retiring hurt and scored 146 not out, and Cambridge astonishingly made the 507 runs needed for victory. It was the highest ever first-class fourth-innings winning total, a devalued record of sorts that lasted for over 100 years. Albert did bowl on the last day, but he didn't use his short ball which had so discomfited Marriott on the previous evening. A few months later, *Punch* of Melbourne mocked the Cambridge batsman in a cartoon with the caption, 'I say, are you sure that's a soft ball? Be very careful how you send them in. A fellah doesn't want to be carried away to the bally hospital, dontcherknow.'

Albert played in the last of the season's trial matches at Lord's, against Oxford University. Close to the Varsity match, Oxford did not wish to risk injury to their bowlers, so the MCC innings consisted of first-rate batsmen punishing third-rate bowlers. Taking advantage, Albert hit a vigorous 67 not out, batting at eight alongside the Somerset amateur Herbie Hewett, who for some reason was batting under the assumed name of Mr Herbert. It was a two-day game, and on the second day MCC bowled the students out twice, Albert bowling a mammoth 66.2 five-ball overs in less than a day's play. He took 10-192, but at times he was hit freely as he tried to inject some life into the game.

This was to be his last first-class match of the season, for in the next two months he played a series of two-day games, largely meeting the minor county teams. Fortunately, most of the fixtures were at Lord's, but this did not stop him murmuring about having to fork out, from his match fees, for his travel and accommodation in Norwich and in Wales. It was part of the experience of being a pro in England. Doubtless the games were all in good fun, with easy runs and cheap wickets in front of crowds keen to see the famous Australian professional in action, but the cricket was second class both in status and on the pitch. One of his best performances came against Worcestershire at Lord's, with the county almost on the cusp of first-class status, where he top-scored with 141. However, although he was in the same country, it was a world away from Test cricket and his brother Harry.

The call had not come for Albert. After their defeat in the first Test, the tourists had picked up some form on better, harder wickets, winning five and drawing one of their matches as they came into the second Test at Old Trafford. The English team selection was in the hands of the county hosting the game. The Lancashire committee picked Prince Ranjitsinhji, the choice of the people too, thus ensuring the financial success of the game. However, the Indian had not been selected for the previous Test at Lord's, because Lord Harris, who had just finished his term as the Governor of Bombay, was unhappy at selecting a player not of British stock. Harry Trott was asked whether he had any objection to the selection of Ranjitsinhji for England. Not only did he have no objection, but he openly expressed the wish to see him in the side. You wouldn't have expected anything different of Harry Trott.

One of the players who had found some runs after a series of low scores was Frank Iredale, who had not been worth a place in the Test at Lord's. At Trent Bridge, Harry had observed the Sydney's man's depression, and taken him to one side and said he needed a tonic to restore his spirits. He mixed something up in a glass and told Iredale to down the concoction in one. Usually a nervous starter, Iredale began his innings with a new-found confidence. The runs duly came, and now Iredale drank down his 'nobbler' before the start of each innings. After a few games, Harry revealed to the teetotaller Iredale that the tonic was a brandy and soda. Undeterred, Iredale continued to take it for medicinal purposes before batting, and in the first innings his 108 was the backbone of the Australian effort after Harry had won the toss. The top order of Giffen (80) and Harry (53) supported him and enabled the Australians to get up to 412.

When England batted, it was a combination of Harry's leg spin and the medium pace of McKibbin and Trumble, topped by some brilliant fielding, that did for them. Opening the bowling, Harry had Grace and Stoddart stumped as they misjudged the spin. If it hadn't been for a 65 not out from the Warwickshire keeper Lilley, and the care of Ranjitsinhji (62), who fell to a good low-down catch at point by Harry off McKibbin, Australia would have dismissed them for less than 231.

England had to follow on, and began their second innings a little after five o'clock. They needed all the help they could get. Ranjitsinhji came to the fore, his innings recalling the Grace of 20 years before, and his short-arm stroke on the leg side had never been matched by anyone before. His score of 154 not out meant Australia had to make 125 to win. Richardson, as tireless as ever, ripped in. When Harry Trott was the third man out for 28, the normally cool Australian captain couldn't stay in the pavilion to watch and was forced to take a cab. Richardson picked up six wickets bowling unchanged, but the Australians made it home by three wickets.

Another series with all to play for in the final Test, and there were still plenty of games to play in this money-making tour, one of them at Lord's against MCC. Once more there was no place for Albert in the team, as MCC relied on their experienced professionals to do the work. The day after the game, Albert turned out for MCC in another game. The Edinburgh club side Grange at Lord's may have been a far less prestigious fixture, but he was paid to play and do his employers' bidding.

Across the Thames, an industrial dispute flared up. In the run-up to the final Test of the series at the Oval, the English professionals initiated a dispute with the selectors, the Surrey committee. Richardson, Lohmann, Gunn, Hayward and Abel refused to play unless their match fee was increased from £10 to £20. Their demand was partially sparked by the increase in gates. The professionals were wearily inured to the custom that amateurs such as Grace were earning far more in expenses than the professionals' match fees, but the fact that the Australian amateurs were making so much money from the tour would have riled. In response, the Surrey committee was irked, not by the fact that the professionals had asked for more money but by the 'clumsy and arrogant' way in which they had acted. If they had gone about it in the right way, the request would naturally have been considered. The Surrey committee dropped the recalcitrant professionals from the team and summoned up some more as replacements. Faced with no match fees, the professionals backed down and Hayward, Abel and Richardson all played. Meanwhile, W.G. Grace threatened to withdraw after some irresponsible statements were circulated in the press regarding the payments made to amateurs, but he was prevailed upon to captain the side. The incident served to emphasise where the balance of power resided in the English game – if anyone had ever been in any doubt. Albert would have watched and learned.

The match was a low-scoring affair on what started out as a soft pitch, and England's 145 in the first innings proved decisive. The English bowlers Hearne and Peel were among the wickets as Australia were all out for 44 in the second innings, and England won by 66 runs.

Although Australia had lost the series, it had been a happier tour for them after the discord of 1893. Harry Trott had led the team well, and his ability as a captain had impressed the host country. According to *The Times*, 'Mr Trott placed his field with remarkable judgement; indeed he is a most excellent captain of a very good side.' Off the field, he had handled the social side with aplomb, dining with the cricket-loving Prince of Wales, Lord Sheffield and Ranjitsinhji in the royal pavilion. One thing he hadn't managed to do, though, was to get his younger brother on to the tour and into the team. There had been some opportunities. Harry Graham had never really got going, and Eady the fast bowler, brought in on Giffen's insistence, had achieved little, writing home to say, 'I am having a great time, but not from a cricket point of view, for I have long since branded myself as a fraud.' But, once the tour had started, it would have been disruptive to bring in someone else, when it was being run on the basis of an equal share of the profits for all players. Harry may also have been mindful of the experience of George Giffen when he had shown a preference for his brother Walter. Never one to ruffle feathers unnecessarily, Harry had sacrificed familial ties in the interests of team unity.

Would Albert have made much difference if he had played? One of his staunchest advocates was Archie MacLaren, who expected Albert to do well playing for Middlesex in England. 'It was a great mistake to have left him out of the last Australian Eleven. I believe that if he had been playing in that great Test match at the Oval when England won by 66 runs the victory would have rested with the other side.' It was a small crumb of comfort for Albert from the great batsman.

* * *

Geniality was one of the most prized virtues of the age and one that ran through Harry and Albert, a disposition perhaps inherited from their father, Adolphus. In September, Harry went off to America for the final stage of the tour, from Philadelphia to San Francisco, as they mopped up the best of what the continent had to offer. The idea, mooted a few years previously, that the Australian cricketers should play a few games of baseball in North America after the tour of England, had been put to one side. Someone asked Harry, 'Why don't you play baseball?' His reply came quickly: 'Running around in circles makes us dizzy.'

The same month, Albert left England for Australia, returning with Jack Harry on board the *Oruba*. When the boat docked at Adelaide, 'Point' of the *South Australian Register* was one of the local reporters who clambered aboard and woke up the two cricketers. While Jack Harry, the former miner, sniffed the air and said how much he loved the climate of Adelaide, it was the younger Albert who was the more talkative of the two. He claimed to feel out of sorts, but Point observed that he was as buoyant and genial as ever, 'tanned by sea breezes', as he told how he had won 16 sports competitions on board. There was a sense of excitement at his return to his own country, but at the same time he was pleased with what he had accomplished in England as he recounted his high scores and improvement in form, and talked of how he would have liked to play some first-class cricket in August. He talked openly of the financial rewards: 'I did the hat-trick once, and ought to have secured it in the next match, but a gallant Captain missed an easy "pot" chance which would have completed the trick. Anyhow, I didn't suffer because he dubbed up a sov from his own pocket. Oh yes, I am satisfied.'

For a man who liked to play cricket, England, with its mass of prospects, was the place to be. 'At the close of the present summer I shall return to London, and probably not come to Australia again for many years. I now have a permanent engagement at Lord's, besides which I believe I shall be able during this next English winter to secure employment as coach in South Africa, which is, of course, handier to London than Australia, and where they pay real good salaries, as the game is booming out there. By 1898 I shall be qualified by residence to play for Middlesex, and I think I shall be able to hold my own in the County Eleven, which, you know, means a fiver a match.'

In the harbourside interviews, he complimented the Australian team. As reported in *The Chronicle* of Adelaide, '"A good team," responded the young Hercules. "My word, they are hot coffee. A bold, dashing batter [like Lyons] might have turned some of the games. ... I was aching to get in and have a hit myself."' He was complimentary about the batting of brother Harry and Gregory in their stand at the Lord's Test, saying it was the best he had ever seen. There was no bitterness, no outward resentment expressed at his non-involvement in the tour – as ever, he was affable Albert Trott.

His intentions could not have been any clearer, and he was now going to abandon Australia, a path that his father had been set against earlier in the year. 'I like London. I like the people and I like the cricket ground.' Nevertheless, for someone who liked to be on the field of play, the immediate future was very much on his mind. The first thing he asked the *Chronicle* reporter was whether East Melbourne had saved a place for him in next Saturday's team.

He needn't have worried. On his return to his home city, Albert received an offer from South Melbourne and one from East Melbourne, but, in the end, along with Jack Harry, he renewed his contract with the latter. And they were pleased to have him back – in the first match, against North Melbourne, he took 7-48. What was of interest was the change in his style of bowling. No longer did he try to bowl every ball fast, Richardson-style, as had been his wont the previous season: instead he relied on breaking the ball and a command of length, with the occasional quick 'snorter' slipped in. According to *The Leader*, 'He seemed to have got it all back and a bit more thrown in, in the form of English experience.'

His innings of 37 gave him the chance to show off the new stroke in his repertoire that he had learned in London. This was a following stroke to leg, which invoked a range of responses from those who saw it from 'undeniably of English pattern' to 'a queer kind of hook shot'. Meanwhile, his hit for six out of the ground and over the gasometer brought down-to-earth approval. His first match on his return to Australian cricket seemed to be a series of cameos, a reel of highlights of the best parts of his game, put on for the benefit of the home audience. 'Look at me and what I have become,' he seemed to be saying to them.

The next weekend, though, the man who always liked to be there was missing: a swelling of the face brought on by a severe cold keeping him from bowling in the second innings. By the final weekend of the game, he recovered enough to bat and made 28. In the next couple of games, the high spot was 7-39 against Richmond in December, where his yorker proved too much for some of the batsmen. Surprisingly, there had been a few peevish murmurs that he had not yet produced a 'sensational' performance.

The first Sheffield Shield game of the season began at the end of the month. Along with Jack Harry, he was selected for Victoria against New South Wales, but he had to stand down after suddenly developing a strain in his leg. He was spotted walking around the East Melbourne ground, evidently very lame and in great pain. He said the strain had first occurred in England, but, whatever its origins, the injury was as convenient as it was conspicuous, and Albert may have been advised informally by MCC that playing in the Sheffield Shield would compromise his two-year qualification period for Middlesex. Albert's medical adviser acted swiftly, and not only ruled him out of the Sheffield Shield game but also out of all cricket for the rest of the season. This suited him, as he didn't want to jeopardise his career by being unable to fulfil his contract with MCC when he returned to England.

Australian cricket was no longer his priority, and he didn't play again that season, as the strain shifted from his leg to his groin to his side, according to which newspaper report you read. No match fees, no bowling to members in the nets: without cricket, he couldn't earn any money. Fortunately, his brother Harry used his not inconsiderable influence and steered him in the direction of a job with the Victorian Post Office. While the exact nature of his duties was unknown, they served to tide him over, and clearly his injury was not much of an impediment. By the middle of the February, he was on the mend and back in the nets, bowling a 'feeler' or two but not fully letting himself go, while his batting was free and powerful.

This new dalliance with full-time employment may have suited Albert in other ways too, freeing up his Saturdays for courting. On 24 February he married Jessie Aveletta Rice, a 21-year-old, whose parents were Catherine and James Rice, an accountant. The marriage took place at her parents' house in Cardigan Street, Carlton, a pretty terrace with a cast-iron balcony. It is not known how long the couple had been acquainted before they were married, but Jessie must have been a brave individual, for she knew that Albert was going to leave Australia for England, and she would have to make her home in a place she knew very little about.

With the important things settled, there was no need to wait for the end of the Australian season. His future lay in England. MCC congratulated Albert on his marriage and sent him £70 and first-class tickets for the new couple's journey to England. His father, Adolphus, had let everyone know how highly MCC thought of his son and what they were prepared to do for him. Albert resigned from the Post Office and travelled down to Adelaide with Jessie to watch the Sheffield Shield match between Victoria and South Australia as they waited for the *Oruba*. Jessie was at his side at the game, and a reporter commented on the difficulty of getting him away to comment on the game. 'Didn't I tell you when I came back from England that if all your cracks got going on the same day they would make a tremendous score?' he said of the South Australian innings. It was to be his final comment on the last match that he was to see on Australian soil for some time. At the end of the game, some of the Victoria players came to the docks to wave off Albert and his bride before catching the express back to Melbourne. The Prince of Jolimont was no more: he had abdicated.

9

Hard as nails

CAPTAIN CYRIL Foley of the 3rd Royal Scots was a man of the Empire who had been around and seen a thing or two. As well as playing in the successful Eton eleven that beat Winchester and Harrow, he also helped Cambridge beat Oxford three times, before participating in the Jameson Raid in 1895. This covert operation by the company troops of Cecil Rhodes was an attempt to overthrow the Boer republic of the Transvaal and bring it under British control, an objective that came with the tacit support of the Colonial Office. With 500 men and eight Maxim guns, the uprising came to grief when the soldiers cut the wires of a Boer farmer's fence instead of the telegraph wire to Pretoria. Alerted by this error, the Boers were able to mount a successful defence of their republic. Foley, along with the other insurgents, had been imprisoned in South Africa but was soon released and lionised on his return to London, where he was able to resume his cricket career, his South African exploits earning him the nickname of 'The Raider' among his teammates.

On a bitterly cold morning at Lord's in early May 1897, Foley, playing for MCC against Yorkshire, observed Albert in the slips, without a sweater, wearing a shirt washed so many times that it was thin and threadbare. One of the fielders looked up at the clouds in the sky and said, 'It looks like it's going to snow.' Albert replied, 'I wish it would. I've never seen snow before.' Albert's comment had more than a touch of the colonial innocent about it, but Foley, the slight and languid officer, who was to finish his career as a lieutenant colonel, didn't see that. Instead, his judgement on Albert Trott was that the

Australian was 'as hard as nails' – a man who didn't feel or fear the cold, a tough man by any standards.

When Albert and Jessie arrived in London, the Middlesex club advanced their new signing £50 towards the purchase of a house. The couple set up home in Willesden, a new horse-drawn tram and railway suburb, which had grown quickly in the preceding ten years, with its population shooting up by 122 per cent. Originally a middle-class residential suburb, it was gradually becoming working class in character as the Metropolitan railway bought land for sidings and workshops and built housing estates for their workers. Among their neighbours were commercial travellers, cabinet makers, clerks, printers, coal merchants – the respectable class with the wherewithal to buy a house. In the days when labour was cheap, the more prosperous of them were able to employ a live-in young or older woman to help with the heavier work, and the young Trott couple were able to do this. Willesden would have catered for the day-to-day needs of the Trott family in terms of food, household supplies and entertainment, and while there would be special shopping trips to Oxford Street and the West End, for the most part they would keep close to home, as people did. The central London theatres and music halls, different to those in Melbourne, were another pull; with a 90-minute ballet as part of the show, the part-titillation, part-folk-art performance had something for everyone. Willesden was Albert Trott's manor, the place where he belonged in London and where over the next few years he would become a well-known figure on the streets and in the clubs and pubs, fame as a cricketer and his convivial nature serving as his calling card. As he settled in, he became a member of the Willesden Green and Cricklewood Conservative Club, the Regency Club in the High Road and the Progressive Club in Church Road. The names and political affiliations of the clubs were only of a superficial importance, as the essential elements were drinking and related social activities.

Then there was the pub, whether it was a small place, barely bigger than someone's front room sitting in the middle of a terrace, or somewhere bigger with aspirations towards the grand, such as the Spotted Dog or the Crown, with its mock-Tudor gables, on the High Road. Many also had a billiards room attached, and Albert was a keen player of the game. The pub was interwoven with every aspect of day-to-day life. It was possible to live a life without it in a working-class district at this time, but for many it featured to a significant degree.

In February 1895, Albert had been described in a newspaper interview as a teetotaller, but this had not lasted and he had taken up drinking to accompany his heavy smoking. His brother Harry had commented on 'his tobacco use, saying that 'our young 'un would smoke anything'

It was usual for people to live near their place of work. For Albert, the advantage of Willesden was its proximity to Lord's, three miles north, within walking distance but with the alternative of trams and trains. Willesden became his home in London, and he fitted in very quickly. In the Australian newspapers of this period, it was still customary to refer to England as 'home', presumably because many of the original settlers had been born in England, and there are many references to Albert 'going home to play' as if Australia was a temporary residence. Today this mindset seems illogical, but in late-Victorian England it may have helped him to settle in London – and, after all, he was half-English, his mother born in Sussex. He was certainly not short of company from Melbourne. Jim Phillips came over to England soon after the Trotts, another leg of the 250,000-mile journey over his last ten years of permanent summers – sporting goods in his luggage, his umpiring and cricketing skills available for hire. The only thing that had temporarily halted his back-and-forth progress in these years was the illness and subsequent death of his wife. Jack Harry did not return to Lord's for the 1897 season, but Phillips had recruited two more players from the Melbourne Cricket Club and the Victorian team for MCC: James O'Halloran, an all-rounder, and Micky Roche, an off-spinner. The latter had lost three fingers of his right hand, but the compensatory strength he had developed in the remaining two fingers enabled him to gain extra purchase on the ball and significant turn. The plan was the usual one: they would qualify for Middlesex while employed on the ground staff of MCC. That summer, Roche even turned out for a House of Commons and Lords XI.

The exodus of sporting talent from Melbourne was not confined to cricketers. In 1896, during the American leg of the Australia cricket tour, Mr Harry Musgrove had made preliminary enquiries about the feasibility of an Australian baseball tour of America. As long as the Victorians could 'put up a fair game of ball', it was fine by their American hosts. Frank Laver, the East Melbourne man, and William Bruce were two of the leading cricketers involved, and the Australian press commented on the need to pay their cricket professionals more if they were not to lose them to other countries or sports. The press need not have worried, for the tour was a disaster from the start. Musgrove went on ahead to San Francisco to make initial arrangements, but then cabled Melbourne to say that the prospects were not good and the trip should be abandoned. The players met and voted and decided to still go ahead, having already made arrangements with their employers. In their first game, in San Francisco, they were not just beaten but outclassed. 'The Australians cannot play baseball,' said the *Australian Star* of Sydney. 'They go in to bat as if they were playing cricket.'

Many reasons were offered for the tour's failure, including takings being pilfered at the gate, a dressing room being robbed, arms becoming ricked from throwing the ball, unfair umpires and a shortage of matches arranged or played. The team travelled on to London in an attempt to recoup their losses. Here the tour was abandoned, after an audit by Laver and the other players revealed a shortfall of £110 in the accounts, and they also announced that Musgrove could not be found. They won the final game against an English team of sorts at Crystal Palace, but Musgrove's failure to promote the game meant that few attended. Stranded, penniless and without return tickets, they resorted to cabling home for money. It was here that the Australian cricketers in London rallied round their compatriots: Laver and Stuckey went to Lord's, where they met Albert and Micky Roche and told them what had happened. Charlie Over, one of the players, had no one in Australia who could cable him money, but luckily help was at hand, 'At Albert Trott's place I met Roche and O'Halloran, the two Victorian cricketers. Mr and Mrs Albert Trott and Laver were very kind to me and they helped me.'

After watching the chaotic events unfold, Albert probably felt glad that he had the security of his contract with MCC in London. Laver and some other members of the baseball team watched him play for an MCC team that included the other two Australian pros. In this game against Hertfordshire, he hit 72 and took 13 wickets. Settled in and growing accustomed to English conditions, his season had gone well from the start, including a sound and quick 62 with the bat against Yorkshire before a deluge of wickets: ten in the Essex game, 12 against Notts Castle, 13 versus Worcestershire and 14 in the Cambridgeshire game. At the end of August, he grabbed all ten wickets in the Oxfordshire first innings, nine of them without the help of any other player: six bowled, two lbw and a caught-and-bowled; and it comes as no surprise that his return included a hat-trick. He became known as one of the best all-round men in England, but it was his bowling that was dominant at this point. Once he had a psychological hold on a team, they seemed to crumble before him, confirming the reputation that had gone before him.

In August, Arthur Conan Doyle looked forward to his arrival at Eastbourne. 'We are playing the MCC today. Albert Trott is coming down so we will have some good bowling against us.' Conan Doyle was one of Albert's victims that day, and in future years they would come across each other at Lord's, where the author was a member of MCC. Albert never shunned these lesser games. MCC liked to win these minor matches, and often the team was made up of amateur club members, supplemented by one or two professionals. In one match, they lost badly, and Albert was mocked by the opposition and asked to give his true opinion of the team MCC had put out. He replied, 'Well, our eleven consisted of four has-beens, six never was-ers and Albert Trott.'

It didn't stop him playing. At the end of the season, he turned out for G.F. Hearne's XI when they played an Ealing Dean XV, scoring 73 out of a total of 163 and grabbing 11 of the 14 wickets. The people who came to see the game expected nothing less of him. And for the players too, there was plenty of foolery and fun in these club games.

It was around this time, and it may have been in this game, that the story was first told of the local club professional who expressed the opinion that Albert was one of the worst ever bowlers to gain a reputation. When the professional came out to bat, he was handed a small piece of folded paper and asked not to read it until after his innings. He didn't have to wait very long to satisfy his curiosity. The first delivery hit him on the body, to the unchecked amusement of the field; the second he hit at with vigour, but missed, and the field guffawed again; the third delivery clean bowled him, and this time everyone roared with laughter. When he returned to the privacy of the pavilion, it all became clear. The note read: 'Trott wins five pounds if he hits you with the first ball, makes you miss the second and bowls you with the third. Is he a good bowler?'

In the first-class game, Albert took 50 wickets and topped the first-class bowling averages, but in other fixtures his tally overall was 300 wickets in all matches for MCC, nearly half of them at Lord's. While some of the opposition was not of the highest standard – the first-class fixture list of MCC was not extensive – it was still an impressive glut of wickets, which had earned him a place in the prestigious North versus South match at the end of the season. In a match ruined by bad weather, he had both of the North's openers caught behind before rain ended the match prematurely. He must have wanted it to go on, so good was his form with the ball. The Middlesex club congratulated themselves on securing the services of a bowler so far above the common run, and in the next season he would be qualified to play for them in the County Championship. When news of his exploits reached Australia, more than one newspaper expressed regret that his non-selection in 1896 had forced him to leave for England in order to use his talents.

But the question arose: what was he going to do over the winter? Albert had renounced Australia, for in the colonies' newspapers he was described as 'the ex-Australian cricketer', so there was no question of him going home and playing in a Test series. In the 1890s, it was relatively straightforward for a successful English pro to find work in South Africa, where the Surrey bowler George Lohmann had paved the way. Albert's plan when he first came to England had been to coach out there, but, by August, O'Halloran had secured a coaching position at Port Elizabeth, while Albert had yet to sign up for any South African club. An unexpected offer had arrived from Middlesex, who were so pleased with his form that they offered to pay him to take a rest in London over the winter. They were not short of money, with investments in government bonds and an ample amount of money in the bank – £1,682 – after all expenses had been met. As well as the £50 they had advanced Albert for his house purchase, they had given him £40 towards his fare, which was in addition to the money paid to him by MCC. When we compare this with the money paid by Middlesex to the other professionals – Jack Hearne £50, John Rawlin £25 and Jim Phillips £15 – we can measure the esteem in which he was held by the county club. And he had yet to play for them.

At first, he considered Middlesex's offer of a winter break, as it would mean he could remain with the pregnant Jessie in their new house – but the idea of rest didn't appeal to someone who loved playing cricket. In September, it was announced that he had been engaged by the Pretoria club in the Transvaal for five months, at a salary of £30 a month plus expenses. It was excellent money, too good to turn down.

In September, A.E. Stoddart left for Australia with a team that included Ranjitsinhji and Albert's teammate Jack Hearne of MCC and Middlesex, for the Test series in Australia. At St Pancras station, Albert, O'Halloran and Roche joined the party that waved them off on the train. Jim Phillips was also leaving to umpire the series, and it may have been the fellow Victorian they were wishing a good journey –

the man who had set them up and done so much for them in England.

Albert's winter employment in Pretoria raised some interesting questions. While South Africa encouraged English cricketers to come to the country to raise standards of play, the welcome was restricted to those with white skin. Bernard Tancred, writing in *Cricket* in 1897, spoke of the omission of the black fast bowler 'Krom' Hendricks from the 1894 South African team that toured England: 'Hendricks is a good fast bowler, but in the opinion of the great majority of South African cricketers it would not be advisable to send him, on account of the colour question, which in England you no doubt find difficult to understand.'

Hendricks, described by the English tourists of 1892 as one of the fastest bowlers they had ever seen, was of mixed race, a Cape Malay. He never played for the South African national team, and eventually he was also removed from the Western Province team. Subsequently, segregation in South African cricket had become more ingrained. Albert would have been aware of this before he went to South Africa, but how much did he know of his own mixed-race antecedents? His father had arrived in Australia 40 years previously with his grandmother Elizabeth McGilvray, daughter of an African slave. He either didn't think about it for a moment or suppressed any thoughts that slipped into his consciousness. There are no direct or indirect written references to his black ancestry, so a silence was maintained, and for all intents and purposes he was of white, English ancestry.

Albert took his good form to the Transvaal representing Pretoria, and he adapted his game to the matting wickets where the surface of the ball became rough and worn on the South African outfields, enabling him to get more work on the ball. The variations in the quality of the matting wickets, some stretched tighter than others, some attracting dust and dirt, worked to the benefit of the bowler, and creases in the wicket offered extra turn. Certainly, that was the view of a batsman like Plum Warner after he was out for a low score. Later, Albert was to say that he preferred bowling on a good matting wicket rather than a hard, true grass wicket. It comes as no surprise when one looks at his returns with the ball. Playing for Pretoria against the Wanderers Club, which included George Lohmann, he took all ten wickets for 22 runs in one innings and scored 59 runs out of 165. In another match, he took nine wickets for eight runs.

In February 1898, he was to play with the man who wrote the article in *Cricket*, Bernard Tancred, along with his brother Vincent, for Pretoria against A. Bailey's Transvaal XI. The latter included George Lohmann, in an attempt to ensure that the teams were of equal strength. The purpose of the game was to provide a benefit for Albert as a reward for his services in the Transvaal. He took 5-84 in his 38 overs, and top-scored in the Pretoria innings with 22 as they were all out for 64.

But, while he picked up these wickets in these lesser club games, he followed the news from Australia on the progress of the Test series and the form of his old teammates, as well as the new ones he had acquired in England. George Giffen was no longer in the Test team, although he lurked in the background as a disgruntled presence. After not being offered enough money to play by Major Wardill of the Melbourne Cricket Club, the 'cantankerous and disloyal South Australian' refused to play against the English touring team. At first, with more than a touch of pique, he announced his retirement from all first-class cricket, but he then 'backed down and condescended to play for South Australia against Victoria'. *The Age* had it right when it said of the Test side, 'It is very certain that *esprit de corps* with Giffen in the team would now be an impossibility.' In the end, he had dropped himself from the team, and now that he had finally departed the Australians had *esprit de corps* in abundance under the leadership of Harry Trott.

And they needed it. In the first Test, they were comprehensively beaten as England won by nine wickets, with Ranjitsinhji making 175. However, the host team came together and won the next four Tests by significant margins. It was Harry Trott's finest hour, and the culmination of his career, in that he led the team to success after the previous four disappointing Test series, where the team had lost their way for a variety of reasons. Now there was plenty to celebrate, as it was only the second time Australia had won a series in the last 13 attempts, such had been the dominance of England. Melbourne's *Punch* summed it up with a cartoon of a contented Harry carrying away an outsize urn, marked 'The Ashes', from a sad and tired group of English cricketers sitting under a weeping willow tree of cricket bats with depressed faces. A sweet moment indeed for Australian cricket.

Albert was outside all of this. It would have been strange if he had not asked the question, of himself if not out loud: why aren't I playing? It's my country, my brother is captain, I have played with these men. In reading the match reports, he would have noted the emergence of a new, young all-rounder for Australia who made his debut in the second Test at Melbourne: one Monty Noble, who took

6-49 to finish off England as they lost by an innings. In *The Argus*, the reporter identified one of the reasons for the young Australian's success: 'Noble appears to have cultivated the knack of making the balls swerve in the air, a trick Albert Trott excelled in when he left Australia, learned from pitching curves in baseball.'

Monty Noble had not just taken his place in the team, but his trickeries too. It was another sensational debut by a young player that was to turn the series, and, what was more, Monty Noble was the same age as Albert. Three years earlier, Albert had been playing for Australia against Stoddart's men in a Test match, while Noble had been playing for the 18 Sydney Juniors against the touring team. How things had changed. With every Test series in which Albert didn't play, he moved further away from the Australian Test team and the prospect of any reappearance grew less likely.

There were other changes too, for when he returned home from South Africa to Willesden he saw his daughter, Jessie Annie Trott, for the first time. She had been delivered at home at Balmoral Road on Christmas Day.

* * *

In England, at the start of the 1898 season, Albert had a chance to show what he could do, now that he was qualified to play for Middlesex. However, the County Championship season began slowly and Middlesex's first game was not until 30 May, so he played for MCC in their opening game of the season against Sussex at Lord's. He hit a vigorous 41, and then, bowling in tandem with Jack Hearne, the pair of them routed Sussex in both innings. Much had been expected of the bowling partnership of the two men, and it was anticipated that Middlesex would be one of the very best teams in the County Championship. J.T. 'Old Jack' Hearne was six years older than Albert, and was experienced at bowling at Lord's, having played for Middlesex since 1890. He was good enough to play for England too, and in 1898 he had just returned from Stoddart's tour of Australia. Tall and lithe, he was around medium pace, varying his speed, bowling an occasional off-spinner, and phenomenally accurate. Having two quality bowlers on at the same time made things easier and brought an added dividend of wickets, complementing each other rather than being rivals. Gentle and kindly by nature, Jack Hearne was well disposed towards Albert, and, as fellow pros, they spent a great deal of time together, in the pavilion and when they travelled to away matches.

Another early-season fixture was against Cambridge University at Fenner's, where he played for C.I. Thornton's XI. This time, he opened the bowling with his old nemesis, the hard-drinking Tom Richardson. Back at Lord's, playing against Yorkshire, Albert took 6-96 for MCC, with Jack Hearne bowling at the other end, and he made an impression on Lord Hawke when he bowled him. Then it was to the Parks against Oxford University, where he played for A.J. Webbe's XI and bowled 58 overs in the second innings to Jack Hearne's 61, taking 5-135 – the professionals demonstrating that it was their job to do the bulk of the work, while the amateur C. Heseltine helped out with 12 overs. This came after a first innings in which the two professionals had bowled 64 overs between them, virtually unchanged. Although this was at only five balls an over, it was still a significant amount. They didn't complain, or even comment on it, because it was what they were paid to do, and while neither of them bowled consistently quick, their workload seems heavy by modern standards, where rest and rotation are the two oft-repeated bywords. It was probably spells like these that finally put a stop to Albert toying with the role of full-time fast bowler.

Finally, after the two-year qualification period, everyone's patience was rewarded when Albert made his debut for Middlesex. It was against Cambridge University at Fenner's, a ground that he knew well in this, his third season in England. A.J. Webbe and Plum Warner were playing for Middlesex, and Gregor MacGregor, who at times had a reputation for irascibility, was the wicketkeeper-captain. MacGregor had lost the toss, so they were in the field in the wet and chill. Albert had been hit a little by Cuthbert Burnup, the Cambridge batsman, who had sent him three times to the boundary, but he came back later and picked up a couple of wickets. By the afternoon, with the rain coming down, he was back in the professionals' pavilion along with the other pros. Jack Hearne, John Rawlin, a fast-medium bowler from Yorkshire, and Jim Phillips – as a player rather than an umpire on this occasion – were all there. Cricket can be an unkind game to play in an English May. No doubt his head ached from too many cigarettes smoked and he had drunk some beer with his lunch, and he was restless before play was abandoned for the day at 4.30. What happened next was to have consequences for the rest of the season.

At some point – and it was reported to be that Thursday afternoon – he cut his right hand so severely that he was not only out of this game, neither batting nor bowling again in the game at Cambridge, but also for the coming weeks. The cut was made with a table knife, it was widely reported in the newspapers. No other explanation or comment appeared in the public domain on the specific events that had led to the cut, other than that he had been unlucky. One thing is certain: it is quite difficult to cut yourself with a table knife accidentally. The only way it could happen is if you were playing a game with someone else, perhaps involving how quickly you could move your hand across the table, and you received an accidental stab. Perhaps it didn't involve a table knife at all. Perhaps the severe cut was sustained by a combination of excessive drink and broken glass. These things have been known to happen. Whatever the actual events, they were likely to have happened in the evening rather than in the dressing room. The chance of there being dangerous horseplay with men such as Jim Phillips and Jack Hearne around seems unlikely.

It can be very easy to gain the wrong impression of the life of the professional during the last decade of the nineteenth century and up until the First World War. Certainly, there were hard-drinking men such as Bobby Peel, fond of a couple of gin and waters before a game, so drunk in Australia that he had to be put under the shower before he could bowl; and then, in a county match, so drunk he bowled a ball in the wrong direction. These are examples of extreme behaviour. Lord Hawke, the Yorkshire captain and president, the man who sacked Peel for his drinking, believed that the life of the professional could be hard. In a speech in Yorkshire, reported in *Cricket,* Lord Hawke commented on the physical demands put on the professional, and on how this was not appreciated by members of Hawke's social class. He said that the professional did not have a servant to throw a coat around his shoulders after a chilly early-morning shooting session. What was more, the professional did not have the same range of footwear as the amateur for dealing with the wet of the spring and the damp of the autumn, and therefore was much more prone to respiratory diseases. Hawke meant well, but the inference that can be drawn from his speech was that it wasn't surprising that so many of the professionals found comfort in drinking.

Not all of them did. In the Middlesex professionals' pavilion, order prevailed, with the successful businessman Jim Phillips and the steady presence of the senior and long-serving professional 'Tireless' Jack Hearne. Every evening, he would sit at the head of the table at dinner and carve the joint of meat, hand round the plates in order of seniority and give himself the carver's portion last of all. When the players stayed together in a hotel at an away game, he would take his gold watch from his waistcoat pocket and check that the other professionals arrived on time for breakfast washed, shaved and on parade. If a player was absent, someone would be sent up to his room to fetch him. Table manners, social order – the outward values of the professional dressing room mirrored those of the amateurs. Hearne enjoyed a practical joke and a game of cards – a friendly one, not those that cleaned out a raw youngster of his cash. He enjoyed a drink, but not to excess. Later in life, he would develop a taste for cocktails, and would order six or seven at dinner at a country house cricket match, but he would only ever drink the first one, confining himself to eating the cherry off the others. As senior professional, the respectable Jack Hearne was above Albert in the dressing room hierarchy.

As for Albert's injury, the cricket correspondent of the *Pall Mall Gazette* tried to coat the incident with a positive glow. 'The rest will not do Trott any harm, for the MCC have been working him pretty well lately, and if he is to be any good to Middlesex this season he required a rest.'

For the county team of Middlesex, though, his absence was a nuisance. They had paid him and waited for him to qualify, and now he was out of the game for some time. In his place they brought in a local lad, the medium-pacer Sidney Webb. But it wasn't satisfactory, for without Albert they fared poorly in their next four County Championship matches at Lord's, failing to win a game, as they drew with the erratic Somerset and Nottinghamshire and lost to Gloucestershire and Yorkshire, the latter by an innings. Stoddart, back from Australia, helped out with the bowling, along with another amateur, Bromley-Davenport. For Albert too, not playing meant foregoing match fees and talent money, so he was as anxious as the club to get back to full-time playing. In the last week of June, when he at last made his County Championship debut against Surrey at the Oval, he was far from fully fit and lacking in match practice. The fixture between the two London teams brought out a large crowd of 8,000. He was brought on as first change, and it was immediately apparent that he had come back too soon as he took punishment from Brockwell and Abel, on a perfect Oval wicket, not the one to choose for a comeback game. He managed a solitary maiden and one wicket as he went for 108 runs in his 26 overs, with Surrey running up 468. The *Pall Mall Gazette*, among others, was blunt about his performance: 'His bowling yesterday was probably the worst that has been seen in a first-class match for a long time.'

When it came to the Middlesex batting, the amateurs held down the top spots and he was never going to bat high in the order, as he had grown used to doing for MCC. Later in the game, though, batting at eight, he did well, in a hard-hitting innings interrupted by rain, to joint top-score with 45 in as many minutes, including eight fours. It was consolation of a kind as the rain terminated the game early.

Over the next two games, away at Manchester and Leicester, he didn't open the bowling but came on later, as he gradually regained what he had lost during his month's enforced inactivity. He also took great care to ensure that he remained free of further accidental injury. Against Sussex at Lord's he found the form he had been looking for, as he carried all before him and took 5-18 off 5.3 overs, and then in the second innings he took 6-72, winning the game for his county. His August began with 11 wickets at Taunton against Somerset, the partnership with Jack Hearne now in full flow; then came nine wickets against Surrey as Middlesex turned over their rivals in the return fixture. His bowling was that of a 'true Australian' said the *Daily News,* and as usual it was the variety of pace and 'a yorker with a certainty that recalls George Palmer' that did for the batsman.

It was the turn of his batting to come to the fore at Lord's, when he feasted on a tiring Leicestershire attack and, his power aiding his luck, he hit 76 in 45 minutes, including a drive off Woodcock into the pavilion seats. At times like this he would say, 'There's plenty of room in the air, Guvnor.' When he bowled, 11 Leicestershire wickets came his way; and he must have taken particular pleasure in bowling Marriott, the Cambridge player who had complained about his fast bowling two years earlier.

Middlesex were the form team in the County Championship, and on 15 August they played Yorkshire, the team at the top of the table, at Headingley. In a low-scoring match, Middlesex were behind on the first innings, and, although there had been rain followed by sun, Tunnicliffe, in Yorkshire's second innings, showed that it was possible to make runs. However, Albert was at his very best. 'Trott is said to be able to make the ball curl in the air,' said the *Nottinghamshire Guardian* as Albert bowled them out with a return of 7-13. The last five wickets came in five overs, and he didn't concede a run. The 10,000 Yorkshire spectators generously applauded Albert and the Middlesex team off the field.

With the defeat of the team at the top of the table, the last few matches of the County Championship had suddenly acquired a new interest. Middlesex had to keep on winning. At Trent Bridge against Nottinghamshire, they did so by an innings. Albert sent down a mammoth 80 overs, picked up 13 wickets and scored 77 batting at eight. It was here that he took the wicket of Arthur Shrewsbury in both innings, the man rated so highly by W.G. Grace and one of the most difficult batsmen to dismiss. Apparently, Shrewsbury knew nothing about the ball that bowled him in the first innings. And on it went, as an unstoppable Middlesex comfortably won their last three matches with Jack Hearne and Albert picking up most of the wickets. He had taken 102 wickets in the County Championship that season, and he had not really started playing until the end of June. Middlesex couldn't have done more to win the championship in August, but in the end Yorkshire held on. The moot question was whether Middlesex would have taken the title had Albert not been injured in the first game.

With the competitive cricket over, Albert, always ready for some end-of-season fun with friends, turned out for the Cross Arrows, the club for Middlesex staff, against Cockfosters, and hit 207 not out – a club record for more than 100 years. When they played Haringey, he took seven wickets, but asked not to bowl in the second innings and instead kept wicket, where he made three stumpings.

For the forthcoming winter, the question of a rest did not arise. Lord Hawke, one of his victims at Headingley, asked him to tour South Africa as part of a team representing England. His cricketing stock could not have been higher.

10

'It's a funny thing'

I N DECEMBER 1898, Albert appeared at Harlesden Magistrates' Court, in front of Mr Bird, on a charge of disorderly conduct. The *Illustrated Police News* reporter didn't mince words and described Albert as 'the prisoner', noting that, 'The prisoner looked well-dressed but older than twenty-five.' The reporter's description is borne out by the photographs of Albert at this period and shortly after, where his face is fuller, the complexion coarser, but he's better groomed and he liked his well-cut clothes.

Two years in London, leading a different life, had changed his appearance, and now the teetotaller, the wondrous skinny colt, the Prince of Jolimont had disappeared. Police Sergeant Billings had seen Albert and 25 or 30 other men walking along Walm Lane, Willesden at 12.30am after a Saturday night out. Walm Lane was a ten-minute walk away from Albert's house at 45 Balmoral Road, but it was not known whether he was gradually making his way home from the pub or on his way to somewhere else in the company of others. The men were walking four or five abreast and making a great noise. When the policeman asked them to go quietly, they did for a few yards but then started to make a noise again. Sergeant Billings went after them and 'the prisoner became sarcastic', marched between the witness and another sergeant, and pushed them with his shoulders. He had been drinking but was not drunk.

"'What have you to say?" said Mr Bird.

"'I am very sorry," said the prisoner.

"'It's a funny thing for a man in your station to find yourself in this position. You are bound over in the sum of 20s to be of good behaviour for six months.'"

In mitigation? There was no mitigation: this was London in 1898, where mitigation did not exist. To excuse, to give reasons, to blame others or to put your side of the story was to show a sign of weakness and run the risk of mockery. Albert had said the bare minimum: all he wanted was to get out of the court as quickly as possible, and doubtless Mr Bird also wanted the matter dealt with swiftly. As far as the magistrate was concerned, a man of Albert's social position shouldn't be doing things like that on the street.

As we know, people deal with difficulties in life in different ways, from confronting things head on, to denial, to sublimation. While Albert had been taking all of those wickets for Middlesex over the summer, his mother, Mary Ann, had been ill. Not just ill, but seriously ill, and her condition was of great concern to all of the family, including brother Harry. On 8 August, Harry visited Mary and Adolphus in the Melbourne suburb of Doncaster with his wife, Violet. When Adolphus left the house to go to a meeting, Harry slumped in his chair for a while and held his head in his hands, not speaking a word. Violet asked him what was wrong, but he writhed out of his chair, collapsed on the floor and started to roll around. Violet was at a loss. However, after several minutes had elapsed, he recovered of his own accord. He responded to questions and announced he felt well enough to take the train home.

Violet thought all would be well, and they caught the train to South Melbourne. After a few minutes, though, the fit reoccurred and he ended up on the floor of the train, seemingly without control of his limbs. Such was the violence of the fit that a large space in the carriage had to be cleared around him, but, with the help of others, Violet managed to get him safely home. Violet called out Dr Thomson, but when he examined Harry he suffered another fit and the doctor had to restrain him as best he could.

The newspaper reports optimistically spoke of Harry being on the road to recovery, but, for the next four weeks, he took no interest in the world around him, barely seeming to recognise Violet or his son and saying little. He was not getting any better and, although the fits were described as epileptic, the cause was more likely to be an underlying anxiety.

It was not entirely unexpected. There had been concerns about Harry's health in the preceding months: he'd lost weight and appeared run-down. Earlier in the year he suffered heatstroke on the cricket field and went blind for a period of time. In the Melbourne Test, a worried Violet had sent a lemon on to the field for him as he was batting in the heat. Then there was the time when instead of fielding, he took a glass of ale and joined the crowd, pretending that he wasn't playing in the match. When it happened, people assumed that it was a joke, but it may have been indicative of something else.

After leading Australia to victory in the Ashes series, Harry had also been forced into more of a public role. In discussions with the Australian Cricket Council, he had represented the players' views and acted as their spokesman in his honest way. He had recommended that the Victorian Cricket Association should withdraw from the Australian Cricket Council, but there had been rumours emanating from the council that his own financial advantage influenced his opinion. There had also been other pressures on Harry, for he had become a member of the Australian Natives' Association, who strongly advocated federation of the colonies. He had become a national figure, in the spotlight with its attendant pressures, and this may have been too much for this, the most obliging of men. For years he had avoided the captaincy on the grounds that Giffen wanted the job, but it may have been that Harry did not feel entirely at ease, and preferred to influence things from second in command.

His health did not improve at home, so he travelled with Harry Graham and a nurse to the town of Woodend for a two-week break to recuperate in the peace and fresh air. There was no question of him returning to work at the Post Office or playing cricket, so a public testimonial was started with a donation of £25 from the Victorian Cricketers' Association, and Mr George Moir added five guineas from his own pocket. People were anxious, as Harry was one of the most liked and popular men in Australia. A North Sydney reader of *The Referee* wondered if these things might run in the family and contacted the paper's resident expert to enquire if Albert had suffered any epileptic fits while playing in England.

It was a matter of public concern, but, powerless to help, and with a visit out of the question, Albert had been playing cricket on the other side of the world while this was going on and his brother Harry's illness was widely reported in the English newspapers.

The news of Albert's court appearance had been syndicated across the English newspapers, and by January it had made its way into the Australian press. Some reported it as coldly and starkly as their

English counterparts, while one took a more jocular approach about Albert Trott appearing before the beak. With the incident so widely known, it couldn't have helped at a difficult time for the Trott family in Melbourne.

As for Albert, his court appearance left him hovering on the threshold of a slightly different world, beyond the suburban respectability of Balmoral Road. Other cases reported in the same jaunty style in that particular edition of the *Illustrated Police News* included the man who had not slept in a bed for nine years who was charged with sleeping under sacks in Hackney Marshes.

A further news item in the *Illustrated Police News* ran as follows: 'In an inquest on an infant the mother mentioned that she had 15 children. The coroner said, "I can't understand how you poor people in the East End who are always complaining about such small wages, manage to keep such large families."

'One of the jurors replied, "Oh they're company for one another; the more the merrier. They're not so particular about here; one eats what the others leave." (Laughter)

'The Coroner: "Oh that's it, is it? It's just as well to know these things."'

No doubt in private, among friends, Albert was able to laugh off the court appearance and rue his bad luck at being prosecuted. But the event was a warning of what could happen if you slipped out of your social position and behaved in the wrong way in public – a glimpse of the harsh and unforgiving world that waited below. There was no formal reprimand from MCC for Albert, and no doubt he was fortunate in that the incident had taken place out of season and far away from the cricket field.

* * *

A few days after his court appearance, on Saturday, 3 December at around five o'clock, Albert left Southampton on board the steamer *Scot* with Lord Hawke's team, bound for South Africa. James Logan of Matjiesfontein, a self-made man who had grown wealthy through wholesale wine and spirits and a dubiously awarded contract for railway refreshment rooms, had financed the tour. An associate of Cecil Rhodes, and an ardent supporter of cricket, he saw the game as a means of bringing the whites of the country together as well as renewing the link between the colonies and the mother country. It was in the same vein as the conservative *Blackwood's Magazine* claim in

1892 that 'the Englishman carries his cricket bat with him as naturally as his gun-case and his India-rubber bath'. It was cricket as the imperial game, the promoter of British values, and Lord Hawke was more than happy to oblige by bringing a team of a strong county standard, backed up by professional bowling, with Schofield Haigh and Willis Cuttell in addition to Albert. Plum Warner and Bromley-Davenport, who played alongside Albert in the Middlesex team, were two of the amateurs. After a smooth journey, broken only by a stop in Madeira for fresh supplies of coal, they docked at Cape Town on 20 December.

The tour was managed by the English professional George Lohmann, formerly a stockbroker's clerk and a financially literate man, who knew his worth and was a shrewd negotiator of his terms with his county, Surrey – on one occasion remarking on his travel arrangements, 'I didn't wish to travel steerage.' He had originally gone out to the Cape to aid his recovery from tuberculosis, and over several years he had played and coached, helping to raise the standard of the South African game, becoming the cricketing confidant of Logan. With his experience in Australia with English teams, he was the ideal man to run the tour, and Albert had played against him the previous year.

After the voyage and his court appearance, Albert must have been keen to get out on the field. The first opportunity was a practice game on 22 December; the first serious encounter began on Christmas Eve against 13 of Western Province. In a low-scoring game, Albert was soon among the wickets, taking 7-68 in the first innings, and the tourists made it home by 25 runs, with a crowd of over 8,000 attending on Boxing Day. The tourists had celebrated Christmas with strawberries and cream, and Lord Hawke presented to each of the professionals a silver card case, while the amateurs received 'charming silver pencils in red or blue enamel cases' from their captain. The social side of the tour was as important as what happened on the cricket field, and on New Year's Day the amateurs enjoyed a picnic at the government farm at High Constantia, before joining the professionals at the Royal Hotel for a joint celebratory dinner.

The second match of the tour was planned to be against a Western Province team bolstered by Jack Brown and other English professionals coaching in the country. Lord Hawke, however, was unhappy with this arrangement. He announced that his team's purpose on the tour was to meet and develop South African cricketers, not to play against the English professionals they knew from home, as it 'nullifies the sporting interest'. Lord Hawke got his way: the professionals didn't play, and the match was scrapped. But, in the lesser matches on the tour, England, aided by an Anglo-Australian professional, ran through the opposition, whether there were 13, 15 or 22 of them. Against a Transvaal XI he had played against the previous year, Albert took 11 wickets and hit 101 not out after centuries from Mitchell and Tyldesley. Lord Hawke saw much of Albert's knock close up, as they shared an unbroken stand of 89, with the Yorkshire man making 31 of them. Lord Hawke was impressed with Albert's batting that day, delaying the declaration until he had reached his century: 'Trott hit it all over the field.' In later years, he would have a different opinion of Albert's batting.

What was not in question was the quality of Albert's bowling, where his experience of the matting wickets the previous year helped him considerably. In the first-class games, he bowled the most overs, 254, and took 42 wickets, the most on the tour, at an average of 13.00. South African cricket was in some disarray, and nowhere was this shown more clearly than in the first Test, which was due to be played in January at Port Elizabeth. Eastern and Western Province and the Transvaal managed to fall out over the method and timing of selection for the match, resulting in its cancellation. As the *Cape Argus* put it, 'The slinging about of all sorts of insinuations, the application of boycotting, and the jealousness of some centres as against the others, are all things that leave a bad taste in the mouth.' In the replacement game against a Cape Colony XI, play was halted on the last afternoon of the match when a plague of locusts visited the ground. They must have known something.

The large crowds at the eventual first Test at the Old Wanderers, Johannesburg, enjoyed a good game and a better performance from the home side than they might have expected at the start of play. Eight of the English team made their Test debut in this game. The ninth English debutant was Albert, his selection cementing his status as an Anglo-Australian. This time there was to be no sensational debut with the bat. Going in at seven, he was run out for a duck in the first innings as England tottered to 145 all out, and by the time South Africa had completed their first innings they were 106 ahead. If it hadn't been for Plum Warner's 132 not out, carrying his bat in the second innings, the England XI would have suffered an ignominious defeat. Despite Warner's efforts, though, this still left South Africa the favourites, with the relatively small target of 132 to win. They didn't get them.

The three professionals, Haigh, Cuttell and Albert, bowled them out for 99, with Albert picking up 5-49. Albert bowled Llewellyn with a ball that sent the bail over the short slip's head. Later, a grateful Lord Hawke rewarded Warner with a gold signet ring that commemorated his innings with an inscription. Albert was doubtless rewarded with some hard cash.

Wherever they went, they travelled there slowly. Pretoria was only 40 miles from Johannesburg, but it took two-and-a-half hours by the fastest train. Lord Hawke complained that 'we were jolted in three Cape carts from Graham's Town to King William's Town'. The heat was taxing too, and Albert described fielding at Kimberley as 'like standing on a boiler'. But, wherever they played, the people wanted to see the players they had heard so much about, and Lord Hawke commented, 'We found our reputation superlative. It was even said that the smoke from Albert Trott's cigarette, broke in from the leg.'

Cricket, and in particular the overseas visits, had flourished on the back of a developing railway system, and this tour broke new ground by travelling to Bulawayo for two matches. The journey called for some fortitude, as the team left Kimberley on Friday at 9am and didn't arrive at Bulawayo until 4pm on Sunday, an excursion of 55 hours. The rudimentary carriages meant an uncomfortable journey, yet there was plenty of time for conversation about cricket. Plum Warner was to say later how he found Lohmann 'a kindred spirit' and enjoyed chatting to him. Unfortunately the air of Matjiesfontein, a favoured spot for those with weak chests, had not worked its magic on the Surrey professional. His health still poor, he did not play any serious cricket that season. When Hayes, one of the Surrey professionals playing in South Africa, saw him, he was to say, 'It was painful to see how poor Geo Lohmann had wasted away and how terribly ill he looked.' Within two years he was dead, buried at Matjiesfontein, the town of his patron, Logan.

The amateurs dined well on the last night of their stay at the Bulawayo club, on a surprisingly extensive menu in this fairly new settlement, beginning with oysters and clear turtle soup, working their way through salmon, chicken, veal cutlets, game, trifle and anchovy titbits before the strawberry cream ices. Meanwhile, the professionals went shopping for souvenirs and Warner was to write: 'One of the funniest things I have seen was Trott, Tyldesley, Haigh, Board and Cuttell boarding the train just before we left Bulawayo, armed to the teeth, like so many stage pirates, with battle axes, assegais, blunderbusses and the like. These murderous looking implements completely filled up the passage of the saloon carriage.'

After the train left Kimberley for Matjiesfontein, it was trying to negotiate an incline when the brakes failed and it slid backwards, crashing into a stationary train behind. Milligan ended up with a black eye and a cut nose, while Albert's thumb was knocked out of joint, and the train windows were smashed. However, they were still able to continue their journey with the African weapons strewn around the carriage.

The second and final Test, at Newlands in Cape Town, took place at the beginning of April. Day two, Easter Monday, attracted a record gate. The South African selectors came in for criticism when they mysteriously included two wicketkeepers, Halliwell and Prince. Hawke's XI were shot out for 92 thanks to six wickets from James Sinclair, who also scored a century. With the first innings completed, the tourists trailed by 85. A century from Tyldesley enabled England to post 330, far too many for the South Africans to chase. Haigh and Albert, operating unchanged, made the ball fizz off the matting wicket and bowled them out for 35.

South African cricket had improved since Hawke's previous tour, the Test match results getting closer, and there were passages of play where they were on top. In the coming decade, they would grow even stronger, and the visits of England teams and the coaching from English professionals enhanced the overall level of play. Lord Hawke's XI had won 15 and drawn two of their 17 matches, so they had never been seriously troubled. What seems strange in retrospect was that the games were given Test match status. While the English bowling was strong, the batting was far short of the best that could be found in county cricket. Test matches they were, though, and Albert had now joined that small group of players who had represented two countries. His ties to London and England had been cemented by his time in South Africa.

Lord Hawke rated Albert's cricketing skills, describing him as the best all-rounder in the world at that time. However, off the field, he thought he found it difficult 'to resist temptation'. In his own mind he was clear that he understood Albert, as he understood all professionals. He wrote: 'Albert Trott had quaint ways. He came to me one day and asked if he could have some money advanced to him to send to his brother in Australia. I complied, but that undoubtedly went to a bookie in Cape Town. At Johannesburg, Alberto repeated the same tactics. I answered that I would send it myself if he gave me his brother's address. I never received it.'

The money may have ended up in a bookie's pocket, or Albert may have wanted to send the money to Harry himself. Lord Hawke might not have realised that Harry Trott's illness prevented him from working and, without funds, other than a meagre pension of £51 a year, he would have to rely on the family or the generosity of others. As for Albert, he had no complaints about Lord Hawke and complimented his captain, saying he 'had no side whatsoever'.

To all outward appearances, Albert enjoyed the tour. He had the company of the professionals in the team and met up with the convivial Len Braund of Somerset, a man who was coaching out there. On the way home, his fancy dress of choice was as a Russian Orthodox priest, and on the dance floor he displayed his stylish footwork. Frank Mitchell, one of the amateurs, offered a perceptive view of Albert. This was the very same Frank Mitchell, the Cambridge University captain who had come out on the field to complain when Albert had hit Marriott at Lord's in 1896, who wrote of his teammate: 'Not everyone is gifted with the temperament, and also, may I add, the stomach of Albert Trott, to whom everything came alike, fair weather and foul, good food or no food, sleep or no sleep; it was all the same to him – an ideal professional for a tour.'

While he had been in South Africa, two significant events had taken place. The first was in January when *Wisden*'s editor, Sydney Pardon, nominated him as one of his five cricketers of the year along with Wilfred Rhodes, William Storer, Charlie Townsend and William Lockwood. This was public recognition of his success in England and proof to the world of what he had achieved since he left Australia. The second was the death of his mother, Mary Ann, in February. It had been two years since he had last seen her.

Albert Trott bowling in the 1895 Melbourne Test. (State Library of Victoria)

Albert Trott in batting pose. Exact date is unknown but this looks to be around 1895. (Getty Images)

1895 Test team. The Australian cricket team in April 1895, somewhat deflated, following their loss to England at Melbourne. Left to right back row: unidentified official, Joe Darling, Jack Lyons, William Bruce, Harry Graham, Harry Trott, Frank Iredale, unidentified official; middle row, seated: Albert Trott, George Giffen (captain), Syd Gregory; in front: Affie Jarvis and Tom McKibbin. (Getty Images)

Three generations of Trotts. Adolphus, Harry and Francis Henry Trott. After the Victoria v New South Wales match in 1895 Albert walked around the pavilion, hand in hand with his four-year-old nephew, Francis Henry, the boy repeatedly saying 'Victoria'.

MELBOURNE PUNCH. AUGUST 13, 1896

ENGLISH CRICKET.—IS IT COMING TO THIS?

[In the match Cambridge University versus M.C.C., played in England recent'y, A. E. Trott was ordered to be take off because a ball of his bumped and struck a University batsman.]

The Batsman.—"I SAY, ARE YOU SURE THAT'S A SOFT BALL? BE VERY CAREFUL HOW YOU SEND THEM IN. A FELLAH DOESN'T WANT TO BE CARRIED AWAY TO THE BALLY HOSPITAL WITH A FRACTURED SKULL, DONTCHERKNOW."

Melbourne Punch **Cartoon August 1896.** After Albert was taken off for bowling short in the match between MCC and Cambridge University, *Melbourne Punch* mocked the Cambridge batsman in a cartoon with the caption, 'I say, are you sure that's a soft ball? Be very careful how you send them in. A fellah doesn't want to be carried away to the bally hospital, dontcherknow.'

Lord's Pavilion 1898. This photo was taken before the cast iron balconies were added to the dressing rooms. The chimneys with the pots are in the centre. Albert Trott struck one of these in 1899, the ball going over the roof. (Marylebone Cricket Club Library)

1901 Players' Team Lord's. Jaunty and in funds, Albert is in the middle of the back row, with Len Braund, his convivial drinking partner, on the right-hand side of him. Photographed in the garden behind the pavilion at Lord's cricket ground before their match against the Gentlemen on 8 July 1901 are: Back row (left-right): G. Hirst, H. Carpenter, A.E. Trott, L.C. Braund, W.A.J. West (umpire). Middle row: W. Storer, T. Hayward, R. Abel, W. Lockwood, J.T. Tyldesley. Seated on ground: W. Rhodes and J. Gunn. (Getty Images)

Lord Hawke's Team Melbourne 1903. Published in *The Australasian*, March 1903. Albert is second left in the back row, in his single teapot pose that he deployed in team photographs of this period. This Australian newspaper followed the English custom of naming the players, according to their amateur or professional status. The amateurs were always called Mr. Back row (left-right): G.J. Thompson, A.E. Trott, Mr E.M. Dowson, S. Hargreaves, C. Over (umpire). Middle row: Mr P.R. Johnson, Mr T.H. Taylor, Mr P.F. Warner (capt), Mr C.J. Burnup, Mr B.J. Bosanquet. Sitting: Mr F.L. Fane, Mr J. Stanning.

Albert at Melbourne in 1903, chatting to three other cricketers. This was taken at the same time as the Lord Hawke's team photo of 1903 in Melbourne. The sideways-on view of Albert gives an indication of his extra bulk. The three Victorian players were not named in the newspaper. Published in *The Australian*.

Albert demonstrating his grip for a particular delivery. Bowling 1905. *Great Bowlers and Fielders. Their Methods at a Glance.* London, 1906. Beldam, (George W) and Fry, (Charles B). (Getty Images)

Three Professionals. Walter Mead, Albert and Jack Hearne walking out from the professionals' pavilion, June 1903. MCC v Gentlemen of Philadelphia.

Albert at point of delivery. *Great Bowlers and Fielders. Their Methods at a Glance.* London, 1906. Beldam, (George W) and Fry, (Charles B). (Getty Images)

Albert taking a slip catch. This George Beldam action shot shows his perfect balance, and his tendency to roll over after taking the catch. *Great Bowlers and Fielders. Their Methods at a Glance.* London, 1906. Beldam, (George W) and Fry, (Charles B).

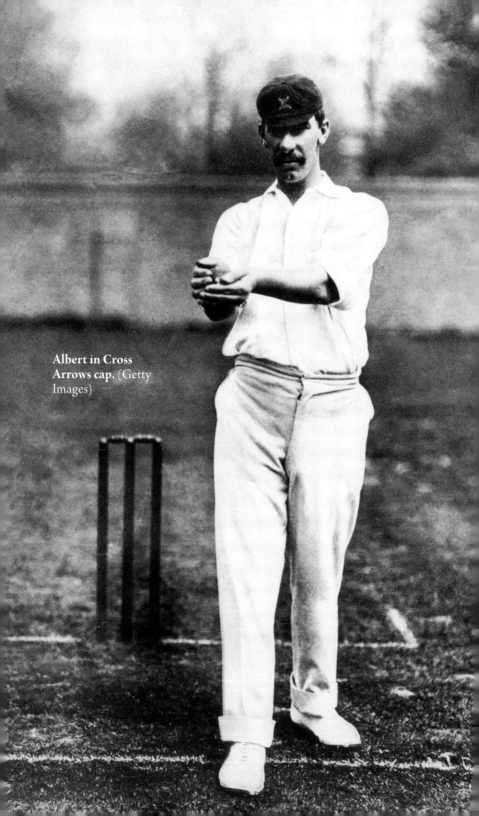

Albert in Cross Arrows cap. (Getty Images)

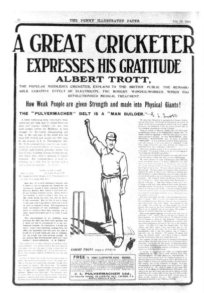

The Pulvermacher Belt. Albert's endorsement of this electrical medical product.

Albert throwing the boomerang in Regent's Park, London. Published in *The Sketch* in May 1907 after his double hat-trick in one innings in his benefit match.

Three Australian Professionals in England. W. Dwyer, Albert Trott and Frank Tarrant, the latter enjoying a cigarette.

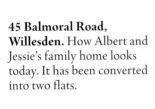

45 Balmoral Road, Willesden. How Albert and Jessie's family home looks today. It has been converted into two flats.

A. E. TROTT
1873 ~ 1914
A GREAT CRICKETER
AUSTRALIA
·
MIDDLESEX
AND
ENGLAND

Headstone Willesden Cemetery. The great cricketer. (Getty Images)

11

'We know more about his tricks'

I N 1899, the Australians toured England, wearing their green and gold for the first time, in their specially made caps and blazers, their colours commissioned by their new captain, Joe Darling. The man who had led their renaissance in the previous Test series was absent. On the day the tour started, Harry Trott was admitted to the Kew Asylum in Melbourne. Bob McLeod, a cricketing friend, oversaw the arrangements for Harry, and it was he, not Adolphus or Violet, who signed the form that admitted him to Kew. The reason given on the form for Harry's admittance was 'supposed dementia'. Harry had been withdrawn, uninterested in recent events, restless, continually moving in an aimless way, and he had made violent threats to Violet.

Despite the fits, the evidence for epilepsy is limited – they may have been seizures or bouts of episodic fainting. In Rick Smith's *Blighted Lives*, clinical psychiatrist Greg de Moore suggests that the violence and the agitation may have been alcohol related, through either heavy drinking or a withdrawal from heavy drinking, contributing to what would be described in modern terms as a 'depressive illness'. Beer to quench the thirst, spirits to pick you up, ran through the age in many ways. One Sydney advertisement asked:

IS LIFE WORTH LIVING?

All depends on the LIVER, and to have a GOOD

Liver one must drink

FOUR CROWN WHISKY

The huge Kew Asylum, built in 1871, was in the Italianate style with rounded windows, balconies and bell towers, set in extensive grounds that also included a cricket field. When they took Harry down to watch a game, though, he showed little interest. It would clearly be some time before he was well.

With Harry missing from the tour, one of Albert's remaining links to the Australian team was severed. He looked forward to doing well against them. At Lord's, in his first game of the season, for MCC against Sussex, he played with exuberance. He took 11 wickets and top-scored in each innings with 64 and 69. He hit the ball so hard that, with Foley as his partner, he scored 69 out of 77 runs in 40 minutes. He was in good form and had represented England in two Test matches in South Africa. Still, if he thought that would earn him a place in the England team against Australia, he was mistaken. As the *Morning Post* put it, 'Trott would certainly gain a place were he not Colonial born.'

Early on in the tour, he had a chance to show what he could do when he was selected for an England XI to play the Australians at Eastbourne. This was not a Test match. The team was originally intended to be a South of England XI, but, when players dropped out, replacements were shipped in from the north. It was the first time he had faced his old team on the field. From the beginning, it became apparent that there was an edge to these encounters between Albert and his country of birth, with the Australians making no attempt to disguise the fact that they did not think much of him. The tourists seemed to be saying he wasn't good enough to get into their team. At Eastbourne, he arrived in good form after taking 6-21 for MCC against Leicestershire at Lord's. On a dampish pitch, he bowled well, with Jack Hearne at the other end, and runs were few. He held a hard-hit shot from Joe Darling for a caught-and-bowled. When he dismissed Trumble, the Australians were seven down for 122. However, Ernie Jones came in at eight and had a slog. A couple of times an over, Albert looked like bowling him, and he was kept on as he tried to tempt Jones. It didn't work, and Jones made 54, not only ruining Albert's figures but also taking the Australians to a respectable 222. Albert had taken 2-105. Going in at five, he made 17 not out by the end of the day, his stand with Gunn rallying his side after the loss of early wickets. He didn't add to his score the next day, though, and Noble bowled him.

In the second innings, he picked up Joe Darling, another caught-and-bowled, but then came up against Victor Trumper, in careful mode, who played some skilful strokes on the on side, particularly to square leg. 'His cricket was of a kind which cannot be played unless a batsman has complete confidence in himself,' said *Cricket* of young Vic, a late addition to the Australian touring team. On the Friday night, the rain fell heavily and ruined the wicket. The Australians declared, and, on a surface favouring the bowlers, they bowled out the England XI in three hours. If one of the running sub-plots of the tour was Albert versus his old country, the first round had gone the way of the Australians.

It was nothing but a minor inconvenience, as Albert was confident he could do well, particularly on his new home ground of Lord's. In a County Championship match lasting three hours and five minutes in total, Middlesex disposed of Somerset on a rain-affected wicket, with Albert's match figures 11-31. The low scores were unusual, and, with Jack Hearne bowling at the other end, the pair helped each other as they developed into a formidable bowling partnership.

The weather cleared by the end of the month, and, at Lord's against Yorkshire, it was the first time Middlesex had come up against a good all-round team – one they would have to beat if they wanted to take the championship. On what was described as a faster track, Albert picked up five wickets in the first innings. When their turn came to bat, Albert came in at number seven to join Warner. He immediately gave a very difficult chance, but was dropped. It may have been this or the influence of his partner that persuaded him to bat circumspectly, and in an hour and a quarter he had made 30, a modest rate of scoring and a longish innings in terms of time by his standards. Through circumstance or design, he had played himself in. A big score was possible. He went after the Yorkshire bowling and made an attack that included four England bowlers – Rhodes, Hirst, Haigh and Wainwright – look simple and ineffective, such was the strength of his drives and the cleanness of his hitting. One of his drives off Wainwright was so powerful that it hit the pavilion seats and rebounded, the ball not stopping until it had nearly reached the wicket. In 175 minutes, he made 164. It was Wilfred Rhodes who finally got him out, and afterwards Albert was to mimic the Yorkshire pro's accent, getting it slightly wrong, saying 'Thy knows' instead of 'Tha knows'.

To make Middlesex bat again, Yorkshire had to score 285. With runs to play with, Albert wasn't afraid to mix up his deliveries, and Tunnicliffe pulled him twice, once on to the covered seats and once into the grandstand, where the ball pitched on the blinds. Both of those hits would have been worth six today. These deliveries were designed to tempt, but there were others that forced the batsman into trouble, and so his captain, Gregor MacGregor, kept him on, knowing that chances would surely come. In his 46 overs he took 4-130, and he was aided by that other Australian import, Micky Roche, who took 5-93, getting much turn on the ball, as Middlesex beat the champions by an innings.

The next time he ran across the Australians was at Lord's at the start of June, when he was selected to play for MCC. After winning the toss, the hosts batted badly and made only 245, with Albert failing to score, bowled by Charlie McLeod. After their performances with the ball on every kind of wicket that season, great things were expected of Jack Hearne and Albert. The Australians batted well, and although the pair of Middlesex bowlers picked up three wickets apiece, Albert went for three an over and the Australians finished over a hundred ahead. His further contributions to the game were slight, and the tourists easily sealed the game, winning by eight wickets. There was some dissatisfaction with the shortcomings of MCC in the field, with the *Bristol Mercury and Daily Post* complaining that W.G. Grace had not handled his bowlers very well, but there was also a recognition that this was a very strong Australian team that, up until then, had lost only one game on the tour.

By the time he played the Australians at Lord's for MCC on 31 July, the game in which he made his big hit over the pavilion, the tourists held a lead in the series, having won one and drawn three of the Tests. The irony about Albert's appearance in that game was that he only played when one of the other bowlers cried off: originally he was selected as a reserve. When he came off the field after the end of the innings in which he had cleared the pavilion, the *Daily News* said that men were dancing all over the place and even the ladies shouted out their congratulations. His only regret was that he had not scored a century. The author portrays him as a backwoodsman with a too-firm handshake and a rolling walk, and as a giant who, when he was not playing, was forever skylarking without a dull care, building up a picture of 'a real colonial type'.

Monty Noble, the man who had bowled the delivery that had been hit over the pavilion, didn't see himself as the unfortunate bowler. He was later to say that when you looked at the height of the pavilion, it was difficult to believe that someone had hit the ball that far, but as

Albert had been caught at third man shortly after, it was the bowler who had come out on top in the confrontation. Noble regarded himself as the victor. It was the satisfaction that came with the end result, rather than the grand gesture of the individual shot, that was important – the eternal conflict between the romantic and the 'look at the scorecard' view of the game.

In this game, Albert had made a brilliant start with the ball, taking the wickets of Worrall, Trumble and Trumper for next to nothing. The Australians had rallied a little, but his bowling had been difficult to play. The next morning, he opened the bowling and it was against Noble – the perfect chance to put one over him. He nearly bowled him with the first ball, and then almost had him caught and bowled. It seemed that a bundle of wickets would soon come his way, 'But his success ended as suddenly as it had begun, and for the rest of the innings he was harmless,' said *Cricket*. In the second innings, the Australians were chasing 92 and he didn't get a chance to bowl. Instead, he competently kept wicket, as Board was injured.

It was a similar story later that month at Lord's when he played for Middlesex in a benefit match for Jim Phillips against the tourists. In his first over, he had McLeod dropped in the slips and then went on to pick up Trumble, Noble, Gregory and then the great prize of young Trumper – well caught behind by MacGregor standing back. For the rest of the time, though, he was less threatening. As Middlesex followed on, he made 43 in the second innings, the top Middlesex score in the match as they struggled to avoid the innings defeat.

On paper, his figures against Australia in 1899 do not look disastrous by any means. However, against the counties his figures soared into the stratospheric. That summer, he was the first player in first-class cricket to take 200 wickets and score 1,000 runs in a season, a feat that had eluded W.G. Grace and many others. At Lord's that summer, in 21 first-class matches, he took 173 wickets: five in an innings on 22 occasions and ten in a match ten times.

His cricket was characterised by an energy that at times touched on violence unrestrained. Fielding at mid-on against Kent at Lord's, he threw down the wicket with so much force that he broke one of the stumps. There were other occasions too. W.J. Ford wrote in *Badminton*: 'I was sitting in the pavilion at Lord's last year watching a match, in the course of which Albert Trott chased a ball to the lower boundary and flung it back to the bowler. So hard and low was the throw that as the ball hummed off the hard ground, the bowler considered it prudent not to meddle with it, whereupon it promptly found the boundary at the Grand Stand side, hitting the seats with a vicious thump.'

Against Fred Tate of Sussex, he made two huge drives in one over. The first hit the wall of the pavilion, in line with the upper balcony, and bounced back halfway to the wicket. The second hit would have easily cleared the pavilion, but went straight to the southern wing, where it hit the 'MCC' monogram on the top of the building. This may very well have been the time when Albert went up to Fred at the end of the day and said, 'Sorry, Fred, but it was really a mis-hit.' It was a story that Fred Tate told against himself with a smile. Albert's hits were not confined to Lord's. At Taunton against Somerset, in his innings of 63, he hit the ball out of the ground and into the river Tone on three occasions. He did get six runs for each of those efforts.

Middlesex thought so highly of him that they took the unusual step of saluting his valuable service to the club during the season, by including his batting and bowling analysis in the club minutes. They also paid him a bonus of £75, while Jack Hearne received £50 and Micky Roche £35.

Throughout the summer, *Cricket* harped about his relative lack of success against his old country, yet the Australians were a good team – some said the best that had ever toured. In Trumper, they possessed one of the great batsmen, something that was recognised at the time with his fine innings of 300 not out against Sussex. They were a tough lot. Ignoring the need to entertain the crowd, the tourists never balked at resorting to defensive play. Against Middlesex, Darling scored so slowly that the crowd began to whistle the 'Dead March', and for a time Lord's was turned into Drury Lane on Boxing Night. Gregor MacGregor asked the police to go into the crowd, and the game was not resumed until the barracking stopped. But, despite their deliberate use of slow play, the Australians had been the better team in the Tests, and obduracy took them through some difficult phases in the games.

After a defeat in a Test series against the Australians, English cricket went through its familiar round of self-criticism, asking whether standards had deteriorated. Albert was one of those asked. His answer was not that English cricket had grown worse but that Australian cricket had improved, and in particular they studied the placing of the field. 'If a man is pottering about, a silly point is immediately put to catch him.' Pottering about: he always managed to resist that trap.

If he felt that he hadn't turned in a match-winning performance against Australia, he never commented on it in public, offering neither excuses nor explanation. Perhaps the clamour of unreasonable expectation climbing on the back of his other extraordinary performances in the season became too much. Perhaps he demanded too much of himself. A couple of years later, Walter Bettesworth, in 'A Chat About Albert Trott' in *Cricket* magazine, said, 'It seemed to most good judges that he failed against them because he was too anxious to bowl them all out at once, and, perhaps disconcerted by his first want of success against them, he never really showed them what he could do.' In other words, he was too excited and bowled with a lack of control.

The Australians, for their part, understood very well why Albert had not enjoyed much success against them, when the normally taciturn Joe Darling said in response to the question, 'How is Albert Trott?':

'There is not the slightest doubt about his being the best bowler in England. He would have been a very useful man to us. Englishmen don't seem to know anything about his bowling.'

'But the Australians played him all right?'

'He always did fairly well at the start, but we know more about his tricks.'

On the surface, 'the best bowler in England' sounds mightily complimentary, but Joe Darling weighted it with a significant rider: Albert was good enough to trouble the English but of no bother to the Australian team.

Late on in the season, Albert said that he felt stale from seven successive seasons of cricket – yet it didn't stop him playing the usual rounds of club cricket into September with the Cross Arrows and others. Jack Hearne went off to India in the employ of the Maharajah of Patiala to develop local players, and a couple of other English pros found coaching berths in South Africa, despite the impending second Boer War. Albert had talked of hiring an iron shed in the Marylebone area, where he would coach those who were looking for something special from the leading player of the day. The iron shed never saw the light of day, but in his pocket was the generous bonus from Middlesex and what remained from his talent money for his exceptional performances in the season. For the first time in a couple of years, he had the opportunity to return to Australia for a family visit. Harry's condition remained unchanged as he recuperated in Kew Asylum, still uncommunicative, a future uncertain, while their father, Adolphus, had fallen on increasingly straitened times. Jessie too must have favoured a Melbourne return that year, with their young daughter. In the end, it may have been the prospect of further expense rather than inclination that led him to winter with his immediate family in the environs of Willesden Green.

* * *

Albert began his cricket of the new century by playing for a different team in his first match of the season, against Surrey at the Oval. London County had been formed a couple of years previously by W.G. Grace, at the instigation of the Crystal Palace Company, as a means of providing first-class cricket for the burgeoning south London population of clerks and other members of the lower middle classes. The enterprise was a way of making money through cricket, with W.G. Grace, no longer in medical practice, the well-rewarded manager. The new-found team largely drew its players from home county amateurs supplemented by some professional bowling. It was another source of income for Albert, but MCC were chary of this upstart scheme and how it would impact on the county game, so he was confined to an occasional appearance when Middlesex and MCC did not require his services.

His form in the 1900 season came close to that of the previous year. He scored a fine 112 against Gloucestershire at Lord's in 135 minutes, which matched the big hitting of Gilbert Jessop for the opposition. At Trent Bridge, for Middlesex against Nottinghamshire, he showed his usual taste for big hitting when, in less than an hour, he hit 74 out of 108, including a drive off Dixon for six. This was the first hit out of the ground since 1893.

At Lord's, in the Gentlemen versus Players match, he revealed that he could be a cool head at the crease when he came in late with Wilfred Rhodes and guided the Players home by two wickets. Against Leicestershire, he was batting with B.T.J. Bosanquet, who was on 99 when the amateur called for an impossible run. Albert gave up his own wicket, and it was sportsmanlike acts such as these that made him so popular.

It didn't always completely go his own way. Against Sussex at Hove, he took 7-204, but, when he worked through his variations, Ranjitsinhji was severe on him in an innings of 202, 'worthy of celebration in verse by a poet laureate', opined *Cricket*. A few weeks later, though, in the bank holiday fixture at Taunton, in the couple of hours of cricket that was possible between the showers, he took all ten Somerset wickets for 42 runs, almost alone and unaided: six bowled, two lbw, one caught-and-bowled and Plum Warner helping with a catch for the other. He liked August in the west country, and against Gloucestershire he took eight wickets in the second innings, all clean bowled. Against the club teams, he plundered mercilessly as ever – at Lord's against a Hampstead team that included Stoddart, Hayman and an ageing Spofforth, he hit 171, with three sixes for hits out of the ground. It may have been the talent money that drove him, or the pleasure in providing entertainment.

In first-class matches he had scored 1,337 runs, and taken 211 wickets and 42 catches – the best all-round contribution of the season. He was second to Wilfred Rhodes in the number of wickets taken, the Yorkshire man having taken 261 wickets. However, for much of the season, Albert had carried the attack for Middlesex, relatively unsupported as Jack Hearne had suffered a considerable and unprecedented lapse in form, 'Tireless' Jack often going wicketless. An additional handicap was the standard of fielding in the Middlesex team: although Albert always seemed outwardly unconcerned, dropped catches had cost many wickets. He had built a reputation as a bowler who was always trying to take wickets. Dr Robert Macdonald, a Queensland dentist who played for Leicestershire for a few seasons at the turn of the century, gave a summary of a typical Albert over: 'His first ball is common or garden, which begets too much confidence; his second is his "fast" ball which comes slow; his third is his "swimming" or swerving ball; the fourth is his "slow ball" which comes fast; while his last is the projectile.'

A few years later, in his chapter in *Cricket: A Handbook of the Game* (a book co-written with W.G. Grace and Archie MacLaren), Albert was to call himself a variety bowler. His account has the feeling of being based on his own words. He described his unusual grip for his off break, the ball between his first and second fingers with his second finger on top of the ball. 'My right hand first finger is much larger than the one on my left hand. I have never seen a bowler that holds the ball as I do.' His leg break was more conventional, but 'I have often to change my mind, and just as I am going to bowl, to turn an off or leg break into a fast ball.'

As for his 'swerver', the ball learned from baseball, it came with an in-curve – 'an off-break but with a lower delivery. When the ball leaves my hand it appears to be going a long way outside the leg stump and instead of it keeping outside the leg stump it swerves into the wicket and keeps on dropping. Also, the batsman, thinking he has got a lovely full pitcher outside the leg stump, generally jumps into his wicket to hit it a bit harder and more surely. If he misses the ball, of course he is lbw. Then again, many a time the ball has not turned a bit, and goes straight; then they think, "Well I did miss a beauty that time." You can well afford to give them one or two, now and again, for if they have the intention of keeping out of their wicket, the straight ball gives them more courage and perhaps they jump in, just at the wrong time.'

The lbw rule of the day, which was not revised until 1935, favoured the batsman and must have been a source of irritation for the bowler. The ball had to pitch in line, wicket to wicket, for the batsman to be dismissed in this way. Anything that pitched outside off stump was given not out. Better pitches and better protective equipment had encouraged an increase in padding up, and, where batsmen such as Arthur Shrewsbury led the way, others followed in taking advantage. The shortcomings of the law were recognised, but attempts to change it in 1902 failed to secure the required majority at a meeting of MCC. The lbw rule that Albert played under may well have encouraged him to go down the path of the 'variety' bowler, so that he retained an element of surprise.

W.A. Bettesworth, the cricketing journalist, believed that Albert could have been a length bowler, like Noble, giving little away, but he chose not to. 'Rightly or wrongly he is credited as a man who is always making experiments.' Sammy Woods, the Australian amateur who played for Somerset, credited the influence of another in making Albert a better bowler. Woods described Gregor MacGregor, his Cambridge University teammate, as the best captain he had ever played under. As the wicketkeeper and captain of Middlesex, MacGregor was in an ideal position to let Albert know what he should bowl. For example, he often stopped him bowling short and made him pitch it up. In Woods' view it was MacGregor who did more than anyone else to make Albert a better bowler.

12

The unknown devil

WHILE ALBERT had been playing in England, brother Harry had also enjoyed some success on the cricket field, for the Kew Asylum XI. He had suddenly rekindled his interest in the game, hitting a score of 90 with some big swipes; and, thus encouraged, he started to play every week, his condition improving, and soon he began to greet friends who came to visit. He picked up wickets and fielded brilliantly at point. The captaincy of Australia, with the concomitant weight of public expectation, had led to his breakdown, but it was playing the game that released him from his condition and brought him back closer to his old self. In June, he was discharged from Kew as cured. By the October, he was captaining South Melbourne against Melbourne in a Pennant match, an indication of the extent of his recovery.

Although Albert remained in Willesden in the English winter of 1900/01, he still retained contact with his Australian family. Fred Trott, the youngest of the Trott siblings, had been working at the Gibraltar gold mine at Adelong in New South Wales, but decided to try his luck and move to England. On the 1901 census, Albert the professional cricketer is ensconced as the head of the family at Balmoral Road with his wife, Jessie, their daughter, Jessie, and Mary Harris, their 60-year-old live-in domestic servant. Fred, 25 years old, is living there too. He may have arrived in London with the offer of a bed and on the off-chance that something would turn up in the way of work. The census record doesn't list an occupation for him, so he may have arrived just before the return was completed. He had played for the cricket team at the Gibraltar mine, and previously for the Coburg club in Victoria. Although a useful bowler, he was not in the same class as his older brothers.

Albert was loyal to his younger brother and tried to put some opportunities his way. In April, Albert took a three-week coaching contract at Essex, working alongside Bobby Peel and Alfred Shaw to prepare the team for the forthcoming season. He took Fred along with him to Leyton, where the younger man bowled some medium pace on a length. *Cricket* kindly tried to latch on to something of what he offered, but in the end had to settle for 'easy on the eye, like his brothers'. With the help of his name, it was not long before he was given a contract on the ground staff. Middlesex agreed to pay Albert ten shillings a week lodging allowance for Fred for 30 weeks of the year. Even at this early stage, it was clear that this was not to be another star Australian bowler coming through the production line to play for Middlesex. Not that it mattered – Fred was always ready to make himself useful around Lord's and MCC as a net bowler, short-notice stand-in, scorer or umpire, and no doubt he kept Albert company of an evening when he was playing a home fixture.

There were plenty of those. The season began on 1 May, and by 23 May he had played in an astonishing seven three-day matches for MCC at Lord's. He was worked hard, bowling long spells, his toil unrelieved by rain. It wasn't only Albert who was bowled so frequently: Jack Hearne played in the same number of games. Although there were different expectations of bowlers, their contemporaries acknowledged the workload of the pro bowlers, with Sammy Woods referring to the pallid Hearne as 'the white slave' because of the number of overs he bowled and the fact that he never got sunburnt. That season, though, it was Albert who was to bowl most overs for MCC and Middlesex.

There was little rest. At this time, the novelist Edwin Pugh watched an MCC match against 'Nonentityshire' at Lord's, 'an occasion for the exhibition of frocks and four-in-hands'. In an essay published in *Black and White* magazine, he described his day at the cricket. After watching Jack Hearne bowl unsuccessfully on the field, he wandered over to the nets, where he found three professionals bowling to a 'languid'. Two of the professionals he knew.

'The other was a stranger to me: a curiously formed man, with a long, thick body and short legs, a face sallow, the features thereof strongly marked and drooping, the expression peevish. He bowled like an inconsistent demon. What the languid exquisite could see or properly reach he tipped up to point or in the slips; what he could not see bowled him clean, every time. There never was such a weird medley of balls as this disagreeable-looking young man in the old yellow flannels sent down. The languid exquisite retired, hurt in the vanity, and then the unknown devil took a hand with the bat. Every ball he got hold of he plunked over the nursery or to the farthest wall, and in five minutes he had sprung his bat.

'"Another guinea to Dark," he said, gloomily.

'"Shouldn't hit so blinking hard," he was told.

'"Who is the man?" I inquired.

'... The man answered: "Albert Trott."'

Edwin Pugh, a member of the Fabian Society and chronicler of working-class life, often runs close to exaggeration and sentimentality in his work – but, beneath the antique varnish, this piece rings true. As well as playing for MCC, the Lord's professional had to bowl in the nets – that was his job. While it could be argued that this net bowling served as practice, others, such as Monty Noble, thought it had a detrimental effect on the bowling of English pros, requiring them to send down deliveries hour after hour. The basic rate of pay for an MCC net bowler was around 25 or 30 shillings a week, and Albert may very well have earned more, topping it up with tips from the members.

In the 1901 season, he sustained a hand injury, incurred when he tried to stop a hard drive off his own bowling, but by the end of the season he had still taken 176 first-class wickets at 21.78 to help Middlesex to second place in the County Championship. His haul of wickets was behind that of Hirst and some way behind that of Rhodes, who took 251, which ensured that Yorkshire were the county champions. *Cricket* commented succinctly on Middlesex and Albert. 'The bowling depended chiefly on Trott, who was hardly as consistent as usual, although on his day he was almost irresistible. Hearne is no longer the bowler that he was.'

As for his batting, he made 880 runs, with his only century coming against Essex in September, where he 'played with more patience than usual at the start' until hitting out aggressively when Rawlin joined him at the crease.

An indication of his approach to batting can be found in an incident in late July at Lord's when Middlesex played Sussex. Joe Vine was bowling leg breaks for the visitors. Albert's method was to swivel around and smash the ball behind the wicket to the boundary. He had done this a couple of times when Harry Butt, the keeper, received a direct hit to the groin. The game was stopped for ten minutes while Butt received treatment, but he was carried from the field and took no further part in the match. Fred Trott came on from the professionals' pavilion and fielded in his place.

'I damn near killed him,' said Albert afterwards. The incident illustrates Albert's unorthodox play, an early version of a Twenty20-style stroke, in the days when such things were unusual – with only primitive protection available for the groin, it was also a dangerous thing to do. Fortunately, Butt, a well-liked player, eventually recovered in time to play the next match. Herbert Strudwick was another wicketkeeper who came up against Albert's habit of hitting the ball pitched outside leg behind the wicket. For him, the danger came from being hit by Albert's big bat when standing up, an experience he described as frightening.

While it was hardly a decline, he had scored fewer runs and taken fewer wickets than in the previous season, and had not achieved his own all-rounder's double record for the third time. With the crowds at Lord's and the Oval, though, he was always popular, referred to by his nicknames of either Albatrott or Alberto. After visiting him in London that summer, Frank Laver spoke of the popularity of his old teammate in England.

Although he had not spoken about them in public, it became clear that Albert still had aspirations to play for England. MCC agreed in March 1901 to carry out the required preparations for an England tour of Australia, including the selection of the team. However, by May the committee, which included Lord Hawke and Lord Harris, decided it was not possible to recruit a team that was truly representative of English cricket. The venture was abandoned by MCC, but their Australian counterparts didn't give up. At the request of the Melbourne Cricket Club, Archie MacLaren took up the task of finding a team that could tour. MacLaren had originally been unavailable. Under another captain, as an amateur, he would have received his expenses and nothing more. But now, under the flag of his own captaincy and management, including the finances, the tour took on a different complexion.

When the Lancashire amateur was appointed, Albert would have allowed himself to hope for Test cricket. His chances of selection for the tour had dramatically increased. MacLaren was the man who had always rated him, who claimed that it was he who had talked Albert into the Australian team six years earlier in Adelaide. A few years previously, Albert had returned the compliment when the Australians toured, describing Archie MacLaren, somewhat extravagantly, as the best fielder in cricket. MacLaren as skipper, with the freedom to choose his own team, could have been the very best of things for Albert. MacLaren had a difficult task on his hands. Two of the leading amateurs, Fry and Ranjitsinhji, were unavailable, with the latter close to bankruptcy. Following the death of his benefactor, the Maharajah of Patiala, Ranjitsinhji needed to visit India to secure his finances by obtaining a new allowance. Further developments proved encouraging for Albert. Lord Hawke, enraged by MacLaren's 'private enterprise' tour, banned George Hirst and Wilfred Rhodes from touring, saying that he did not see why the Yorkshire players should go, 'to put money in the pocket of Melbourne Cricket Club'. When MacLaren approached Surrey, he found that Bobby Abel, Bill Lockwood and Tom Richardson were similarly unavailable. As MacLaren ran up against barrier after barrier, it seemed that he would have no option but to take Albert.

However, MacLaren didn't pick him. Instead he chose Sydney Barnes, a professional from Burnley in the Lancashire League with relatively little first-class experience, after a successful net session in which Barnes struck MacLaren on the glove. Although the selection of Barnes proved to be an inspired choice, at the time it seemed more like an act of desperation than of genius.

So, why didn't he pick Albert? Archie MacLaren explained, 'Mr Wardill wrote me and expressed surprise that I had not included Albert Trott in the team but I replied, "If we could not beat Australia with Englishmen, we could not beat them with Englishmen and Australians." Mind you only for the fact that Trott was an Australian was he left out, otherwise he would have been the first trundler I would have chosen. His variety of bowling is just what we want for you Australians, and I wish we had a few like him.'

C.B. Fry, too, argued that Albert should be included as the best possible choice for bowling in Australian conditions, but he also regarded Albert as an Australian, which ruled him out. There is no record in MCC minutes of any discussion about Albert's eligibility – they had already disowned this private tour. Despite his English residence, his Middlesex qualification and his appearances in South Africa for Lord Hawke's England, the climate for dual national cricketers had suddenly altered.

* * *

Albert's response to his non-selection was the same as when he had been rejected by Australia in 1896. He looked for another offer from elsewhere. England and Archie MacLaren's loss was Hawke's Bay Cricket Association's gain. The energetic president of this New Zealand association, the wealthy solicitor Mr H.E. Williams, visited England in his search for a new coach to raise the standard of cricket in his district. Hawke's Bay had employed Jim Phillips as a coach in the past, and no doubt it was he who had led them in the direction of Albert. The signing of a player of Albert's stature was hailed by 'Poyntz' in the *Evening Post* of Wellington as 'one of the greatest strokes of enterprise in New Zealand cricket' and put Hawke's Bay ahead of other areas of the colony.

Albert left England on the *Waiwera* in October, delaying his departure to New Zealand by a couple of weeks. Hawke's Bay would pay his fares and were agreeable to his wife Jessie accompanying him, but he decided to travel out alone. What was more, when he boarded the ship he gave his marital status as single. Mr Williams was returning to New Zealand from London at the same time, but they travelled on separate ships. No doubt Albert wanted to enjoy the long sea journey before arriving in New Zealand in December.

Mr Williams was proud of his new acquisition, but was anxious that the association should draw up a programme for the use of Albert's time. In the morning, he would coach school games or give private coaching, and in the afternoons, bowl for practice. The arrangement was for one season in the first instance, but Hawke's Bay would have first call on his services for the next season. Albert was suitably cool about returning, saying he would 'if the work suited him'. Mr Williams, though, wasn't going to let him get away: 'We must make it our aim that he will be so satisfied with his position that he will return.' Albert would 'endeavour to remain until the end of March', but he had to get back for the start of the English season in May.

When he arrived, he was in good spirits and said he would return to New Zealand for the next three seasons if he found 'the change congenial'. If he didn't, he already had an offer to go to America the next year. But he was keen to make a start, and on his first afternoon he had some net practice at the Basin Reserve. As for coaching, he said, 'There is nothing I like better than to bring a youngster on. I could stay with him all day so long as he will listen to what I say.'

New Zealand must have come as a surprise to him after the sprawl and clamour of London. He had only ever lived in big cities, playing his cricket among those he knew well. In New Zealand, he was on his own. At the turn of the year, he played three first-class matches for Hawke's Bay against Wellington, Otago and Canterbury. Despite significant contributions from Albert, Hawke's Bay were comprehensively beaten in the first two games. The final match they won thanks to Albert's 11 wickets and 80 not out in the second innings.

Later, in interviews with the local press, he gave his impressions of New Zealand cricket after his three weeks in the colony. He did not approve of cutting the grass before the second day's play, as the rules of cricket only allowed for the wicket being rolled for ten minutes before the start of the innings. Such a thing was never done elsewhere in first-class cricket. Another curious custom he noticed in Dunedin was that the association allowed one innings to be played on a certain wicket, and then gave the players the option of changing it in the next innings. As for the players, Sims of Canterbury was correct in his play while Downes of Dunedin was a good bowler, but Albert doubted the absolute correctness of his action. (Sims had taken 13 wickets in the match, including Albert's in the first innings.) The losses he blamed on the state of the pitches, but Hawke's Bay's sole victory was entirely down to merit. It was also cold on the field – almost as cold as he had ever known it, and, suffering from a touch of sciatica, he had had to bowl with a sweater on.

He then turned his attention to his own Hawke's Bay team. Some of them, he thought, should still be among the juniors. Their fielding was below the mark. Not enough attention was paid to this department in the game of cricket. New Zealand cricket on the whole was fairly good, but in every province he visited there was an evident want of coaching, both at the wickets and in the field.

His allegations regarding the grass cutting in Wellington caused intense indignation in cricket circles in the city. The officials denied that the grass had received an extra cut and said that Albert had been confused by the steering roller in front of the main roller making a separate impression on the turf, such impression being about the same width as the roller would make. Albert was accused of using this to make excuses for Hawke's Bay's defeat. But it was also the tenor of the rest of his comments, and in particular the criticisms of his own association, that caused an outcry. The *Otago Daily Times* disputed all of his statements about New Zealand cricket, saying he may be a first-class cricketer but, 'He would also make a first-class novelist, judging from the way he draws on his imagination. What he lacks in fact he makes up in fiction.' He was wrong about everything, just wrong. The paper went on to say with regard to his comments about the Hawke's Bay players that 'they would resent the belittling opinion of a man who was brought out specially to teach them, and paid by them, being broadcast all over the colony'.

His comments, as they were reported, were certainly undiplomatic. In essence they were the lament of the pro abroad, forced to play an inferior standard of cricket on oddly prepared wickets, in strange places, but at the same time seizing the chance to bolster his own credentials as coach. The comments seem out of character, not from the mouth of the genial Albert Trott. This was an irritated man. Naturally good-natured, up until this point his public utterances had shown that he was savvy to circumstance and how he might be interpreted. Perhaps too much drink had loosened his tongue and the words had tripped out unrestrained by tact. In the rest of the interview, when the questions turned to himself, he talked about not playing Test cricket. 'Trott regards his own position in England as peculiar. He is disqualified through being an Anglo-Australian from playing for England against Australia, likewise from playing in Australia against England, but he is qualified to play for the County of Middlesex against Australia.'

The Ashes Test series was being played in Australia while he was out in New Zealand, playing at this standard. In the last of these matches for Hawke's Bay, he had come up against Syd Callaway, the man who had partnered him in their epic stand against England in Adelaide. The match and the innings that had made his reputation must have seemed a long way and a long time ago. Perhaps the pair of them complained about their lot together.

There were rumours that he had resigned. However, after Mr Williams had returned to Napier, his timetable came into operation on the Monday morning, beginning with a 6am start coaching tradesmen in the nets. The earliness of the hour delighted the *Otago Daily Times*, as Hawke's Bay aimed to keep him busy throughout the day and he also had to coach schoolboys. The coaching for them was free, but few took advantage. 'The services of the professional have been enlisted at some considerable expense,' grumbled the *Hastings Standard*; 'we trust that young cricketers will evince more interest.' Albert was approached to represent the North against the South, but Hawke's Bay refused to let him play, as there was only a limited time left for him to coach. And, for good measure, he was not a bona fide resident of New Zealand and was therefore not qualified to play in a representative match.

Albert's three months in Napier were beleaguered by difficulty, yet things must have improved by the end of March, when he was due to return to England for the cricket season. Somewhat surprisingly, before he left he said he would return in November so that he could devote more time to coaching. Mr Williams had persuaded him and drawn up a contract, which Albert had signed.

When Albert arrived back in London in May, he was to learn that Lord Hawke, always ready to promote the game, proposed to take a team of English amateurs out to New Zealand at the end of the season. Their numbers would be supplemented by a series of professional bowlers, and Lord Hawke approached Albert. The proposition was tempting when compared with a further stint of coaching. However, he had to secure his release from his contract with Hawke's Bay. He contacted Mr Williams, but the Napier solicitor held firm. A contract was a contract and Albert, said the *Otago Daily Times,* had to 'grin and bear it'. In England, when the touring team was announced, it came with the afterthought that Albert's services could be called on if needed. He obviously hoped that Mr Williams could be persuaded. When it was revealed that the party would travel on to Australia to play some matches after the New Zealand tour, it increased his desire to get out of his Hawke's Bay contract.

Knowing that they were anxious to have him back coaching in Napier, he kept them waiting. New sports had arrived with the new century and were being promoted, including Vigoro, which Albert wanted to play. Vigoro came from Canada and was similar to cricket in scoring, but the batsman and fielders had rackets with which to score or stop the soft rubber ball. The wicket was 3ft high and 2½ft wide. MCC allowed a trial match to take place at Lord's in October 1902. The composition of the teams was uninspired: the professional cricketers against the amateurs. The amateurs did play a ringer in that their captain was Eustace H. Miles, the tennis and racquets champion. With the advantage of his presence in the team, they scored 73, which proved to be a match-winning total. The professionals, led by Bobby Abel, made 18 and 39, losing by an innings – but Albert, with his natural eye for the ball, had the satisfaction of being the top scorer in both innings, with 5 and 18. MCC were not impressed, and when another trial match was proposed two years later, they refused permission to stage it at Lord's.

Albert's outward journey to New Zealand was unusual. He boarded the *Sophocles*, and once again his boarding details show that he declared himself to be a single man. At Cape Town, the Australian team who had toured England that summer joined him on board. The weeks spent on the sea voyage with his old team, as they returned home well paid, may well have caused him to reflect on his itinerant life as a cricketer and what might have been. The *Sophocles* docked at Melbourne and he disembarked at Sydney, finally back on Australian soil. Immediately he went out on the cricket field and bowled some curly stuff, for the benefit of a few spectators and the press.

Albert didn't reach New Zealand until mid-December. No sooner had he arrived than he left Hawke's Bay, turning up at the Auckland dockside to welcome the touring party from England, led by Plum Warner, as Lord Hawke was absent through illness and injury. Despite the lack of bowling, the English tourists won their games fairly comfortably.

At Napier in January, Albert turned out for a Hawke's Bay team of 15 against 12 English tourists. The ground was ridiculously small, and Warner and Bosanquet, Albert's Middlesex teammates, took advantage of the short straight boundaries with some drives. Albert finished with 6-255 off 41 overs. When it came to batting, he scored two in the first innings, out to a miscued big hit, and was bowled for a duck in the second innings. In a post-match interview, Plum Warner, perhaps sensing that the Lord's pro needed some help at a local level, suggested that New Zealand cricket could be improved by two or three English professionals going out there in the winter. Warner seemed disinclined to be drawn on what he saw as the strengths of the New Zealand game, but he did speak very highly of the form of Albert Trott's two colts, Macassey and Cotterill.

When the game had finished, Hawke's Bay agreed to release Albert a week early from his coaching contract in March so that he could join Lord Hawke's XI on the Australian leg of the tour. They must have sensed there was no point in trying to hold on to their reluctant recruit.

Albert left Napier for Wellington to join Warner and the tourists. The express train on which he travelled had barely left the station before the Hawke's Bay Cricket Association announced that they would not engage him again. The progress of the players under his leadership had not been rapid, and they felt justified in terminating his contract. However, the *Hawera and Normanby Star* did say, 'During his visits here Trott made himself very popular and nothing would please his friends better than to hear of his success against the teams which the English combination will meet in Australia.' Friends: wherever he travelled, he found friends.

It was left to *Free Lance* to suggest that Hawke's Bay's expectations of progress under Albert had been unrealistic and that they should employ more coaches, 'It seems to me that one man cannot affect so much when he has to attend to many players.' Later in the year, Mr H.E. Williams, the man who had been so pleased when he signed up Albert, was trenchant in his criticism of him at the annual meeting of the Hawke's Bay Cricket Association. He reportedly said, 'He did not believe that Trott ever took the slightest interest in his work from the time he came till he left, and on one occasion the speaker had to speak to him very severely, much to the president's regret, on the unsatisfactory way he performed his duties.'

Mr Williams and Albert were diametrically opposing personality types: the man who liked to button things down versus the harum-scarum man of genius. It was never going to work out. Albert had spent little more than six months in the colony over the two years, but they didn't forget him easily in New Zealand. Six years later, the young cricketer Bert Bailey was still referred to as Albert Trott's 'pet pupil'.

* * *

In a photo of Lord Hawke's XI taken in Melbourne Albert stands out. Not just because he's the only one not in a striped tour blazer, his white sleeves rolled up to the elbow, but it's his stance. The amateurs are relaxed, some of them slightly suspicious as they fix their glances on a camera positioned to one side. One of Albert's hands rests on his hip, single teapot style; the other leans on the chair in front. His moustache is well trimmed, and he looks in good nick, in funds, broad-shouldered and ready for action. It's his standard pose of the period, in the back row of a team photo, similar to the one taken of the 1901 Players' team at Lord's.

He stayed at the Oriental with the other two English professionals, while the amateurs enjoyed a warm welcome from their hosts at the Australia Club. Several members of the Victorian team were at the Bijou Theatre for the opening night of 'Boy Jim' by Conan Doyle, and Albert joined them. Doubtless he diverted them with stories of how he knew the author from Lord's and had been a guest at his house in Sussex. Albert found himself an object of interest, said *Punch*, 'not so much for the "brilliancy" of his complexion as for the fact that his is the only face in the English team that is known to us.' *Punch* wasn't joking. For the rest of the team, this was their first game in Australia. As for the Victorian team, Albert had played with a few of them, but there were many new faces, a sign of how time had moved on.

A good crowd turned out for the game, and he had plenty of friends among them who wanted to see what he could do in his first game in Australia for six years. When he came to the wicket, batting at eight, it was the signal for applause all around the ground. He hit at Armstrong's leg-side deliveries, and twice in succession despatched them to the fence at fine square leg. But he didn't show anything like his old Australian form, and, ever the showman went for the big hit, holing out to Harry Graham in the deep for 17. In the field, he came on second change, and picked up four top-order wickets but was on the expensive side. With his style of bowling, he always needed a decent keeper. His faster deliveries proved too much for Taylor behind the stumps, and the byes mounted. In the second innings, he made a second-ball duck as the English batting collapsed, and in the end the Victorians won comfortably by seven wickets.

Before he left Melbourne, he met Harry and Adolphus. The reunion came at not the happiest of times. His brother was playing cricket for Bendigo, where he had adopted a big-hitting style and was among the runs, but his recovery was still fragile and it was doubted whether he was ready to play first-class cricket. The other strain on Harry was the lack of money, and he had been declared bankrupt. Having spent his savings of £1,000, he had resorted to selling his cricket trophies. Now he was supporting himself by working for the Post Office again, sorting letters, and a ghosted column of cricket tips in a newspaper provided some income. The Melbourne Insolvency Court took a compassionate view of his circumstances, and in April of that year they gave him an unconditional discharge from his debts.

The precariousness of Harry's finances had also affected Adolphus. A few days after the end of the match between Victoria and Lord Hawke's XI, Albert's father was admitted to the Melbourne Benevolent Asylum at Hotham on the grounds of debt. This neo-Gothic asylum had been built as a place of refuge for those who couldn't support themselves. Benevolent in name, it was less so in nature. This was no place for distressed gentlefolk – with its wards and corridors, it was more in the style of an English workhouse. In 1902, the medical staff had reported that the bathing facilities and sewerage were inadequate, and the air became foul and unpleasant on the wards if the doors were shut for any length of time. There was neither discretion nor sympathy about the plight of the residents. The antics of an amusing inmate were discussed at the committee and duly reported in *The Argus*. Little had changed by the time the widower Adolphus was admitted. It was a huge fall for him, for a man who had aspired to middle-class respectability and to riches, with his shares in gold mines and with his two sons who had played cricket for Australia. He was admitted temporarily for a week in the first instance, but then indefinitely. At the asylum's next committee meeting, letters from Albert and Harry were read out, in which they agreed to make a contribution towards the support of their father. It would be some time before the opportunity to escape from the asylum's benevolence presented itself to Adolphus.

For now, Albert couldn't do any more for his father, as he travelled on to Sydney for the next match. Here, Plum Warner was at his engaging best, bordering on the unctuous, at a dinner at the Australia Hotel after two days' play in the match against New South Wales. He praised Trumper and Duff and said that Monty Noble would get first place if an eleven of the world were chosen. As for the present game, he said, 'They required an Australian bowler to get rid of Australian batsmen,' to great cheers and laughter from the gathering. Albert had taken 6-88 in the first innings, with Duff, Gregory and Trumper among his victims, the latter caught at mid-on. *Cricket* acknowledged that this time he had enjoyed great success against Australian batsmen. In the second innings, his nine overs cost 76 runs, with Warner relying on Bosanquet for much of the work. Lord Hawke's team struggled in the field in the heat. With the game in an interesting position, rain on the fourth day meant that it was abandoned.

In Adelaide, they looked forward to his arrival, the local press anticipating some big hitting that had not been seen in Australian cricket since Lyons had retired. For Albert, the tour became a royal progress: 'The greatest attraction to Australians is Albert Trott,' said the *Evening Journal*. Wherever he went, he was greeted by old friends, and he enjoyed this to the full; as the *Adelaide Register* said, 'He smiles in the same old way; one can never forget the Albert Trott smile.' As for the match, he made little impact, with his one-time nemesis, the 44-year-old George Giffen, taking his wicket. Lord Hawke's team contrived to lose after making South Australia follow on. After their easy tour of New Zealand, the Englishmen had come up short, which demonstrated the strength of Australian cricket.

It was a subject he elaborated on in an interview he gave just before he left when he was asked about the ascendancy of Australian cricket.

He said it could only be put down to sheer ability. The Australians enjoyed a longer dry season, but England had better grounds, a more liberal patronage of the game and a wider number of players for selection. The enthusiasm for cricket had not diminished in England. As for himself, he said he was in the best of condition and had no intention of returning to Australia and residing there permanently – as a professional, he enjoyed better security in the more settled conditions in England.

From his conversations with the players, Albert well knew that the life of the Australian amateur cricketer could be extremely rewarding. As Perth's *Sunday Times* put it, 'There is a pleasing fiction in Australia that the professional cricketer is purely an English product.' Syd Gregory was another Australian cricketer in the bankruptcy court, even though he had done well out of the game. In court, he revealed that he'd earned £700 and £800 on his last two tours to England. The lower of these two sums was about twice as much as a professional in England could have earned on a tour of Australia, with £300 plus expenses being the standard remuneration at this time. (A fee of £800 would be roughly worth £80,000 in 2017.) The article went on to say, 'The fact is that there is no such thing as amateur cricket in Australia after the player has attained to a certain degree of excellence. Yet in the English cricket reports Albert Trott is just Trott, but Gregory is Mr. Gregory. Why the distinction?'

In essence, Albert had to say that he was better off playing in England than in Australia because this was the path he had been forced to take. The well-paid life of an Australian amateur Test cricketer was now forever beyond his reach.

13

'All he's got to do is to keep his head'

ALBERT HAD slipped between the distinctions of nationality. The selectors of both countries had found it difficult to decide whether he was Australian or English, but one thing was for certain: his home was in London and he was a Londoner. The city had changed in the time he had lived there as it took on the energy of a new century. Roads were dug up all over London for the laying of electric cable, as the new technology ousted the gaslight from the streets. It was the time of cinema as mainstream entertainment, with the 'electric' theatres and the Bioscope attracting crowded audiences for the silent films. By 1902, the electrification of the Underground had shoved aside the steam trains from all of the lines, and the twopenny tube of the Central Railway had opened in 1900. Motorbuses, lorries and cabs jostled with horse-drawn vehicles for space on the roads. The populace had an appetite for entertainment. There were 12 music halls and 23 theatres in the central London area, with another 47 just outside. Fred Karno's Fun Factory provided them with stars and sketches. Boxing matches and football attracted large crowds. There were soda fountains, revues and Blue Hungarian waltzes in the dance halls. Shops and restaurants grew in size as a greater range of food became cheaper and more available. New newspapers such as the *Daily Mail* and *Daily Express* started up, aimed at clerks in offices, but there was a strong demand for titbits – easily digestible pieces of information for a newly literate working class. Advertising had grown, with omnibuses covered in hoardings and newspapers extolling the virtues of food, drink and patent medicines. As Peter Ackroyd summed it up in *London: The Biography*, 'London was, in a phrase of the period, "going ahead".'

Albert embraced the spirit of the new age. He was part of it as a professional sportsman, but he also took advantage of the fresh openings, enjoying himself and cashing in on his reputation and famous name. He knocked about in the Lord's nets with one of the leading lights of the music hall, George Robey, who was always good for ten bob, a few funny stories and a drink in the bar afterwards. He gave hints to young cricketers in the *Boy's Own Paper*. He took on a ghosted column that was syndicated in newspapers such as the *Western Chronicle*. The columns had little of his voice, and, beyond collecting his fee for the use of his name, he had nothing to do with it. Along with W.G. Grace, he endorsed the John Wisden 'Special Crown' match ball: 'You may like to know that it was one of your "Special Crown" match balls I hit over Lord's pavilion in 1899.' By the standards of the twenty-first century, it may seem commonplace, but the use of a sportsman's name to sell products was relatively new at this time. While writing a newspaper article or a book was acceptable, many of the amateurs, with the notable exception of W.G. Grace, shied away from the vulgarity of advertising. It was also difficult to see some of the northern professionals under the watchful eye of Lord Hawke becoming public figures in this way. Albert was able to do it because of his connection to Lord's and to the capital. He was a metropolitan cricketer, someone who attracted stories, a personality. His public persona was that of a sporting man, bold and attacking when he came out to bat and always trying to get the man out when he bowled. He was the superb, athletic fielder who pulled off spectacular catches, slightly larger than life. The greater use of images, such as photographs and cartoons, in newspapers, and the rise of the cigarette card, helped to spread the fame of sportsmen. Then there were his nicknames: Alberto or Albatrott, evidence of his popularity and his given name, with its curt repeated consonants, Albert Trott.

In 1903, a young P.G. Wodehouse referred to him in a short story, 'Now, Talking About Cricket', in a Surrey versus Middlesex match at the Oval. 'How well I remember that occasion. Albert Trott was bowling (Bertie we used to call him); I forget who was batting.'

His fame brought with it friends: those who wanted the reflected limelight of his achievements on the field, and those who wanted to be seen out and about with a character. And then there were those who wanted to take advantage when he was in funds. He had carried this attention around with him, ever since his telling debut for Australia in 1895, and he enjoyed it, his gregarious nature meaning that he shunned time alone. As Lord Hawke pointed out, 'The trouble was not the player but the hangers-on, who, mainly for the sake of being seen talking to a famous cricketer, pestered professionals with their attentions and, worse still, by their offers of wholly unnecessary drinks.' Later, another professional was to remark, when looking back on his own career, that he would have preferred it if his well-wishers had given him the money instead of buying him a drink, but it was the fans' need to be seen 'treating' the pro that was important. Never one to refuse a 'cooler', Albert took what was on offer, for the teetotaller of 1895 had long disappeared.

In the 1902 season in England, between the two winter spells in New Zealand, he had not proved as effective as in the preceding seasons. He came close to 1,000 runs with the bat, and, although his bowling average remained more or less the same, his tally of wickets had dropped to 133. By the standards of today, it seems an impressive haul, but more games were played at that time. After his two sensational seasons, much was expected of him and he was judged by the highest standards. Before the season began, *Cricket* encouraged him to achieve great things against the touring Australians: 'All he's got to do is to keep his head.'

His chance came against them fairly early on, when he was picked for an MCC team in a match at Lord's in late May. *Cricket* judged that the MCC bowling 'left a good deal to be desired', even though it contained Jack Hearne and Len Braund as well as Albert. The reason for *Cricket* naysaying the bowling attack was that it included Albert, and while he was deadly against English batsmen, 'he failed with a disheartening regularity against the Australians'. In the first innings, he took the wickets of Darling, Gregory and Noble, with two of them bowled and a caught-and-bowled. In the second innings, he bowled Trumper as the Australians won easily, but he had been expensive, going for more than five an over. He hadn't done disastrously, but what people talked about was the brilliance of Trumper's batting, which overshadowed everything else.

In his second game against the Australians for Middlesex, his 'once invincible' bowling was largely ineffective, and his knock of 21 came with some luck before he was caught. But he did redeem himself, when he threw himself full length to take a magnificent catch at slip to halt another fine innings from Trumper. He always managed to find his moments in a game.

As for his batting, early in the season he took 103 in 65 minutes off a Somerset attack that included his friend Len Braund. Here he completely outscored his partner Hunt, who contributed 33 runs to the partnership and let Albert simply get on with it. When his batting came off it was spectacular, such as in his innings against Leicestershire at Lord's, where he hit 40 in 11 minutes. And it was in this season that he managed to send the ball clear over the Tavern pub and out of the ground.

In July, he wasn't selected for the Players' team against the Gentlemen at Lord's, with *Cricket* very specific on the reason for his omission, saying he had been 'hardly up to form' that year. No Albert Trott would have been unthinkable a couple of years previously. The team was selected by the MCC committee, which included representatives from Middlesex, so they may have decided to allow him a rest.

There was certainly some disquiet about his form with the ball within the county club, and it may have been Gregor MacGregor or Plum Warner who talked to the *Daily Telegraph*. The club was disappointed in how he had bowled that season, saying that he hadn't fallen off in skill but had lost some of the keenness and energy that he had shown when he first played for the county. They would have been better pleased if, instead of bowling so much to be hit, he had more often shown the concentration of purpose that characterised his work against Yorkshire, when they found it a hard matter to get the 68 runs required for victory. In the seven overs he had sent down that afternoon, he was entirely himself, and nothing could have been much better than his bowling. He was still a young man and should have been at his best for years to come.

One factor in his falling-off mentioned by the *Daily Telegraph* was that, in some matches, he had not bowled his fast ball often enough and instead had relied far too much on a slow, looping leg break that was immensely hittable. His workload in that period makes interesting reading. In the three seasons between 1899 and 1901, he had bowled 25,713 balls in first-class cricket and carried the Middlesex and MCC attacks. Jack Hearne, in the same period, had bowled 20,103 balls, that is 5,610 fewer. (Wilfred Rhodes sent down 26,286 balls of slow left-arm in the same period, while George Hirst's workload was relatively light, with 14,834 medium-fast deliveries. Lord Hawke often referred to the need to rest the Yorkshire bowlers.) If we then consider the immeasurable number of balls Albert had sent down in the nets at Lord's and the overs he'd bowled in Napier that winter, it's hardly surprising he lacked energy. Bowling fewer fast balls was a way of conserving himself during long and frequent bowling spells, as he had little chance to rest between games as the fixtures came thick and fast.

Another reason for the lower number of quick deliveries could have been the change in his physique. As far back as 1899, Howell of Australia had observed that he had grown fleshy in England, but during the tour of his birth country that winter, his extra weight was much commented upon. When he had stopped off in Sydney in 1902, it was said that he looked much stouter than when he had last appeared in Australia. In Melbourne in 1903, *The Australasian* announced that Albert had filled out a lot. A few days later, *The Register* in Adelaide described him as having 'filled out considerably, and when in his flannels will almost look a giant'.

These descriptions seem fanciful when you examine the team photo of Lord Hawke's XI from 1903 at the Melbourne ground. Albert looks far from huge and in reasonable condition. What must be remembered is that those who now encountered him in Australia had not seen him for many years and back then he had been slim, touching on the skinny. There had been a big change. The team photo, though, is also deceptive. Albert's pose is one for the benefit of the camera, holding in his midriff as Taylor's head in front masks the lower part of his body.

Another photo taken shortly after at the Melbourne ground is more truthful than the team one. He was caught on the field, somewhat unawares, side-on to the camera, chatting to three of the Victorian players. The photo reveals how he had thickened at the waist and the rear compared with the gangling youth of the East Melbourne club. He may not have had the dimensions of W.G. Grace, but it was not difficult to see in which direction his physique was going. His face put him closer to 40, but he'd only just celebrated his 30th birthday. His bat is at his side as he dominates the photo, the other three players listening to what he has to say. Cricket photos at this time were usually posed, or, where there was a shot of the action, it was far too distant for the viewer to discern what was going on. This photo is unusual for the period – more modern, part of a photo story on the visit of

Lord Hawke's team, with its close-up shots of the players and an air of naturalness.

When Albert had first enjoyed success in England, the Australian newspapers would comment on how they had lost the services of such a valuable player, blaming George Giffen and the lack of foresight shown by the selectors. However, although everyone sought his company when he toured with Lord Hawke's XI, and he enjoyed a warm reception as formerly one of their own, it was nothing more than that. When they saw him bat and bowl, there was no huge outcry about what they had lost. The Australian team, with its new faces, had grown much stronger than England, and they had no desperate need of him.

Towards the end of his time in Australia, he was asked about his poorer form in 1902 in England. He blamed it on a bruised hand, which he had injured in August when he'd slipped on the floor of the dressing room. It had caused him to miss a few matches, and he felt that it had affected his bowling. He didn't see any reason why he couldn't return to his old self in the coming season.

* * *

There was another consequence of the game in Melbourne, when a young Australian professional bowled at Plum Warner in the nets. Frank Tarrant made such an impression on the amateur that he invited him over to England, with the promise of a place on the MCC ground staff and the prospect of qualifying to play for Middlesex. Albert had played with Frank's uncle, Ambrose Tarrant, in the Australian Gentlemen versus Players match in Melbourne and in the same Victorian team. But he played no part in the recruitment of the 22-year-old all-rounder, and barely knew him until he arrived in London at the start of the 1903 season. Tarrant turned up with a 40lb marble clock, awarded to him for topping the Fitzroy bowling averages, a little money and a change of clothes. The two Melbourne cricketers became friends, and later Frank moved into a house in Balmoral Road with his wife and young son, a dozen doors away from Albert and his family. The friendship seemed to have extended to the wives, as when Albert's second daughter was born in 1904, she was named Hilda May Kathleen, after Tarrant's wife, Kathleen. Frank Tarrant returned the compliment a year later when he named his son Albert. As the boy grew up, he must have been relieved that his father had become friends with Albert, as his elder brother had been named after the French Emperor, Louis Napoleon Bonaparte Tarrant.

Frank's first-class experience in Australia was no more than three games for Victoria, in lesser matches against Tasmania and New Zealand. His introduction to the English game was quiet, almost anonymous, without the fanfare and interest that had greeted Albert on his arrival. Far from the finished article, he was quick to pick up how to be successful, developing his batting and his left-arm spin to English conditions. However, learning about the game was not confined to the technicalities of batting and bowling. Frank Tarrant was to say later that he learned his cricket from Albert Trott in the school of hard knocks. Early on, playing for MCC, he was to come up against W.G. Grace playing for London County. He had Grace caught wide out at second slip, clearly out, no doubt about the catch or the hit. Tarrant waited for him to walk, but Grace remained at the crease. When Tarrant gave him a glare, Grace made no attempt to move, but merely walked down the wicket and patted it. Albert, fielding at midwicket, said, 'You'll have to appeal, Frank. The old — won't move unless you do.' Frank, astonished that he hadn't walked, said nothing, and in the end it was left to Albert to appeal. Given out by the umpire, Grace walked with evident surprise back to the pavilion. As Frank told it, 'He got away with a bluff like that, time after time.'

In MCC's early games in the 1903 season, an early sign of Albert's changing status came when he didn't always open the bowling, only coming on as second or third change. On a rain-affected wicket at Lord's, the first two days washed out, he had to watch impatiently as Jack Hearne and Charlie Llewellyn, operating unchanged, bowled out London County for 72. In the second innings, he opened the bowling and showed what he could do, picking up 7-27 from the Pavilion End as MCC won the match in a day. This time, he had used his fast ball much more than he had of late, and it was too much for the lower-order batsmen.

When the county season began, Plum Warner, team captain in the absence of Gregor MacGregor, used Bernard Bosanquet's leg spin to open the bowling against Sussex, and later he was to use George Beldam. On his return, MacGregor also changed the bowling around. The old opening pairing of Hearne and Trott, once so deadly, could no longer be assumed.

As for his batting, he seemed to have resolved to rein himself in and not throw away his wicket cheaply. In the early part of the season, he had scored a useful 37 for MCC against Yorkshire at Lord's, when runs were hard to come by. An unusual feature of the match was that it was played on the Nursery ground, as the area in front of the main pavilion was flooded. Later in the month, the weather changed, the grounds becoming drier and harder, and against Gloucestershire, Middlesex scored freely with centuries by Plum Warner and Leonard Moon. Albert came in at number eight after a mid-order collapse, including the dismissal of Lord Gordon-Lennox – out for a duck in his sole first-class appearance. Partnered by Gerard Griffen, Albert had made a half-century when Jack Hearne came to the wicket, last man in. Ably supported by a steady 20 not out from his fellow professional, Albert went on to make a chanceless 103. As the stringer for the *Lichfield Mercury* put it, 'No professional at the present time is a greater favourite with the crowd at Lord's than Albert Trott, and when towards the end of the afternoon he completed his century there was quite a demonstration.' For *The Times*, this was the best innings he had played for many years and showed that he was not a 'wild hitter' but a 'batsman possessed of a remarkable number of strokes all around the wicket'. This was to be his highest score of the season.

Middlesex's prospects at the start of the season had not been particularly bright, as they had finished 12th in the 1902 season, but under Warner they had made a good start. Against a Yorkshire team that was struggling through Hirst's absence and Rhodes' inability to take a wicket, they won by nine wickets. Albert chipped in with three wickets in the first innings, but it was Hearne's ten in the match that did for the county champions. Individually and collectively, with Hearne's re-emergence and a variety in their bowling attack, Middlesex had grown stronger.

This time, Albert was selected for the two Gentlemen versus Players matches. At Lord's, he was cheered to the wicket by the crowd but was bowled first ball by Walter Brearley, too late on the stroke to a quick delivery. In the second innings, his 20 overs went for 120 as Fry scored an unbeaten double century. In a prestigious match, his overall contribution had been three tail-ender wickets, and the only redeeming feature of his play had been his usual excellent fielding. The next game against the Gentlemen came straight after. When he came to the crease at the Oval, his steady approach from a month before had been abandoned and he was in a reckless mood, hitting out in search of runs but finding few. In the second innings, he reverted to his more measured approach as the Players chased down a total, and he started well, but then mistimed one from Bradley. Yet again, a few tail-ender wickets was the extent of his contribution.

As Middlesex took on their rivals Surrey at Lord's, the game attracted much interest, with Middlesex unbeaten. Form with the bat still eluded him, but his interventions in the field were timely. He caught Holland in the slips and, immediately after, bowled Walker and Miller. On this occasion, he bowled impressively, as well as he had all season, going on to mop up the tail as he took 6-66.

At Old Trafford on a sticky wicket, Lancashire could do little against Albert and Jack Hearne. Rain had restricted the amount of time in the game, but MacGregor still boldly went for victory, opening the innings with Albert and Bosanquet as they tried to chase down 259. With runs still difficult to score on a tricky pitch, the game ended in a draw, with Albert on 35 not out.

In the next match, against Essex at Leytonstone, it was back to switching the bowling around. Albert sent down just two overs in the first innings, and took three wickets in the second as Middlesex used five bowlers. If a bowler didn't take a wicket, the ball was quickly thrown to someone else. His days of operating unchanged with Jack Hearne had gone.

By the time they played Somerset at Taunton, Middlesex were still unbeaten. Albert came on third change and bowled five expensive wicketless overs. Demoted to number ten in the batting order he made a characteristic 40, twice hitting the ball out of the ground. In the second innings his 20 helped Middlesex get home by a couple of wickets. Against Gloucestershire his bowling had become peripheral to the success of the team, as had Jack Hearne's. Middlesex won by 272 runs, bowling out Gloucestershire twice, but Albert only bowled two overs in the match. The amateurs had taken on the bowling work with Bosanquet, Hunt, Wells and George Beldam carrying the attack.

At Headingley, they suffered their sole defeat as Yorkshire took their revenge, their win comprehensive, this time having the benefit of Hirst and Rhodes, back in form. Albert's contribution was minor, as he took a couple of wickets coming on third change in the second innings.

After a couple of rain-affected matches at Lord's, Middlesex played their final County Championship match of the season against Surrey at the Oval. He came to the wicket when Middlesex were 182/6, and every ball he looked like getting out. Somehow, though, he managed to survive. He played to stumps, and the next day he was out to a good one-handed catch at third man off Richardson, his 40 runs coming in an hour. In the field, it was like it had always been in the past, when he and Jack bowled unchanged, dismissing Surrey for 57. His analysis read 12-5-19-6. Two hours' bright sunshine had made the pitch more difficult, and Albert, in control, varied his pace, the ball breaking several inches. As the *Yorkshire Post* put it, he was 'at one time simply irresistible'.

Middlesex were county champions for the first time since the competition had been formally organised in 1890. While the team had been successful and Albert had made significant contributions, his form had not touched the heights of three or four years previously. He had taken 105 wickets, but had only been called on to bowl half as many overs as he had sent down in 1900. His best return had been 7-28 against Cambridge University, when the students were at a loss against him. His other good returns had largely come on rain-affected pitches drying out. With the bat, a third of his 604 runs had come in three innings, with too much hitting out. *Cricket* listed his name among other batsmen who had suffered a 'more or less disappointing season'. As for his bowling, it said, 'It is sad to be obliged to chronicle a great falling-off in Trott.'

In the hope of buying a wicket, he had often resorted to serving up something hittable. It was left to the *Illustrated Police News* to defend him, under the headline 'Trott's Bad Balls': 'I was much amused to hear the other day, to hear a critic say, after watching Trott bowl for a time: "What a lot of rot that man is sending down." Two batsmen, however, were well set – one of them F.S. Jackson. The orthodox stuff was being hit all over the place, so Trott tried some "rot". It certainly was not academic bowling, but Jackson was tempted to hit at it, and retired caught and bowled. There cannot be anything very rotten in getting rid of a batsman of Jackson's calibre.'

The problem for Albert was that the English batsmen had grown wise to him, like their Australian counterparts. And he also had to win back the confidence of his own captain. He was still only 30 years old, with time to overcome these setbacks.

In the autumn, Plum Warner led an England team to Australia in an attempt to regain the Ashes. A committee selected the team, but the captain had the final say on who was included. In his book *How We Recovered the Ashes*, Warner discusses the players he selected, and, for him, the leading all-rounders in England were George Hirst and Len Braund. Despite him being good enough to represent the Players at the end of the season, Albert's name was not mentioned by his erstwhile captain as one that was even remotely under consideration.

14

'How weak people are given strength and made into physical giants'

THE ARRIVAL of the South Africans in England in 1904 enabled Albert to renew some old acquaintances, formed in the two seasons he had spent out there. One of the players on tour was Louis Tancred. Albert knew the three Tancred brothers well – Bernard, Vincent and Louis – as he had coached at the Union Cricket Club. During Albert's time as a coach, Vincent had developed into a fine batsman making some good scores. He played in one Test against Lord Hawke's XI and had then been unlucky to be left out.

In 1904, the younger Louis had been selected for the touring team, while Vincent, a year older than his brother, had been omitted yet again after poor scores against the Australian touring team in 1902. In early June, with the tour well under way, Vincent, an ex-soldier who had fought on the side of the British in the Boer War, was playing billiards with friends at the New Club in Johannesburg, outwardly in the best of health and spirits. In the bar chatting with friends, he borrowed a Webley service revolver from one of them and returned to his rented room in the lake suburb of Florida. He shot himself three times in the head. His brother Bernard, hearing that Vincent had taken a revolver and concerned about his fragile mental state, took a train out to Florida, where he found his brother unconscious on the floor of his hotel room. He died four hours later. His suicide came as a surprise, and different theories have been offered to explain why he did what he did. It could have been disappointment at his non-selection, money troubles or the disposition towards melancholia that was stated at the inquest. It could have been that he had not achieved as much as his brothers on the cricket field. But it came as a shock to men such as Albert, Bill Brockwell, Len Braund, Cyril Foley and others who had played cricket with him. It must have made a strong impact on them, although doubtless they did not say very much about it, in either public or private. His brother Louis stood down from the tour for nine days, before returning to make a series of big scores, ostensibly in memory of his brother.

Vincent's death was not mentioned in *Cricket* – only 'the wonderfully good innings' of his brother Louis. The taboo around suicide was just too strong, and it was left to *Wisden* to record the bare fact that he had 'shot himself'.

Albert had played in the same MCC team as Louis Tancred earlier in that season. The South Africans had arrived early, to get used to playing on turf wickets. MCC selected an eclectic line-up against Kent, including Louis Tancred and three other members of the touring team along with Albert, Frank Tarrant and Sir Arthur Conan Doyle. Louis Tancred made a well-compiled 45, and Shepstone, another of the South Africans, made a similarly careful 45. They were making the most of the occasion to get used to English wickets. On his home turf and unrestrained by this need, Albert hit 43 out of 59 in half an hour, with *Cricket,* perhaps somewhat sardonically, noting that 'Trott's innings was of the kind that is vastly admired by spectators'.

Later in the season, Albert played for Middlesex against the tourists at Lord's, where Frank Tarrant was in the team by special dispensation, having not yet completed his two-year qualification period for the county. In the first innings, Middlesex came up against a very quick Johannes Kotze, who ran in off 22 yards with the wicketkeeper, Halliwell, standing well back. The combination paid off, and Tarrant, unready and discomfited, found himself at the crease earlier than he had expected, with Middlesex two wickets down and no runs on the board. It was unpleasant from the start. A ball came in from the off and hit him on the elbow. A similar ball came in, this time striking him in the heart, knocking him out cold. It took ten minutes and a large brandy before he could resume. He tried to run himself out to get away from Kotze, but Plum Warner was equally reluctant to face the South African. Tarrant was relieved when he was eventually skittled for 31 and could return to the pavilion. W.G. Grace, a spectator at the game, examined his arm and said he was seriously hurt and needed to see a specialist. His arm went black from the shoulder to wrist, and later in the game he tried to bowl but found it difficult.

This was how Tarrant remembered it 30 years later. He approached his good friend Albert Trott and promised him the biggest drink in the pavilion if he could exact some sort of revenge on Kotze for him.

With seven wickets down in the second innings and 14 more runs needed to win, the South Africans looked to be in the strongest of positions. Warner put Albert on to bowl and he picked up a couple of wickets, as the score reached 202/9. As Kotze walked to the wicket, Tarrant reminded Albert of his promise and 'he grinned in a knowing way'. The other batsman, White, managed to score five, and three extras were scrambled, bringing the scores level. Kotze, though, was now on strike. Albert's first ball to him was a full toss that swung in from the leg and knocked him to the ground. The next ball sent the middle stump flying, and the game was a tie. Albert had taken 6-75 off 22.3 overs.

Albert's batting that season revolved around the usual themes. There were times when he hit well, and there were times when he took more care. At the Oval, he managed to resist the underarm lobs of Digby Jephson, making a useful 42, perhaps remembering from the 1899 Gentlemen versus Players match that it was not a good idea to try to hit the amateur out of the ground. Now he rarely batted up the order, usually going in at eight or nine, and at his best there were cameos for Middlesex and MCC – useful thirties and forties rather than bigger innings.

He had to score runs or take wickets, as he was on talent money, and doing well on the field meant living well. Around this time, Plum Warner wrote that Albert was paid five shillings for every run that he scored in May. 'Trott made a splendid drive for £1, which he followed up with a brace of half-sovereigns, and a well-timed leg glance for fifteen shillings.' In the pursuit of a whimsical tone in the article, Warner may well have exaggerated how much Albert was paid, as the amounts are generous for the time. Harry Lee reckoned that the pre-1914 rate was ten shillings for a fifty, and £1 for a century or five wickets. It used to be said that a major disadvantage of the talent system was that the professionals played for themselves rather than for their side. This was always difficult to pin down, but it may have been one explanation that was offered for those short deliveries sent down in an attempt to buy a wicket. A few years later, Warner, ostensibly an amateur, persuaded the Middlesex committee to award him a liberal £3 and ten shillings in expenses for every game he played, home or away.

Gregor MacGregor had introduced a merit mark system for professionals the previous year. Each merit mark earned was worth five shillings and was paid in November alongside a bonus. The merit mark system smacked of the old school, the senior prefects keeping the younger boys in line. The committee warned the professionals that this bonus was not to be regarded as winter pay and they should not rely on it being paid every year. In 1904, Albert picked up £72 15s, merit marks and bonus combined, while Jack Hearne came away with £62 10s. A few years later, the Middlesex committee decided to pay the November bonus in instalments, a form of compulsory budgeting for the professionals that, at the same time, improved the club's cash flow.

In the Essex match at Leyton, Albert came up against the amateur Edward Sewell. According to Sewell, who described this incident in 1940 in *The Scotsman*, under the headline 'Albert Trott as the Originator of Body Line', Albert set a field with the wicketkeeper standing back, four slips, an extra slip behind and between first and second slip, a deep third man, a fine long leg and 'a short leg deepish behind the wicket'. The only two players in front of the wicket were Albert and Plum Warner, the captain, at cover. This field was reminiscent of some of the ones Albert had set in Australia in 1895 when he was experimenting with becoming a full-time fast bowler. Sewell said, 'I had three overs of this rubbish and not even one yorker in the lot, that being one of Trottie's best when he was bowling very fast. And he was not slow that day! I was not hit, nor was my wicket, and I gave no chance. My chief surprise was that Plum stood three overs of it. Plum did call a halt, saying, "That's not bowling, you go off," to Trott.' Sewell added, 'It would have been on the posters of the evening papers had any bowler done the same thing these last ten years or so.'

The reason for this spurt of fast bowling against this particular batsman was all down to an article that Sewell had written. Sewell said, 'I had made the innocent, and perfectly true statement that some cricketers questioned the fairness of Trott's delivery when he let go the swerve from leg to offside. He was a not very brainy, although extremely brawny, mortal and he read into this an accusation of throwing. I never saw Trott throw a ball when he was bowling, nor did anyone else. But when he bowled that particular swerve, with off break spin on the ball, on a perpendicular axis, there was a bending of the elbow which the uninitiated almost invariably believe to accompany unfair or illegal delivery.' Sewell seemed to be saying that it looked like he was throwing the delivery, but he actually wasn't.

Albert made a respectable 747 runs over the season, his average dropping by a couple, but there were no centuries and his top score was 67. Against the Gentlemen at the Oval, when the Players went down by an innings, he must have enjoyed hitting about his Middlesex teammate Bosanquet, paying him back a little for the punishment he had received at Napier. Bosanquet, a powerful hitter and successful with his leg breaks and googlies, had taken over from him as the leading all-rounder at Middlesex.

Nevertheless, while Albert's bowling was not as devastating, he still picked up 108 wickets, including a couple of ten-wicket hauls. *Cricket*'s praise was faint yet fair: 'Trott was at times most successful.' In one of the most important fixtures of the year, Middlesex versus Yorkshire at Lord's, his first innings analysis read 5.2-2-7-4 with all of his victims clean bowled. Middlesex won by 77 runs. Later in the season on the same ground against Lancashire, MacGregor brought him on as first change at the nursery end. He clean bowled Tyldesley with a beautiful ball and then had Archie MacLaren caught behind. *The Times* noted that while he had been 'generally rather expensive', on this day 'he kept the runs down as well as taking wickets'. It was another one of those 'his best for some time' performances. His final analysis read 31.4-10-59-6. Following on, Lancashire only escaped defeat with the help of the weather and preserved their unbeaten record, finishing as county champions.

Middlesex finished fourth that season, the consensus being that they were best in August when their amateurs were all available, and they were also short of an up-and-coming bowler.

But Albert's personal stock remained high, as an entertainer and a personality, touching all sections of society. Prince Edward and Prince Albert, ten and nine years old, grandsons of Edward VII, were keen followers of the game. They played it at Windsor Park and watched games from the secretary's box at Lord's or the Oval. The *Evening News* reported that the two princes were leaving Lord's in a car one evening when they passed Albert. He lifted his cap to the boys, and they saluted in return. Their tutor spoke to them immediately and evidently mentioned Albert's name. Prince Eddie put his head out of the window again and smiled and saluted Albert. 'There was at any rate, one proud professional at Lord's last night.' The word 'proud' gives it away: it was highly probable that Albert, with his connections to the paper, was the source of the story.

Off the field, he always sought diversion and entertainment. At the season's end, he had done enough to be included in the Players of the South team who were playing the Gentlemen at Dean Park, Bournemouth. On Friday, 2 September, the members of both teams were staying at the Grand Hotel in the town. A Mr Cowley, a manager of the Bournemouth Trading Company, invited Albert and Len Braund, along with a Mr Masterson, to a ride in his Gladiator car in the New Forest. They returned to the hotel at 9pm for a late dinner, and, the night still being fine, a further ride was suggested. The party was driven for several miles in the area of Poole, and, on returning from Branksome, a sewer cart approached them at about 2am. They successfully overtook the vehicle, which was carrying the town's night soil, only to hit a second sewer cart behind it. Len Braund and Albert were thrown out by the impact, with Cowley bruised against the steering wheel, while Masterson landed on his head. Severely injured, he was taken to hospital in an ambulance but eventually recovered. The next day at the cricket, still shaken from his nocturnal exploits, Braund put himself down the order, and the Players offered little resistance as they were bowled out in the fourth innings.

There were no sanctimonious rebukes in the press for staying out late and drinking in the course of an important game. Alcohol restored the spirits and celebrated good company, and the Gentlemen versus Players matches, for example, were often characterised by heavy drinking. When the fixture was played at Lord's, MCC always provided champagne for the Players team at the end of the game. This was discontinued in 1907, after Arnold of Worcestershire behaved so badly. While there were no restrictions on players drinking, being worse for drink in public and inappropriate conduct was frowned upon. A man had to hold his drink.

Meanwhile, in Melbourne, Harry's mental health had improved and he had played cricket for Victoria again, although he now heftily topped the scales at 16st. His financial affairs had still not rallied sufficiently for him to take care of his father. Adolphus had to engineer his own escape from the Benevolent Asylum, where he had remained for over a year. Described in *The Argus* as an elderly man 'well-known in cricketing circles', he was detected by the matron in the act of 'courting' one of the 'female inmates'. The matron took steps to prevent a repetition of the behaviour, but a few days afterwards the 'female inmate' left the asylum, and the next morning her 'elderly lover' also left. The woman was Josephine McMahon, and she married Adolphus shortly after. Josephine, a Catholic born in Ireland, had money of her own, and when she left, the Benevolent Asylum pursued a claim against her as she had already made a will in their favour. Adolphus had been awarded a state old-age pension, so the two of them must have had enough to pay the rent on a house in Peel Street, Prahan where they set up home together. The treatment of the story in *The Argus* indicates how times have changed, as the story was told under the headline 'Pauper Romance'. If people lacked money and relied on charity, that was their fault, and their dignity was of no importance. The article was based around the minutes of the committee meeting of the Benevolent Society, and although Adolphus and Josephine were not named, their identities could be easily surmised by the newspaper's readers.

When Albert's daughter Hilda was born on 29 May, he would have been around for this family event, as he had a day off between two games at Lord's. No doubt he was pleased with the new arrival, but a growing family and the need to fund his convivial lifestyle meant that extra money was always needed. He had either loaned for a fee or sold the ball that he had hit over the Lord's pavilion in 1899, and it was now on display in John Wisden's shop window in Cranbourne Street. Attached to the ball was a letter from Albert confirming its provenance, the ball that he 'hit over the pavilion in 1899'. In a letter to *The Field*, 'Old Blue', an MCC member, said he had been at the top of the north-west tower of the pavilion at the time, and while the ball had cleared the front-facing roof, it had hit the sloping roof that faced the garden, before dropping into it. As far as Old Blue was concerned, Albert couldn't claim that he had fully 'cleared' the pavilion, and that feat remained to be accomplished.

Another source of income came from an unexpected quarter, when the Pulvermacher Belt Company approached Albert. The company tapped into the new wonder source of energy, electricity, and manufactured belts that, when worn under the clothes, cured all kinds of nervous and chronic diseases. Made of copper and zinc, the belts were dipped in vinegar before being strapped to the body, where they sent an electric twitch to nearby muscles. In a full-page advertisement in the *Penny Illustrated Newspaper* in July 1905, there is a line drawing of Albert about to bowl, under the headline, 'How Weak People are Given Strength and Made into Physical Giants'. The advertisement begins by listing his cricketing achievements for Middlesex, and then goes on to say: 'Mr Trott, although from time to time undergoing severe physical strains, is a man who is youthful, light-hearted, possesses nerves like bars of steel, dauntless courage, tireless energy, and elastic step – truly a specimen of superb manhood.'

In short, he is a hero. The advertisement includes a concocted letter of endorsement from Albert, where he says that 'when I finished a day's cricket I felt done up. My limbs ached, my back was bad …'. But the Pulvermacher provides the cure, and it's so convenient that he can even wear it on the playing field and in bed.

The text refers throughout to manliness and the 'manly man', vigour and courage, qualities that are evident in a man like Albert Trott. It also talks about 'vigour' and 'vitality', the turn-of-the-century code words for sexual energy. There was a great fear at this time about the effects of masturbation on young men and how it depleted the life force through untoward ejaculation. There were different models of the Pulvermacher, and some of the ones for men included a little pouch so that the testicles could get the full benefit of the electrical twitches. Other models were advertised with a bare-chested classical man in a throbbing belt, hands thrust behind his head, homoerotic style. The exact model that Albert was endorsing was not shown. The readers, though, would have got the message: if men like Albert Trott use the Pulvermacher, it must be a good thing. Perhaps he even gave it a try after a long stint in the field and strapped it on when he went to bed. The advertisement ran throughout the summer in a variety of forms and publications in the popular press. Doubtless his fellow professionals ribbed him for endorsing the belt.

If the Pulvermacher had any magic, it failed to work for Albert in the 1905 season. Middlesex had a poor time of it, with Hearne, Bosanquet and others falling short, but Albert's season was worse. In the previous years, there may have been a decline, but an occasional stand-out performance had always saved him. In 1905, there was scarcely a sniff of his past glories. *Cricket* was blunt in its summing up: 'Trott, who for some years was the mainstay of the side, is no longer much use with the bat or the ball.' An average of 13.80 with the bat, with a top score of 45, and 62 wickets was the limit of his achievement.

A mere suggestion of what he could do came against Essex at Lord's, when he hit 43 not out in 30 minutes while Tarrant, now qualified for Middlesex, laboured over 48 in a couple of hours. While he may have been disappointed when his innings was cut short by a declaration, it was the manner in which he'd played that enabled Warner to set Essex a target. Although Albert picked up a couple of wickets, Middlesex couldn't bowl the visitors out, and Essex chased down the 254 in 53 overs for the loss of three wickets.

Against their rivals Surrey at Lord's, he took eight wickets in the game. In the first innings, he bowled a young Jack Hobbs and in the second innings he forced him to hit his wicket. But Middlesex's win over their neighbours was one of the few bright spots in the season.

Albert played only 21 first-class matches that season, compared with the 36 he had played in 1900, and he played little for MCC. He was not selected for the Gentlemen versus Players matches or for any other representative games. In July, he was down in Wiltshire at Heywood House, playing country house cricket against Westbury United. This was the kind of fixture against the vicar, the head gardener and the groom in the outfield that he used to play at the end of the season. This was also a year in which the Australians toured and England were on top in the series. As the Australians struggled in the Tests, it was facetiously suggested that Darling should try to call up some of the Australians playing in England, 'even Albert Trott'.

The concerns about his batting were hardly new. In 1902, playing for MCC against London County at Lord's, he came in at number five. He arrived at the crease, outwardly in a desperate hurry to get at Llewellyn, the bowler. When the umpire asked him what guard he would take, he said, 'Oh anything will do for me.' Llewellyn clean bowled him first ball. The newspaper story said that he didn't take a guard because he wanted to get on and hit the bowler, but his refusal was also a case of not respecting his own talent, of not taking the game seriously. It may have been an occasion such as this that prompted Lord Hawke's remark that 'Trott was rather like Tom Emmett, full of drollery and too apt to take his batting lightly'. The incident where he didn't take a guard was forgotten at the time, because his lapses could be compensated for by a powerful display of hitting as he quickly returned to his best form. When runs are just around the corner and the game comes easily to you, then you can take it lightly. But when runs are hard to find, and you swing between playing your natural game and playing yourself in, and neither approach brings results, then you can only wait for form to return. By 1905, he was struggling.

Sammy Woods always said it was the hit over the pavilion in 1899 that ruined Albert's batting. He spent the rest of this career trying to repeat it, rather than trying to bat properly. 'Poor chap, he never did much in the batting line afterwards; it can't be done with a bat that weight.' As we have seen, Albert did play some useful innings after 1899, and there were times when he took it steady at the start. But perhaps Woods had a point about the bat. He had moved away from the conventional-weight, ready-made James Cobbett bat that he'd used in 1899. Woods and others reckoned that one of Albert's bats weighed over 3lb, and it was described as 'a savage beast of a thing' by A.E. Knight. Walter Warsop, a batmaker based in St John's Wood, made it to Albert's specification, with a special bulged back, the first of its kind. 'See if you can get a bit more wood behind it, Walter,' you can hear him say. It was a big bat by any standards. Frank Tarrant too felt that his friend still had it in him to play a good innings, but with the caveat, 'Albert could bat as well as ever, if he would give up trying to hit the first ball out of the ground.'

Throughout the season, Albert's name appeared above his column in the *Weekly Dispatch*, his contribution probably confined to the occasional chat to his ghost. This profitable arrangement was ruffled when it came to light that the column was not all Albert's own work. In the column, he supposedly wrote about the batting of Lionel Palairet, but 160 words of the article were identical to the words of C.B. Fry published in a book, *Giants of the Game*. Albert had to explain away his error in the sister paper, the *Evening News*: 'I have been taken to task for not stating that my opinion of Mr Palairet's style was really Mr C.B. Fry's expressed opinion. It was an omission on the part of my typist. Like all cricketers I do make mistakes, and I ought to have read my "copy" more carefully. But I know C.B. will forgive me. P.S. By C.B. I mean Mr Fry and not Campbell-Bannerman.'

Of course C.B. would have forgiven him. It's likely that Fry had recycled some of his own earlier copy (the article had originally appeared in the *Windsor Magazine*) and published it under Albert's name in the *Weekly Dispatch*. Fry had probably written the apology too. Fry, late at night, in his flannel suit with sleeves rolled up, tapping out copy for a myriad of publications while everyone else played cards, is an abiding image of turn-of-the-century cricket. Later in the year, further evidence suggested that Fry was Albert's ghost when a column in the *Evening News*, published under Albert's signature, gave a list of those players who had been invited to tour South Africa with MCC. The composition of the touring party had not been disclosed elsewhere, and *Cricket* seemed surprised that Albert should be privy to this advance information. He would not have known the composition of the party. Fry was one of the amateurs invited, he knew the names of the other players who had been asked, and it was he who had written Albert's column.

In November, James 'Dimboola' Phillips, the umpire, wrote to MCC saying he was retiring from the game. For some time he had been studying, finding odd moments around the cricket to consult algebraic tables, so he could become a mining engineer in Canada. He had stood in 29 Test matches, respected by both teams as a man who would give a fair decision. As an umpire, from beneath his deerstalker hat, he had been fearless, taking on the chuckers at the behest of MCC. He had no-balled Ernie Jones, Tom McKibbin and C.B. Fry. At one time, until his weight got the better of him, he had been able to play all year round for Middlesex and Victoria, something that had become difficult to do. But Phillips always knew how to do things the right way, as he wrote to MCC and thanked them for all they had done for him. In return, they recognised his contribution to the club and to the game, and they were sorry to see him go. For Albert, Dimboola Jim was the man who had encouraged him to come to England, someone who had been around in London as a mentor, part of the group of Victorian expatriates who had visited Balmoral Road. When he was in London, Phillips would have been a good influence as Albert tried to negotiate the trickier pathways at the end of his career.

His finances were a recurring pressure. In November, Albert wrote to Middlesex and asked whether he could have a benefit in the 1906 season. But the Whit Monday benefit match was under the control of MCC, and the county club had no claim upon it. Albert's request was turned down. He would have to wait.

The next year, the Middlesex club finished 11th in the County Championship, failing to improve on their finish in the 1905 season. Their fall was 'inexplicable' after they had done so well in 1903 according to *The Times*, but the team was chopped and changed around. Bosanquet was often unavailable due to business commitments, while others could not play regularly. It was an unsettled team, the batting order often changed as the captains tried different things, hoping they would came off. Their bowling was not especially threatening and Albert took only 62 wickets in all first-class games, always too erratic to be relied on.

A new personal nadir arrived for him in the match against Surrey, a team he had always enjoyed playing against. As Surrey scored 419, he was used for only six overs, which went for 12 runs. In Middlesex's second innings, MacGregor relied on a series of nightwatchmen, who lost their wickets. Albert was last man in and made 15 not out, barely given the chance to contribute to the game as Middlesex lost by an innings. To be underused in this way, in front of his home crowd, must have hurt his pride. The time of his great all-round successes seemed distant with this change in his status.

After this debacle, he had a chance in the next game to put things right. It was probably better that MacGregor was not available to captain the side. Plum Warner gave him the opportunity to show what he could do with the bat when they travelled up to Headingley to play Yorkshire. He put him up the order to five, hoping it would give him a sense of responsibility. After kicking his heels for the first day waiting for the rain to clear, he went in and, as *The Times* said, 'succeeded in changing the aspect of the game'. He top-scored with 83 off Rhodes, Hirst and Haigh, and he 'hit hard, showed restraint and good judgement'. In the very last match of the season, he played an innings similar in character against Surrey at the Oval, this time making 75. At this point in his career and this late on in the season, he needed these runs, just to remind people of what he could do. His final total of 952 runs had a respectability about it. Now that his bowling was on the wane, perhaps he could become a full-time batsman?

In October of that year, MCC decided that the next year's Whit Monday match should be given to Middlesex for a benefit, and Lacey, the secretary of MCC, recorded the following note in the minutes: 'They having nominated A. Trott.'

15

His last bow

THE MCC committee, keen to improve the facilities at Lord's, had been spending money on making changes to the pavilions. Frank Verity, who had continued his father's architectural practice, added white cast-iron balconies to the lower dressing rooms. These distinctive features, so familiar today and seemingly ever present, gave the amateurs a better view of the game. The professionals' pavilion was extensively remodelled, providing more space for the ground staff, including a larger changing room. Albert always liked playing at Lord's. He must have welcomed the extra space, as the pavilion was not just used by the home-team professionals but also by the visiting pros, as well as the ground staff. However, the changes weren't to everyone's taste, as Leo McKinstry explains in his biography of Jack Hobbs. The Surrey professional never liked playing at the ground, because the professionals' pavilion offered a poor view of the game. He didn't like the food at Lord's either, and always found Surrey more of an egalitarian club than Middlesex.

Although Albert's performances had dipped, he still could live off his reputation, his presence greater than his current on-field performances. In 1906, he had appeared in George Beldam and Charles Fry's *Great Bowlers and Fielders: Their Methods at a Glance*. The book, with its use of action photographs, gives some indication of what he was like as a bowler, as he demonstrates his various grips, his face stony and impassive, worn beyond its years. Captured at the point of delivery, with his head low, there is the delivery where his front foot is slanted as he bowls across his body, and another delivery where his front foot is straighter and his head even lower. He is almost frowning in concentration as he releases the ball, the peak of his cap pulled down low, shielding his eyes, his head leaning away. 'A bowler of several kinds' is how Fry describes him before listing his different deliveries. 'He is not all these bowlers during one spell, nor even during one particular match, but in the course of a season he is all of them.' In the photos of him fielding at short slip, you get the sense of his athleticism and the size of his hands as he moves down low to take a catch. 'For almost every catch at second slip Trott uses two hands. He prefers falling to the ball to using his feet, and he has brought falling almost to an art. He often rolls over after making a catch.'

If he felt any trepidation when he began the 1907 season, he put it to the back of his mind. There was an element of pressure, knowing that his benefit match came early on at the end of the month. It was the last chance to make a lump sum. The game was over the Whit Monday bank holiday weekend – a sought-after slot for a benefit, with the prospect of a decent-sized crowd if the weather was fine. England in May: rain was never just a possibility. Precautions had been taken, with the Whit Monday gate insured for £500.

As was usual for him, he began the year with a run of fixtures at Lord's. After his inconsistent bowling of the previous season, he knew that he needed to knuckle down early on to try to find the form he had lost. Experiments shelved for now, this was Albert Trott, the man who put the ball on the spot. Against Yorkshire for MCC, he kept a good length on a wicket slowed by rain and finished with match figures of 10-77. Against Derbyshire, he was the bowler who got the batsmen into difficulties, and another ten wickets came his way. It was a batsman's wicket against Hampshire, but all were agreed that he was the pick of the Middlesex bowlers. He was Albert Trott as he should have been, the one his critics wanted – not trying to buy wickets with tempting loose stuff.

The next match against Somerset was his benefit. Different newspapers gave him a thumbnail profile to speed him on his way: well-known Anglo-Australian – was sensational – of late, not so good – but has done well this season – worthy and popular – this is his benefit, so do turn up. Albert would receive the takings from the turnstiles and, as with other testimonial matches at Lord's, no collection was allowed among the crowd, but there was a collection box either side of the gate.

To celebrate Albert's performance in the game, the sporting Sammy Woods presented him with an individual souvenir – a straw hat woven with a hand-painted ribbon, with three rabbits on the front and four on the back.

There were those who found other means of fashioning a story from the man of the moment and his double hat-trick. In a display of opportunistic photojournalism, *The Sketch* photographed him in his tweed suit and cap, practising throwing the boomerang in Regent's Park. The headline read 'Learning to Swerve?', and the brief news item confidently stated that Albert was an expert boomerang thrower. It seemed to link his mastery of swerve as a bowler with the mystery of the boomerang. It was probably the first time he had picked one up. A couple of days later, on the Saturday, he helped out the Paddington Cricket Club when they played at Marlow for the first time. The Buckinghamshire club didn't seem to know that he was 'assisting' their visitors, so few were there to see him take six wickets and knock the ball around for 32.

His feat against Somerset had lifted Middlesex from the gloom of the previous season. In his next game, against Gloucestershire, regaining the accolade of the main bowler, he was given first use of the ball. Even in Albert's best years, Jack Hearne had taken that honour. He was economical and picked up six wickets, but it was Tarrant who cleaned up with 13, the Victorian developing into a fine all-rounder. The two Australians bowled as a pair. Against South Africa, a rejuvenated Albert reeled off six successive maidens, and he ended up with a total of 50 first-class wickets in May.

Throughout his time in England, Albert's fielding had never lapsed. In the slips, he was as good with his left hand as with his right; whether the ball came low or wide, he seemed to catch it, defying a creaking back. His success was attributed to his quick reflexes and the size of his hands. In the slang of the day, the latter were referred to as 'landing nets' or 'carpet bags'. At Lord's, when the touring South Africans arrived to play MCC, Albert was introduced to Arthur Nourse. When they exchanged greetings, Albert's hand was enveloped in the South African's grasp so that it disappeared from view. In the mitt stakes, Nourse was in another league. Undeterred by any feelings of inferiority, Albert went on to take three fine catches in the game. Around this time, it was Bobby Abel who pointed out that, irrespective of his batting and bowling, Albert had always been worth his place in the Middlesex team on account of his fielding alone.

Middlesex were a notoriously poor fielding side. Walter Mead, the Essex pro, always felt sorry for Albert and Jack Hearne because of the number of catches that were put down. Mead understood how they felt, because he suffered the same problem at Essex. In public, neither Jack nor Albert complained, but there must have been times when they lamented their luck in the earshot of the other professionals. For some players in the golden age, fielding was classed as a voluntary activity.

The match reports were always fairly discreet about dropped catches, the comments in the press either non-existent or restrained. Warner, for example, dropped an easy catch off Albert against Sussex, *The Times* confining its comments to 'He ought to have been caught by Warner.' It wasn't just Warner. There were plenty of others in the Middlesex team who let Albert down, and 'he was not helped by his fieldsmen'. MacGregor, behind the stumps, suffered from inconsistency in what was to be his last season in county matches. In his autobiography, Warner was to say that the team's fielding was dreadful at this time. If you did drop a catch, you were not allowed to smile. The only time you could do that was if you dropped a catch off your own bowling, but, as Albert said, 'You have to be as good a bowler as me to do that.'

Playing for MCC against Oxford University, Albert had another ten-wicket haul in his match figures. In the second innings against Hampshire, he batted gamely with a bruised thumb, making 42 in an effort to save the game. The injury had restricted him to a couple of overs in the second innings, and now it kept him out of the next few games. By the time he returned to the team in August, he was able to rediscover some form at Old Trafford. On a wicket made difficult by rain, he went in at four and hit out, top-scoring with 52 as Middlesex made 182. On this pitch it was enough to win by an innings, and in the second innings he took 4-7 off 5.2 overs.

After the disappointments of the previous season, he had come back with the ball and taken 96 wickets at 16.67, his best return for three years. His performances later in the season, after suffering his bruised thumb, had fallen short. Early on, though, concentrating more on pitching the ball on a length, and that excellent return against Somerset, had helped him. With the bat, he'd made 549 runs and shown that he could adapt to the circumstances and play to the requirements of the team. But what really concerned him at that point was how little he had made from his benefit. At 34 years old, he must have wondered how many more overs he had left in him, and time was running out to make a pot of money to ease him along in his retirement from the game.

Although many newspapers commented on how Albert's feat with the ball had cost him money because of the premature end to the match, in reality it had made little impact. Few would have been likely to turn up after lunch. Tasmania's *Daily Telegraph* quoted an English paper as saying, 'The gate money for Albert's benefit amounted to £325, but with subscriptions it will reach between £500 and £600.' Albert had insured the gate for £500. Although it rained for a couple of hours on the Monday and play was curtailed, the insurance company refused to make up the difference between the amount received and £500, on the grounds that there had been a significant amount of play during the day.

The sum of £600 would be worth around £60,000 in 2017. For a tour of Australia in 1903, an English professional earned a fee of £300 plus expenses and a possible bonus. Even with its greater purchasing power in 1907, £600 wasn't a great deal of money, and not enough to provide long-term financial security. It's worth comparing it with other benefits for professional cricketers of the Edwardian era. In 1907, David Denton of Yorkshire's benefit was estimated to be in the region of £1,800 to £2,000, aided by crowds in excess of 20,000 on the first two days of the game. A few years earlier, George Hirst, a player of similar stature to Albert, had picked up £3,703, made up of the gate money, collections and £1,000 in subscriptions.

In 1903, MCC granted the Middlesex versus Somerset match as a benefit to Dick Attewell, former England player, a member of the MCC ground staff and an umpire. The loyal servant Attewell had already picked up a benefit of £1,000 as a Nottinghamshire player in 1899. His second benefit brought in £500 from the gate takings, but MCC retained the right to ensure that any benefit monies from matches at Lord's were used in a proper way, to stop players squandering them. This went back to 1899, when Lord Hawke had proposed, and the MCC committee had agreed, that the counties should have 'direct control over investment or disposal of benefit monies'. In prudent mode, MCC decided that 'the proceeds of Attewell's benefit might be used for the purpose of liquidating his debts'. Dick Attewell had enjoyed a career at the top level, touring Australia three times, but the financial mess into which he stepped when he stopped playing gives an inkling of what life could be like for the ex-professional.

But these amounts begin to rattle like loose change when we consider what W.G. Grace made from the game. His first testimonial, in 1879, had brought in a useful £1,458, while his second, in 1896, collected by MCC, Gloucestershire and the *Daily Telegraph* under the auspices of the 'shilling' for W.G. fund, amassed the gargantuan sum of £9,703. The latter alone is close to £1m in 2017 purchasing power.

With the low takings on the gate, it was down to the subscriptions from generous individuals or organisations to boost the pot of benefit money. Middlesex contributed £50 to Albert's fund, while MCC contributed £10. The latter was an amount unequivocally on the low side, considering that he'd represented the club so well over the previous 11 years, bringing in the crowds to Lord's, as well as sending down deliveries in the nets hour after hour. But MCC never donated huge amounts to professionals' benefits, with their usual contribution being £10 to £25 at this time. They were consistently careful in their attitude to spending money, whether it was refusing to pay expenses for amateurs to play in important matches at Lord's – and then, after requests, capping the amount to £1 a day – or spending time considering whether Lambert was worth 25 or 30 shillings a week as a net bowler. Without question, they thought they were being fair, and what they feared most was the nightmare of all committees, that of setting precedents. Nevertheless, men such as A.J. Webbe, Lord Hawke and Plum Warner, committee members all, had played in the same teams as Albert, knew him well and must have had an inkling of his financial circumstances.

The intention, no doubt, was that subscriptions from those who valued Albert would swell the final sum. The snag was that there was another man simultaneously in need of funds. John Murdoch, the assistant secretary to MCC and to Middlesex, had managed the MCC side that toured Australia in 1903/04 under the captaincy of Plum Warner. Murdoch suffered from cancer of the throat, and *Cricket* intimated that there had been a hope that the months in the Australian climate would improve his condition. Murdoch lived in an MCC-owned house in Elm Tree Road, and in 1886 he had received part of the profits from the England XI versus Australia match at Lord's. But, with doctors' bills to pay, Middlesex realised that he was in pressing need of financial assistance, and the takings from their match against Essex at Lord's were set aside as a benefit. This took place a fortnight after Albert's benefit and brought in £54, far short of what was envisaged. Determined to help one of their employees, A.J. Webbe, former Middlesex captain and a member of the MCC committee, then moved that 'further assistance' was required for Murdoch, and MCC voted a further sum of £500 for their assistant secretary. The extra money may have brought Murdoch some peace of mind, but it did nothing for his physical health. By the end of the month, he was dead, and a trust was set up for his family, administered by MCC.

Both MCC and Middlesex acknowledged that the amount collected for Albert's benefit was insufficient, and that more needed to be drummed up. Both clubs felt that the timing of his benefit had been unfortunate, and that Murdoch's testimonial 'somewhat interfered with Trott's list in the pavilion'. However, there does seem to be an imbalance between a £10 donation to one of the leading professionals and £500 for an assistant secretary. The matter came to a head at Middlesex's annual meeting at the end of November, when the club stated in public that the amount of the benefit was inadequate to recompense Albert Trott for his contributions to the club. Shortly afterwards, Middlesex announced that they would be making up the amount to £800. The club did have money: for some years they had invested in Bank of England consols, and there was £4,500 in their account.

While £800 was less than a third of George Hirst's benefit, it was still a useful sum for Albert. Invested properly, it could provide a pension and supplement other earnings. James Murdoch's benefit was invested in this way, and, by 1931, with the advantage of the high 1920s interest rates, it was still paying out an income of £99 a year to his descendants. Albert's money was put on deposit in the London and South Western Bank under the control of Middlesex. Within months, however, he was eating into his capital. He asked the club to advance him £115 that he owed on his house. They agreed to pay this from his benefit money, and to pay his medical bill of £3 5s out of club funds.

16

Scenes from a life

AFTER HIS couple of lean years, Albert's double hat-trick in his benefit game had propelled him back into the public eye, and there was a renewed appetite for Albatrott news. A brief account of his life appeared in the English sporting papers and was repeated in the Australian press.

'The "Albertrott" is a strange bird. He is a cricketing genius, with all the eccentricities of genius strong upon him both in action and speech.'

The profile continues in the mock-heroic mode:

'If Albert Trott drove a ball from Lord's Ground into the Great Central Station, at Marylebone, with his bat of 2lb 9oz, no one would be surprised. If Albert Trott turned a Catherine wheel as he saw a batsman pose for his stroke, and made a wonderful catch as he was regaining his natural upright position, no man who knows him would be astonished. If Albert Trott dismissed eleven men in less than two overs people would just shrug their shoulders and whisper: "Trott again", or "wonderful man, Trott. Never knows what he can do!"'

The profile was written in July of 1907 by Jimmy Catton, better known to his readers as 'Tityrus', of the *Athletic News*. Almost 20 years later, he recalled the eccentricities of Albert's speech when he had interviewed him that day. 'How Trott did orate, how he told me everything he ever did, the date on which each event happened, and the exact figures he established. What a marvellous memory, thought I, because as a rule, cricketers are too casual about their deeds. When I came to write Trott's story I discovered that it was teeming with inaccuracies, and that scarcely a date or a figure was correct.'

Jimmy Catton, as he freely admitted himself, was not above manufacturing interviews with non-compliant cricketers, but his account of his interview with Albert suggests that at the very least they had met. Someone who knew Albert well was Plum Warner, although the view was distant and limited across the amateur–professional divide. Warner wrote many books about the game, including several versions of his autobiography, as well as writing for newspapers and founding *The Cricketer* after the First World War. His ample writing on cricket, described by Marina Warner, his granddaughter, as 'fluent', focused on games, tours and personalities. But he did also write about Albert's ghosted column:

'He gave his name to articles in a weekly paper but he never wrote a single word of them. He was not a literary genius! On one occasion the newspaper in question stated "the beer gave out before lunch on Whit Monday." Albert was hauled before Francis Lacey, Secretary of the MCC.

'"I see you have been criticising the club," said Lacey.

'"I never wrote it, sir," said Albert.

'"So I understand. As a matter of fact, what was written is not correct … and in any case, you cannot be both a servant and a critic of the MCC."

'"I know nothing about it, sir."

'"Well, that's all right, but you must ask your friend, whoever he may be, to be more accurate in future."'

'Just comes of having a "ghost!"'

Another of Warner's stories about Albert is in a similar vein. This took place in 1903, when they returned from Lord Hawke's tour of Australia. After the boat had crossed the Mediterranean, some of the players took the land crossing, in order to avoid the rough seas of the Bay of Biscay. Warner said:

'At Marseilles I gave Trott his ticket, on which was marked the price of it – PRIX, so many francs – when the following conversation took place.

'Hargreave: "What's the first stop between here and Paris, Albert?"

'Trott (looking at his ticket): "Why PRIX" (which he pronounced "Pricks") "you fool."

'Pricks was good but, "you fool" was even better.'

Some of Warner's stories about Albert revolved around him being stupid, not understanding something, saying the wrong thing or bowling the wrong delivery at an important point in a match, 'giving us all heart disease'. When Middlesex fell away after winning the championship in 1903, it's easy to sense Warner's frustrations with Albert. In his *Book of Cricket*, he offered a considered view of his abilities on the field:

'When he first came to England, and for three or four years subsequently, he had that "curl-in-the-air ball" to a very marked degree; and during those years he was qualifying for Middlesex he had great fun with this ball. He not only curled it from leg, but he made it drop in the air after the manner of the baseball pitcher, and over and over again have I seen an apparent full pitch to leg land on the batsman's toe. He was the sort of bowler who required supervision, for if left to himself he might work a theory to death and lose a match in four overs. On the other hand, he could win – and often did win – a match in a quarter of an hour ... A certain perversity of genius prevented him from being the best all-round cricketer in the world.'

The phrase 'perversity of genius' resonates, suggesting a man fighting with his own talent, his ability to do different things with the ball proving a hindrance as much as a help. But it also suggests someone who never quite did what was expected of him, and therefore someone who could never totally be relied on. Warner was always fairly forthright about the shortcomings of the professionals in the team.

One of the others to attract his ire was Ted Mignon, a right-arm fast bowler, and a decent enough field at mid-off, who had taken those two catches for Albert's hat-trick against Somerset. Warner felt that Mignon could have made much more of himself, but the Kilburn-born professional became the butt of the Middlesex team, with stories about his shortcomings. In *My Cricketing Life*, Warner described the following incident on the field that involved Albert:

'He [Mignon] sometimes used to lose his head when fielding, and on one occasion when we were playing Yorkshire two batsmen found themselves in the middle of the pitch with the ball in Mignon's hand. All he had to do was to throw the ball quite gently to Albert Trott, who was bowling, and one of the batsmen would have been run out by at least six yards. Instead of that he threw the ball with all his might feet wide of the wicket, and it went to the boundary. We were all furious with him, and when at the close of the day's play he went back to the dressing-room he was solemnly held down and given six with a hairbrush, as hard as Albert Trott could lay on.'

The regular exchanges between Albert and Ted Mignon provided an uninterrupted stream of entertainment for the Middlesex team members, as Albert played on his psychological hold over the younger player. On one occasion, Mignon was fielding at mid-on when the ball sailed around eight feet above his head. 'Catch it!' yelled Albert. Mignon replied, more in sorrow than in anger: 'I'm not a — airship, Albert!'

Plum Warner and the other players also relished the times when Albert riled a professional from the opposing team. Tom Wass, the glaring, muttering fast bowler from Nottinghamshire, was one of their favourite victims. In a match at Trent Bridge, Albert had bet him that, if he was on at the time, he would clean bowl him first ball. Everyone knew of the bet as Wass walked out, the number 11 bat, scowling at the field that grinned and waited for Albert to deliver the ball. Wass frowned and took up his stance in a determined and defiant manner, the field silent when the delivery came down, a fast yorker that bent back the middle stump. Wass turned around and knocked over the three stumps with one strike of his bat.

The spectators laughed, and Albert rubbed it in, saying, 'Bad luck, Tom,' as he picked the dirt out of his spikes the while, a habit of his after bowling anyone.

Harry Lee rated Plum Warner as the greatest captain he played under, but he was strict with the players and 'not personally popular'. He would sometimes consult a senior professional about the state of the game, such as Jack Hearne, but if others had an opinion it was better if they kept it to themselves. There was no captaincy by committee. When things were going well, the players were 'Jack', 'Frank' and 'Albert', but when the game was in a less promising position he reverted to 'Hearne', 'Tarrant' and 'Trott'. This was a habit he retained throughout his time in charge at Middlesex.

Around this time, an 18-year-old, Patsy Hendren, was on the ground staff and had started to play for the Middlesex and MCC teams, originally as a slow bowler. He would have known Albert from around the nets at Lord's. Later he was to say about Albert, 'For a few years he was the most talked about player in or out of the pavilion. When old players get together there's always at least one yarn about Albert.' One of the stories that Hendren tells is that of Albert saying, 'I've bowled myself into the workhouse,' after his performance in his benefit match which had 'cost him hundreds of pounds'. The line about the workhouse has come to the service of many a professional after his benefit, and perhaps Albert did say it, but his bowling that day didn't cost him hundreds of pounds. Other stories reveal a more playful, mischievous side to Albert, such as the incident with Mignon and the hairbrush. The teetotal, non-smoking Surrey wicketkeeper Herbert Strudwick remembered the first game he played with Albert, at the Oval in 1903, when he stood up to the stumps to him.

'Then there was the occasion of my first Gentlemen and Players match when I asked Albert Trott how I could find his fast ball, which he disguised so well. "You'll soon find it," Albert told me. It was some time before he bowled it and when he did it just missed the leg-stump and hit me full toss on the left foot. I was hopping round in great pain when Albert came up to me. "You found it all right then," he said.'

David Frith, in his profile of Albert in *Silence of the Heart*, tells how Harry Bates, who played a couple of games for Middlesex in 1909, pioneered the trick of spitting pellets of paper at unsuspecting batsmen or umpires. Albert, his competitive nature pricked, responded by filling his mouth with dozens of pellets, firing them off messily in all directions.

Harry Lee was another who saw the playful side to Albert. Lee played in the same team as Albert at the start of his career, and remembered his antics. 'He was a practical joker, whose favourite trick was to get a novice in the dressing room, and play him at pitching with a lacrosse ball. He could spin the ball so that it leaped off the table and hit the other fellow's nose, or stand up straight and spin right back to him, so that the other man could not get it. With his big, powerful hands, he could do almost anything with a ball, and he never tired of experimenting to find something he could not do.'

The fun came with a price, and Albert had to endure a retaliatory trick or two in the professionals' pavilion. When he was given a locker, he wanted his name painted on it in the dignified Lord's manner. But there were wags about. His name appeared as 'Mr Albert Trott Esq.'. Albert didn't seem to mind, or perhaps he didn't notice it, but then another member of the team altered the lettering to: 'The Right Hon. Mr Albert Trott Esq.'. It was then that he went to Mr Lacey, Secretary of MCC, to complain.

Despite his liking for practical jokes, Albert did help the younger players in the nets. He taught Harry Lee how to bowl his famous slow swerve ball, and Lee gives some first-hand insight into Albert's technique with regard to swinging the old ball: 'When he was bowling an outswinging off spinner, for instance, his arm would be lower and he would impart body-check to the ball. Body-check is not easy to describe, but very roughly, as he ran up he would thrust his right shoulder forward with his left foot on the ground, his arm would go over quickly, and the ball leave his hand, slightly behind his head.'

Difficult to describe and difficult to do. It must have taken many hours of practice in the nets before he could get Lee to bowl this delivery. It shows a patient side to Albert, and his interest in the technicalities of the game, as well as providing a link to his past, playing baseball in Melbourne almost 20 years previously. 'Trott helped me considerably to master this slow ball, which nine times out of ten swings as an outswinger and comes back as an off-break,' said Lee.

In Taunton, they were still telling stories about Albert Trott in the 1960s. He played regularly at the County Ground for Middlesex for many years, the fixture usually coinciding with the August bank holiday. The story goes that he enjoyed a steady carnal liaison in the market town, visiting one woman in particular whenever he played there. Apparently, he, and possibly she, was also partial to an encounter while playing in a game. At one stage, he disappeared for a considerable length of time without explanation, and was found out when Middlesex were dismissed earlier than expected and had to take the field. At some point, it is said, the unidentified woman was murdered, and the police questioned him in connection with her death, although he was never an actual suspect. David Foot, the west country writer, recalls being told the story by an elderly member at Taunton, a man who was usually reliable in what he said. The man undoubtedly told others too. This is the extent of the tale, and there are no further details, but the account has often been repeated. David Foot followed up the conversation with the member by researching the local newspapers of the period, but found nothing. I have also found no record of the murder of a woman in Taunton at the time that corresponds to the story.

Murders in Taunton were and are very rare, and when they do happen they attract a great deal of attention – even when the victim had only a former connection with the town. Albert may have visited a woman when he played there – he wouldn't have been the first or last cricketer to have found this way of occupying himself in the quiet town – but there is no evidence that he was even slightly connected with the murder of a woman in or near to Taunton. The story has passed into Albert Trott folklore, but, in the absence of any corroborative evidence, it has to remain in the realms of 'that would be interesting if it were true'.

* * *

The off-season months were an uncertain time for the professionals at Lord's, as they were paid by the game in the summer, with the prospect of a bonus in October if they had done well. They envied the Yorkshire professionals, who were on regular winter money. If they'd had a good season with Middlesex, they could stash away a little to tide them over, and a good season for Albert, Frank Tarrant or Jack Hearne was if they made £175. When September came, it was useful to have something to supplement their earnings over the coming months, something more regular than the odd bit of coaching. Some could get work with their families, while Rawlin went back home to Yorkshire to work down a mine.

In 1907, Frank Tarrant, in pursuit of some winter work, returned to Victoria. When asked about Albert, he loyally said his friend was doing fine, and was as good as he ever had been with the bat if only he'd play himself in. Frank played some Sheffield Shield cricket, but also turned out for an Australian XI and Victoria against MCC, scoring 159 in the latter match. The Australians felt that this was perfectly reasonable, as Tarrant was born in Melbourne and had lived there for 21 years. In London, the MCC committee viewed the matter differently: Tarrant was qualified to play only in the English first-class game. On his return to Lord's for the summer season, he was told that he had offended public opinion in England by playing against MCC and was asked for an explanation. This stance from MCC effectively closed off the opportunity of making an all-year-round living by playing the first-class game in the two countries, something that Jim Phillips had been able to do ten years previously. It was an indication of the tight control that the English game had over its professionals.

Qualification difficulties aside, the chances of Albert ever returning to Australia to play cricket had disappeared, and he knew he would be unlikely to get a first-class game, with his loss of form and physical fitness. After the debacle of his winter coaching stints in Hawke's Bay, no offers arrived from elsewhere. Invitations to tour overseas had also dried up. Despite his success with Lord Hawke's XI in South Africa, he was not selected for an under-strength MCC side that toured there under Plum Warner in 1905/06, with several professionals in the party. It was a case of waiting to see what did turn up.

In February 1908, the theatrical press announced that Oswald Stoll would be putting on a cricket match, tip-and-run style, at the Coliseum in St Martin's Lane. The theatre had the benefit of one of the largest stages in the West End, and, with the game so popular, Stoll hoped that many would turn out for this novelty production. It was Middlesex against Surrey, four-a-side, and Albert was there with Jack Hearne, Ted Mignon and a young Patsy Hendren. For the players, it was all a bit of fun and a few pounds in the damp winter. The leading Surrey pros sensibly declined the offer, and it was left to the not-so-well-known Alan Marshal, Len Gooder, Bill Davis and Bill Hitch to represent the county. A mesh net was lowered to protect the audience from hits into the crowd, but the highlight came on the night when it failed to come down properly, and people in the stalls joined in as fielders.

Play lasted for a set amount of time each evening, and the ongoing score was posted outside the Coliseum on a blackboard in order to pull the people in. After six nights, it was Middlesex who took the trophy, a polished-up tankard from a nearby pub, and it was presented to Albert, presumably as the Middlesex captain for the first and last time in his life. The players made £5 each for their efforts, but Stoll never repeated the experiment of putting cricket on the stage.

Albert began the 1908 season playing for MCC, but began poorly against Yorkshire and 'sent down some exceedingly poor stuff'. At one point in the game, he was bowling so badly that it was difficult to set a field to him. In his first game for Middlesex against Hampshire, he sent down seven expensive overs for 45, *The Times* saying, 'Trott is but a shadow of his former self.' Yet he held on to his place in the team and tried to get some form together. Against Gloucestershire, he bowled well but without much success, and that was put down to poor luck. In the Yorkshire match, he managed a couple of good overs against Hirst but wasn't at his best. With his batting, he tried to be more cautious, but in his innings in the Nottinghamshire game he 'scored rather more slowly than the state of the game rendered advisable'. This was probably the first and last time that *The Times* or anyone else had ever said anything like that about him. It sounds as though it was hard work. Nevertheless, Middlesex won the game and Albert's bowling was 'exceedingly good' as he picked up three wickets, opening the bowling with the fast man Ted Mignon.

When Mignon was injured playing against Essex, Albert rose to the occasion and sent down more than 80 overs in the match, with his length and variation of pace reminding everyone of his best days. And everyone said his slip fielding was wonderful. Despite not appearing in the leading bowling averages, he'd done enough to get into the Players team to play the Gentlemen at the Oval. His contribution to the game was minimal, though, and he wasn't called upon to bowl in the second innings. Once again, he appeared to have lost his length when bowling against Surrey, sending down six overs of dross for 48 runs. A game against Kent was abandoned without a ball being bowled, and that gave him some rest. An easy match at Lord's against the Gentlemen of Philadelphia gave him the chance to find some form, and he picked up nine wickets in the game, to restore his confidence.

By the end of July, he was playing against Gloucestershire in Bristol, and, trying his luck around the wicket, he bowled Board with, in the words of *The Times*, 'a beautiful ball', the newspaper going on to say, 'Too much praise cannot be given to Tarrant and Trott for their untiring energy. It was their bowling more than anything else which won the match for Middlesex.' It was no flash in the plan, for at Trent Bridge too he bowled admirably as Middlesex won by an innings against Nottinghamshire.

Throughout this season, though, he struggled with his batting. The only high point came in the Lancashire game at Lord's. With Bosanquet in charge, he was put up the order to four and responded with his best innings of the season, a well-made 49, in partnership with his new captain. Mostly he wavered between excessive caution and excessive aggression. In the Surrey game, he started with confidence and judgement but then hit out blindly at a rising ball, seemingly losing his head. A further rush of blood ruined what had been a promising innings against Yorkshire at Bradford. 'Trott batted with sound judgement up to a point,' said *The Times*, 'but one fine drive off Haigh spoilt him, for from that moment he went wildly at every ball, and was twice missed from high catches.'

His season with the bat had brought a paltry 295 runs at 9.21, and he'd taken just 54 wickets at 29.79. 'Trott had a deplorable season,' said *The Times*, his only redeeming feature 'his wonderfully fine slip fielding'. He'd taken 38 catches and could still get down for the low ones.

Now 35 years of age, for many years he could easily have passed for a man in his forties. He must have wondered how much cricket he had left within him. While he was aware of how poorly he had played by his standards, he remained in limbo, as there were no written contracts from Middlesex, no clear-cut 'retained' or 'released', only verbal agreements, and a financial insecurity hovered over 45 Balmoral Road. He could be sure of being on the MCC ground bowling staff, but nothing else, and that only brought in a little. It was probably a cocktail of hope, denial and drink, bolstered by dips into the benefit pot, that got him through the winter, but he always had those who wanted his company.

Always a companionable man, he attended the dinner of the Hendon and Cricklewood Rifle Club. The club attracted a range of social classes, including army officers, and had recently opened some rifle ranges where members practised. Albert is listed as attending the dinner, so presumably he was a member, as guests were listed separately, and he must have used the club's facilities for some target practice. While some members attended the dinner with their wives, Albert went there unaccompanied. Another of his engagements at this time was at a funeral at New Willesden Cemetery, for John Smith, who worked for Francis, Day & Hunter Ltd, publishers of popular music, originally set up by music hall artists.

In February, it was the new version of the game of Vigoro that came to his rescue. The take-up of the game had been poor in England following the trial matches at Lord's and the Oval earlier in the decade. John Grant, a commercial traveller who had trademarked the name of the game, had now developed an indoor version. There was a new long-handled wooden bat too, and cricket-style bowling had replaced tennis-style serving. The improved game was demonstrated at the Aldwych Rinkeries, the new roller-skating venue in London, in a game between Middlesex and Essex. Albert was probably the man who pulled the teams together. He managed to persuade Ted Mignon to come along – the spanking incident with the hairbrush now presumably forgiven by the Kilburn fast bowler – together with a couple of Surrey players to make up the Middlesex team. There was little value in it as a spectator sport, and *The Times* got it about right with, 'One imagines that it would be the players who got the chief amusement.'

What must have been galling was that while Albert was trying to make a little extra money from this trivial game, the Australian players, led by Monty Noble, were in dispute with the Australian Cricket Board over the financial arrangements for touring England. Noble wanted the tour to be run on previous lines, as a private financial speculation with the players retaining the right to choose a manager and distribute the gate money among themselves, accountable to no one but themselves. The Board wanted full control of the tour, handling the gate money and accounts, retaining a share of the profits for assisting the state associations and strengthening the fund for old cricketers. They estimated that the players would still earn around £700 each, with £1,800 accruing to the Board's general fund. Albert guessed correctly that Noble and the others would eventually settle with the Board, and the tour went ahead, accompanied by ongoing acrimony, as the Board took their controversial slice of the profits. In the final event, bad weather hit the tour and the players made only £473 each. Even this would have seemed like riches to Albert, and he would have been privy to what was going on through the tour manager, his old East Melbourne teammate Frank Laver, a visitor to Balmoral Road.

Albert's own expectations had dropped and little was expected of his bowling, 'seldom effective these days' according to *The Times* in its preview of the 1909 season. His sole aim was to play as many matches as possible so that he was picked and paid. Where once he was picked by MCC for every possible fixture in May, as the man who drew in the crowds, he now got a game against Kent only because Mignon and other professionals had been delayed in Ireland. When he came on to bowl, his start was not propitious, as he sent down some very poor stuff. He redeemed himself partly with some hard, clean hitting as he made 45 in the second innings, but was out to an excellent catch in front of the pavilion as he aimed to clear the ropes. In this May, late on in his career, he proved capable, mixing sound defence with clean hits, without ever going on to make a good score. Meanwhile, his bowling was steady rather than spectacular, doing enough to hold on to his place. But a big crowd of 14,000 at Lord's at a benefit for J.E. West, a member of the ground staff, saw him throw away his wicket.

With his bowling, he drew on his primal guile, making use of the air to tempt the batsman down the wicket to play at him. It worked well against Essex, the batsmen duped as he took ten wickets for 123 in the match, his victims largely bowled or stumped by Murrell. He followed it up with a 5-97 in the first innings against Nottinghamshire on a difficult pitch at Lord's. 'Trott has recovered his form to an astonishing degree,' said *The Times*. He seemed to repay the confidence shown in him, when he was sent in up the order to five against Hampshire as Middlesex tried to force a result. He did exactly what was asked of him, picking the right balls to hit and making 77 not out. No doubt he needed a rest from his efforts, and his joints may have stiffened after what was a long time batting, so Warner didn't bowl him in the second innings. For a few weeks, he struggled to find his length and found it difficult to put an innings together. In August, however, he hit 93 at the Oval, coming in at eight. Although he was beaten and nearly bowled on a couple of occasions, it was his square cuts and off drives that brought him the runs. He wasn't yet done. In the next match, against Lancashire at Old Trafford, he smashed 50 out of a partnership of 58 in 38 minutes. Late on, he played for Middlesex against the Australians. As he waited and watched Noble, Trumper and Armstrong in the field, he probably knew this was the last time he would come up against them. The encounter was an anti-climax: in a game curtailed by rain, he neither batted, bowled nor fielded.

He had played a complete season and it hadn't been a disaster, and he had helped a Middlesex team short of batting. There were, though, a couple of ominous signs. People now observed that he was very slow at running between the wickets. And, while he had taken some difficult catches, it was noted that he missed some relatively easy ones.

The accepted wisdom was that a professional could carry on playing into his forties – Jack Hearne was six years older than Albert, and George Hirst touching 40. Experience, and conserving energy, could get a player through the long days in the field. However, the 1910 County Championship began badly for Middlesex, with Kent rolling them over by an innings at Lord's. After that, Albert barely played a game; and when he did, in his final match for Middlesex against Essex in July, he didn't even get to bowl – they didn't need him. His final wicket for the club had come more than a month earlier against Somerset at Bath, as he bowled Jack 'Farmer' White. The feeling was that Hearne had picked up a spot of late form, and he was preferred out of the two of them. Albert helped out for MCC – substitute fielder, a couple of games against the minor counties and a game with Conan Doyle down at Littlehampton. He was now so far out of the picture that it would be difficult to ever get back in. While nothing had been said in public, some were to say later that it was clear that Albert was struggling with the physical demands of the game. Or, as *The Times* put it in June, 'Trott is now out of date.'

The Times was correct. In June of that year, the Middlesex committee met to discuss Albert. In order to make up his benefit money, the club had invested £400 in India stock. When that investment was realised, it made up the amount he received to £745. The minutes read as follows: 'It was decided that Middlesex should add £55 to this amount to make the money up to £800, clear on the understanding that Trott's connection with Middlesex should cease.'

Or, in other words: take your money and go. They had paid him off. He was sacked. Eleven years before, they had recorded his bowling figures in the minutes; now they wanted him out of the place and nothing more to do with him.

17

And when they are in their cups, they forget their love both to friends and brethren

ONE EVENT follows another, and even if the second is not quite hard on the heels of the first, it seems that it's a natural consequence. The inevitable upshot of Albert's truncated 1910 season was financial, as he'd played so few matches and not earned any money. His benefit money was under his control now, but had been reduced by the £115 used to pay off his house. In November 1908, Middlesex had advanced him another £100 from his benefit. He was living beyond his means, and, if he had taken out further loans, using his house as security, he may not have had much of the benefit money left. He had also been fired. These events had a far-reaching impact on his personal life. In January 1911, his wife, Jessie, left their home in Willesden with their daughters, Jessie and Hilda. They travelled to Liverpool, boarded the *Afric* and by mid-February were back in Melbourne. She had known what he was like for years, but it was at this particular moment that she decided to leave. Whether she had left him because of his drinking or errant ways, or simply because he was not earning enough to support them all, she thought she and her girls would be better off back in her original home of Victoria. She must have been determined, or perhaps just desperate, to return to an uncertain future in Australia, knowing that Albert was unlikely to send any money from England. Her return home in steerage class was far different from her arrival 14 years previously, when she had travelled first-class, the wife of a successful cricketer, with her fare paid for by the Middlesex club. A year later, she was living with her daughters in South Yarra.

For Albert, the house, sold or repossessed, went the way of his wife and family. In 1911, he was still registered as a property owner on the electoral register for Balmoral Road, but by March he had moved out of the house and it was empty. There is no census return for 45 Balmoral Road for March 1911, and neither is there any trace of Albert. He wasn't staying with Frank Tarrant, who had moved with his growing family from Balmoral Road to a larger house in Linacre Road, around the corner. His brother Fred wasn't around to provide temporary accommodation. He had left in 1906 and was now married, living in Scotland, where he worked as a professional playing for Peebles.

Eventually, Albert was to move into lodgings in 14 Denbigh Road with his landlady, Mrs Mary Crowhurst. His new home was in Harlesden, still in the borough of Willesden, just over a mile away from the old one, but still within a reasonable distance of the Lord's ground and convenient for the Progressive Club in Church Road. The bulk of the household furniture was sold off, and it may have been at this moment that he sold his framed broadsheet from 1809 of *The Laws of the Noble Game of Cricket as revised by the club at St. Mary-le-Bone*. The note of provenance on the back of the picture, signed by Thomas Harris, reads, 'The above Cricket Picture originally belonged to Albert Trott. I gave Albert Trott £1 gold sovereign 25 years ago.' One item that he did keep and had delivered to his new address was his wardrobe, for he always liked his clothes, the need to look good when going out and about, so it was essential to have them stored properly. It was his last vestige of the successful cricket professional, something that he did not wish to give up. Otherwise, his move represented a shift in social class, from home owner to lodger, and it presaged a retirement of sorts, cutting costs and maximising resources.

In March 1911, *Cricket* announced, 'It is said on good authority that Albert Trott contemplates returning to Australia at the close of the approaching season.' He was tired, but for now his day-to-day life carried on in the same pattern, turning up at Lord's to bowl, still employed on the ground staff. There was still the possibility that he could be picked for matches, and he was always ready to oblige, good man that he was. He was picked for MCC against Leicestershire and contributed with match figures of 9-89, and he took 11-113 in a match against Hertfordshire, bowling for extended periods in both matches. However, it was an effort, and each game took that little bit more out of him; his figures didn't reveal the true physical cost.

The next week, at Lord's, Albert was selected to play for MCC against Cambridge University, and it's in this game that we can get a glimpse of how it must have been late on in his career. It was here that Henry Grierson came across him, and he describes the scene in his book, *The Ramblings of a Rabbit*. Grierson, a decent cove, self-deprecating about his own ability, had been enjoying his early summer playing for the Cambridge University XI. They had beaten Yorkshire, coming across the good-natured pro in David Denton: "'Don't keep on bowling that length stuff, Mr Grierson. You pitch 'em up and I'll have a go all right and you'll get me out." And then there was the bad-natured pro who was a bit of an outsider and nobody liked him, "No names!"'

In an evening at the music hall, one of their party threw an orange at the wire walker and hit him on the nose, and it ended in 'the last throes of hysterics'. It's all breezy stuff, with barely a backward glance until Grierson plays against Albert: 'He took a blob first innings, and the same second time. I was trying to bowl swingers with the leg side packed and poor Albert was in dreadful trouble with them. Finally he walked towards point, leaving the sticks clear on the leg side, and was quite happy when he was bowled behind his back. Ireland commiserated with him on bagging a brace, but Trott said, "That's all right, sir, and it's the third pair I've got this season." Rather pathetic from a man, who only a few years before, could have hit us all into the pavilion at will.'

Grierson understood the poignancy of the event, and the other salient detail that he added to the account was, 'Albert Trott played … but was obviously in dreadful health.'

His only other appearance for MCC that season was a two-day game against the Royal Engineers, making the Cambridge University game his very last first-class appearance. Albert was suffering from dropsy, nowadays classified as oedema, resulting in a build-up of fluid in the body, often in the lower legs and ankles. It can also cause swelling in the lungs and abdomen, leading to a discoloration in the face, tenderness in the limbs, stiffness of joints and weight gain. Some of his symptoms were exacerbated by playing a great deal of cricket over the years, with its wear and tear on the body, combined with a regular intake of alcohol, and it may have been difficult to isolate the precise causes and effects.

At the end of the season, he didn't go back to Australia but remained in his new lodgings. This time, knowing that his playing days were definitely over, he applied to add his name to the list of umpires and was accepted. If he thought the commitment would largely involve home fixtures at Lord's, he was mistaken. Although he could umpire MCC matches at the ground, it was policy for ex-players not to umpire their old clubs' matches. His season was fairly extensive, involving much travelling, more than he had ever done as a player, mainly through the southern counties standing in County Championship matches. He was in company, still spending every day in the game with the people he knew. But, with swellings in the legs, the pain that came from standing for long periods, the shifting of the weight from one foot to the other, it was not really the type of work he should have been doing.

The same conditions of service applied for umpiring as for playing: payment by the match. He was on the ground staff still, and so he had to bowl in the nets. It's difficult to see how he could have fitted this in on top of the umpiring, but he toughed it out and did a full season. Albatrott wasn't going to give up. His last match of the season was at Scarborough, where he umpired Lord Londesborough's XI against the touring Australians. With the exception of Syd Gregory, the members of the team were strangers to him, ten or 15 years younger, and they would have had no memories of the man standing at square leg and his exploits on the field. It was another sign of how things had shifted on.

The following February, he was in hospital, with the press reporting it in the usual discreet way. 'Cricketers will be sorry to learn that Albert Trott is lying ill at St Mary's Hospital Paddington.' The cause of his confinement was gastritis, an inflammation of the lining of the stomach resulting in upper abdominal pain. Nausea, vomiting and bloating are further symptoms, and causes can include alcohol or heavy smoking. The *Nottingham Evening Post* said optimistically, 'Albert Trott, the cricketer, is not likely to have to stay in hospital for more than two or three weeks, and there is no reason to think he will not be able to undertake his duties as umpire during the coming season.' One can almost hear Albert saying this in a cheery voice to the reporter; after all, he had a job that he wanted to keep, and he couldn't give an indication that he was not fit to carry it out. It was a significant length of time to spend in hospital for a man who had previously enjoyed good health, and also a further drain on his financial resources. There is no record of Albert applying for help from MCC at this point, so perhaps he had enough to manage.

While he was in hospital recovering, a sudden spat broke out in Australia between his brother Harry and Matthew Ellis, one of the Victorian selectors, in the letters column of *The Age*. The public disagreement continued for several letters and days, until the editor refused to print any more letters from the two men. The dispute primarily focused on Harry's criticism of the Victorian selectors, but Ellis also brought up Albert's non-selection for the 1896 tour: 'His brother Albert, one of the best all-round cricketers Australia ever produced, was left out of the Australian Eleven by selector Harry Trott, who since confessed that he ignored his brother's claims because of the close relationship, yet knowing full well his cricketing ability. England received a great cricketer; Victoria lost one, through the Poo Bahism of Mr. Trott.'

Harry's reply was immediate and published in the next day's paper: 'What a grand slap he gets at me when he tells the cricketing world that Harry Trott, selector, left his brother out of an Australian Eleven! I have often been blamed for it, so I now know where it comes from. I might inform Mr. Ellis that the three gentlemen who selected the team were T. Garrett (N.S.W.), W. Bruce (V.), and G. Giffen (S.A.). I had nothing at all to do with the selection. I knew more about my brother Albert's ability as a cricketer than Mr. Ellis, and his own performances that year in first class cricket should have gained him his place. No one was more disgusted at his omission than myself. So much for my Poo Bahism!'

Harry's comment is, of course, correct in so far as it deals with the initial selection of the touring party, but what he doesn't mention is why he didn't bring Albert into the team in 1896 after he was elected captain. Harry's letter reveals that he had heard this accusation before and there must have been many, not only in Victoria, who presumed there was an irreparable rift between the two brothers after the 1896 tour. Patsy Hendren of Middlesex recounted the following incident:

'Harry came over here with an Australian eleven, and unexpectedly met Albert in Oxford Street. This was their conversation:

'Harry: "Hullo, you young beggar!"

'Albert: "Hullo!"

'And Albert passed on, grinning at the brother he had not seen for years.'

Far from providing an answer to the relationship between the two brothers, this story warrants further probing. The only time the two brothers were in England together was in 1896. Far from not having seen each other for years, they had travelled from Australia on the same boat and run across each other on the tour. Patsy Hendren would have been seven years old at the time, so someone else must have witnessed the encounter. The story has probably been amended in the re-telling, but if it does illustrate anything, it is the strange, pared-back way that brothers sometimes communicate with each other. There is no evidence of a major fall-out between the two brothers. They had simply grown apart, not having spent much time together in the preceding 16 years. Albert had returned for a few months in 1896/97 and had been at the match in Melbourne on Lord Hawke's tour, a matter of a few days. That was the limit of their contact. As someone else once remarked, 'Brothers, like umbrellas, are easily forgotten.' The pair of them had liaised over providing financial support for Adolphus in the Benevolent Asylum. Albert had also supported Fred when he came to England. The fact that Albert had even contemplated returning to Australia a year earlier suggests he was not concerned about renewing contact with his family, which, as well as Harry, included his sisters Anna and Mary, and his brothers Gus and Walter. Harry was struggling for money – a couple of testimonial funds had been set up for him – and he wasn't in a position to help Albert financially if the latter returned to Melbourne. The former Australian captain was back playing cricket for South Melbourne, yet also working night shifts for the Post Office from 11 till seven, and his weight had shot up to 18st. Harry, with his own concerns, had enough to worry about.

By May, Albert was seen at Lord's, having recovered from what was described as a 'sharp attack of gastritis', and was able to resume umpiring games. In terms of travel, his schedule was around southern England, only going as far north as Nottingham, but he often had to stay in boarding houses. With considerable grit, he managed a full season, but he found it difficult to stand for long periods and was eventually given a run of fixtures closer to home, at the Oval. At Lord's in May, there was an incident that demonstrated the pressure on umpires and the spirit in which the game was sometimes played. In a match between MCC and Kent, classed as a friendly game, Ted Dillon, the amateur Kent captain, looked to be caught close to the ground by 'Young' Jack Hearne at third slip by a rising ball from Buckenham.

Dillon didn't walk. When the bowler appealed, umpire Harry Butt said he was unsighted and referred it to Albert, who was standing at square leg. Albert gave him out. Dillon asked Hearne whether he had caught it, and the fielder expressed a doubt – he probably said he wasn't sure. MCC captain Johnny Douglas then overruled Albert's decision and said 'Not out', and play resumed with Dillon carrying on batting. It's interesting that the umpires made no attempt to tell Dillon that he had to go and left it to the two captains. Although Albert had lost face, the two umpires probably thought they had done best by letting the gentlemen captains sort it out between them. But they hadn't. At their meeting the next month, the MCC committee said that after Dillon and Douglas had reinstated Dillon, the umpires 'were wrong to allow the batsman to continue without protest'. If nothing else, the incident showed the putative power of the amateur captains over the paid officials on the field of play.

Another who questioned Albert's ability as an umpire was Jack Hobbs. He said of Albert, 'He was a fine cricketer but he was not a good umpire. I say that without any feeling. Once when I had 83 against them [Somerset] Albert gave me out lbw. This was a very, very bad decision. On another occasion, I had scored over 80 when he gave me out lbw to a ball that I had hit.'

According to Hobbs, he was not the only one who suffered from Albert's poor umpiring decisions.

'Another instance I remember was in a Sussex match at Horsham when Razor Smith was bowling round the wicket. A.E. Relf was batting. Razor sent down an off spinner and appealed. It looked a case.

'"Not out!" says Albert Trott.

'Razor was disgusted and showed it. His next delivery was a fast one, with no spin – a fair length ball. Again he appealed.

'"That is out," cries Trott and everyone smiled. Relf gave Albert Trott a look fit to kill as he retired to the pavilion. We chip Relf about it to this day.'

The physical demands of umpiring took their toll on a man who found it painful to stand on swollen legs. One of the basic treatments for oedema is to avoid standing for long periods of time. Concentration probably didn't come easily to Albert, and what he had must have been difficult to maintain in these circumstances. Nevertheless, the verdict of *The Times* was that as an umpire he had proved 'a most capable one'. Perhaps the instances where he didn't get it right were the ones that were reported and remembered. Hobbs' comments about

Albert's umpiring didn't surface until the 1920s. And he wasn't only umpiring, for despite the ill health he was still on the ground staff in 1914. How much he actually bowled at this point is open to question. His appointment may have been due more to unchallenged habit than genuine need on the part of his employers, but there was no doubt that the staff wanted him around. As for Albert, he needed to be at Lord's, to have that contact with his ground and his old teammates.

There had been a further significant event that must have affected Albert as he went into the 1914 season. In the previous year, the health of Adolphus had been of increasing concern to his wife, Bridget, and to the rest of the family. Possibly suffering from a form of dementia, he had been admitted to the Kew Asylum in the August, but had been discharged a few days later. Not long afterwards, he was readmitted, and this time he remained, dying on 11 November in Kew. When Harry visited his father it must have reminded him of the days he had spent there, suffering from depression. Adolphus was the third member of his immediate family to be treated at Kew. His half-brother Julian Nanton Trott, who had arrived on the *Seringapatam* with him, had also been a patient in 1895, enduring a depressive illness. Adolphus could never have anticipated the kind of life he would lead all those years earlier when he had been a boy in Antigua – a life transformed by cricket, father to two Test cricketers. His sons' deeds on the cricket field had provided him with the public platform to be a personality in cricket circles. Adolphus was the one who had wanted Albert to remain an Australian, the man who had told the Melbourne newspapers of his son's cricketing feats in England when they had been slow to acknowledge them. But then there had been the other side: the financial worries, the mental health of family members, and the vicissitudes that drag people down. When he considered the life of his father, did Albert think, this is how it all ends? It has been said that when a man's father dies, he becomes a little boy again. Adrift from his family but never short of company, Albert must have felt the weight of his circumstances.

Shortly after that lbw decision in the Somerset match that so irked Jack Hobbs, Albert had to pull out of his next allocated match as umpire, Hampshire against Yorkshire at Southampton in May 1914. The abruptness of his withdrawal made people realise the critical nature of his illness. He was admitted to St Mary's hospital in Paddington. This time, he came under the care of Sir John Broadbent, a cricket lover who had treated the late king, and one consoling factor was that the doctor took a personal interest in Albert's case. He was in and out of hospital, but the main problem was that the oedema was not confined to his legs but was also present in his upper body. The swelling in his abdominal cavity would have made it difficult for him to sleep, with the fluid pressing on his internal organs. The build-up of fluid there, and in his legs, may have been a result of damage from cirrhosis of the liver. The volume of fluid was significant. In mid-July he was 'tapped' and a gallon and a half of fluid was drained from his body.

What did Sir John Broadbent tell him while he was in hospital? Did Albert know that his condition was more or less incurable? The other pressing concern was the lack of money, and while some of the treatment at St Mary's could be funded by charitable donations, there was a limit. With his money running out, he knew that the only 'free' medical service was that provided by the workhouse. Broke and broken, he had had enough. Announcing that he was tired with the tedium and routine of hospital life, he borrowed some money from an orderly for his taxi fare back to 14 Denbigh Road. Better out of the hospital than in, had been his calculation, but as soon as he was in his lodgings he had difficulty in sleeping, as the fluid in his body gradually began to return.

This was the time of the July crisis, as the threat of war loomed. A month previously, Gavrilo Princip, armed with a pistol, had assassinated Archduke Franz Ferdinand of Austria–Hungary and his wife Sophie in Sarajevo. In an attempt to provoke a war against Serbia, Austria–Hungary issued an ultimatum with ten unacceptable demands. It was an uncertain time in the world, its impacts felt on the streets of London as people wondered whether the alliances signed by European countries would come into play and bring about a large-scale war. On Tuesday, 28 July, Austria–Hungary declared war on Serbia, and the following day, Russia mobilised its armed forces. If Germany and France became involved, it would be inevitable that Britain and the Empire would be drawn into the conflict.

In the days before the bank holiday, people debated whether to go away, perhaps sensing the last chance for a holiday for some time. People hushed their voices in train carriages and on the streets, conspicuously avoiding speaking about the crisis, as if talking about things would make them more likely to happen. However, every news item said war was in the offing. There were telegraphic delays in Vienna, with the offices swamped. Steamers turned back on the

Dardanelles. Orient Express services beyond Austria were cancelled. The troops of the Paris garrison were confined to barracks. In Britain, the mobilisation of the First and Second Fleets was almost complete, and there were armed guards at Portsmouth. The headlines on the newspaper placards were relentless.

For three nights, Albert tried to get some sleep. On Wednesday, 29 July, he managed to get some rest with the aid of a sleeping draught, fetched by Mrs Crowhurst from the chemist. The next morning, he told Mrs Crowhurst that he hadn't slept all night, and he asked for another sleeping draught, but the chemist refused to provide one. Albert left the house and walked the short distance to the Progressive Club in Church Road in search of company or fresh air, anything to get out of his room, to stop thinking. It was a cold, blustery kind of day, but he could be heard singing in his room and in the street. He came back to the house at lunchtime. The sequence of events that follows was noted in court, and reported in the newspapers with minor variations. Just after 2pm, Mary Crowhurst was standing by the front door of her house when she heard a sudden sound. She went upstairs and found Albert lying on his back on his bed. He had shot himself in the temple, with a Browning pistol still resting in his right hand – the great hand that had bowled 71,549 balls in first-class cricket, the hand that had gripped the bat and hammered the ball over the Lord's Pavilion.

Dr Carson Smith was called to the house, along with the police, but death had been instantaneous and nothing could be done. A search of the room revealed £4 in cash and a will written on the back of a laundry ticket. He had left some photographs to an Australian friend and his wardrobe to Mrs Crowhurst. His body was taken to the mortuary, where someone placed a wreath on his coffin saying, 'With love and deepest sympathy to Dear Old Trottie.'

The inquest took place on Saturday, 1 August, held by the experienced Middlesex coroner, Dr Gordon Hogg. Fred Trott cabled from Scotland to say that he couldn't attend and that Albert's family were in Australia. Two witnesses were called. Mrs Crowhurst explained that Albert had been depressed for some time but had never spoken of taking his own life. Dr Carson Smith said he had found Albert dead on the bed, and that the dropsy had prevented him sleeping and caused his depression. A police inspector said that Lord's owed Albert £6. The inquest was over in a few minutes, and the verdict was 'Suicide during temporary insanity'.

MCC agreed to cover the funeral expenses and made a payment of £10, but it was Jack Hearne who took on the job of making the necessary arrangements. The funeral director was a personal friend of Albert's, Frank Crook of James Crook undertakers, their premises on Willesden High Road. The funeral took place on Wednesday, 5 August at 4pm at Willesden New Cemetery. No headstone was erected at the time.

The next edition of *World of Cricket* devoted several pages to his life. J.N. Pentelow had brought in Archie MacLaren as editor, the man who had talked Albert into the Australian team all those years ago. In the obituary, Albert's death was briefly compared to that of Arthur Shrewsbury, who had shot himself in 1903. Shrewsbury was a more introverted character, who had killed himself because he believed he was suffering from an incurable disease – very different from 'the genial good natured Albert Trott'. The tribute pointed out that Albert 'was no one's enemy but his own'. But then it went on to say, in a flash of insight, 'He may mean harm to none; but the man who is his own enemy must inevitably cause his friends endless trouble.' It gives the impression that, without meaning to be difficult, Albert did pose problems for those who knew him, and presumably that included his wife and family. The piece goes on to talk of Albert's wide circle of friends: 'The man had his faults like the rest of us; but he was a man for all that. A very likeable man.' It points out that he had not liked stepping out of the limelight, and that, bored with the hospital, 'he discharged himself while those who wanted to help him protested'. This suggests that, far from being alone, he was still in contact with friends, and against their wishes he had chosen to follow his own path. The article also said, 'We remember him in his prime, a great cricketer, big of heart, full of individuality, getting the utmost out of the game, never sparing himself.'

Another who knew him well was P.J. Moss, sports editor of the *Daily Mirror*, who had played with him in the Cross Arrows. He pointed out that 'even the fell disease dropsy could not quite subdue his exuberant spirits'. Moss also emphasised Albert's 'kindly spirit' on the field, and how a youthful cricketer would receive a full toss to complete his first century, and only then get the one that spreadeagled his stumps. 'Poor Albert – a good fellow and a pal.'

External events, though, were now taking everyone's attention as Britain walked in to a European war. In the same edition of *World of Cricket* was an editorial warning that 'Armageddon may well be at hand. As one writes the talk is all of War – War – War!' The writer speaks of the debt the nation owes to cricket, in bringing the races and creeds together, and how the different parts of the Empire will come to the aid of the mother country in the battles ahead. MCC tried to set up a Cricketers' Battalion to go out and fight. A marching company of soldiers came on to the field at Hove while a match was in progress and halted the game. Cricket and Albert Trott were to be forgotten for the next few years.

18

The great cricketer

HARRY TROTT died in November 1917 from Hodgkin's lymphoma in Melbourne. A large monument was erected at Brighton Cemetery over his grave, paid for by public subscription and the Victorian Cricket Association. He had never commented in public on his brother's death, obviously finding it difficult, with the stigma and silence that surrounded a suicide. As for Jessie, she never divorced Albert, and neither did she re-marry after his death. She lived with their two daughters for many years, running a boarding house in Melbourne, dying in 1955. Hilda became a typist and married in 1942, while the younger Jessie remained at home with her mother.

In Australia, the memory of Albert slipped away, as he had not played there since 1897 and the achievements of his older brother as captain loomed larger. Albert was not completely forgotten in England, despite the nature of his death. After the end of the war, Plum Warner was to write about Albert in *The Times* and in his books – mainly anecdotes from the field of play, but he also said, 'Poor Albert. He was a good soul. He had a heart of gold and was as simple as a child, and he was one of those people who compel attention. He ought to be playing still as he had a wonderful physique.' But what kept his memory alive more than anything was the big hit over the pavilion in 1899. He became completely identified with the event, the yardstick by which the efforts of others were measured as they came close, or threatened to come close, as the design of bats changed. Someone else will completely clear the pavilion at some point, and it will be televised, but Albert Trott will still be mentioned. In 2016, Eoin Morgan, James Fuller and a group of Middlesex players faced a bowling machine for an hour and tried to clear the pavilion, but even with an endless supply of hittable deliveries they were unsuccessful. In some ways, Albert's reputation as a cricketer has come to rest on his big hit, and his other cricketing achievements tend to be overshadowed by that August day in 1899.

In the 1970s, Middlesex finally placed a monument on his grave, where he is described as a 'great cricketer'. Some have suggested that the word 'great' is not deserved. Big hits aside, his other achievements include 8-43 for Australia against England, the best ever analysis on Test debut. His intervention in that game brought a series to life and helped to establish the Ashes as a contest. He was the first player to score 1,000 runs and take 200 wickets in a season in England. He was the first to take a double hat-trick in the same innings in a first-class match, a feat that has been accomplished on only one occasion since then. One of these achievements, taken by itself, would be an outlier – but, taken together, they demonstrated a formidable player, especially when we add in his ability as a fielder.

When we consider Albert Trott, the notion inevitably comes to mind that, with his natural ability and skill, he could have achieved far more in the game and avoided his untimely end. This relies on the 'what ifs': what if he had kept his fitness, what if he had not fed the batsmen with tempting deliveries, what if he had batted with more restraint? And what if he had remained in Australia in 1896 rather than come to England? With his best years still in front of him, he could have won back his place in the Australian team and enjoyed a successful Test career. But these are alternative histories. It couldn't have been any other way. His life was shaped by his character and temperament, the man within, as much as his skills with bat and ball. Over the years, he was someone who struggled to come to terms with his own cricketing talent. In the process, he brought about his own downfall, suffered a reverse of fortune, losing everything – a last desperate act, the life of an Edwardian cricketer tinged with shades of the Shakespearean tragic hero.

Yet his apparent shortcomings were only part of his story. Leaving aside matters of character, there were other obstacles, external to him, that hindered his career. In particular, Albert was unlucky in that, during the era in which he played the game, MCC tightened its control of the registration of players. If Albert had returned to play first-class cricket in Australia, he would have compromised his Middlesex qualification. This meant he suffered the double bind of being unable to play Test cricket for either England or Australia and was denied the opportunity to show how good he was at the highest level. The professional cricketer effectively experienced a restraint of trade, and even Plum Warner was to admit at a later date that the strict qualification system was unfair on the Anglo-Australian players. It was a world away from the players of the twenty-first century who operate as free agents, moving between countries, teams, competitions and formats in search of the highest rewards for their efforts.

Cricket was unusual in England in that, unlike rugby or football of the period, it didn't have separate competitions for amateurs and professionals, but attempted to accommodate both on the same field of play. The ostensible division between the two was that the bowlers were professionals paid to do the work while the amateurs, for the love of the game, provided the style and artistry in the batting. The period from 1895 to 1914 was hard on the professional, particularly those like Albert who relied on the game for nearly all of their income. They were paid far too little – £175 a year would be worth around £17,500 in 2017 – and, in search of money, he played too many games for MCC, on top of his Middlesex commitments, in addition to the long hours bowling in the nets. If he had been allowed to pace himself a little more, he would have performed better on the field and enjoyed a longer career. The lack of winter pay at Middlesex also posed difficulties. If you were going to make money as a professional, enough to keep you going throughout the year and on your retirement, you had to be good at 'the business of cricket'.

This could be done, as was shown by Albert's fellow professionals Jack Hearne and Frank Tarrant. Hearne, with his upright character and gentle manner, earned the respect of the amateurs and on his retirement became the first professional to become a member of the Middlesex committee. He lived on the money he had made from the game, from coaching at schools and from his winters in India with the Maharajah of Patiala. Away from the lure of metropolitan delights, he lived modestly in Chalfont St Giles with his wife and became a churchwarden, a respected member of the community. Tarrant, with an eye on the main chance, made the most of what came his way in a slightly different fashion. He had a shrewd sense of his value as a cricketer in England and was ready to negotiate a better deal for himself. At one time, in the winter, he worked in the office of Stileman, the accountant to Middlesex. When MCC prevented Tarrant playing in Australia, he found winter coaching work with Jack Hearne's contact, the Maharajah of Patiala. By 1914, he had an offer of £600 a year from the Maharajah to stay in India all year, but he told Middlesex he would reject it if they could guarantee him £300. Middlesex turned him down, and the committee privately decided that it was better for the club if they didn't rely so much on professionals. He would have to wait for the end of the war before he made some serious money, buying thoroughbred racehorses for Indian maharajahs and others. Cricket opened up circles in which those deals were negotiated. Albert struggled, lacking Jack Hearne's disposition or Frank Tarrant's business acumen – his resources outside the game were limited to his genial nature and many friends.

After the war, the leading professionals were able to carve out better pay and lucrative endorsements for themselves, with men like Jack Hobbs and Herbert Sutcliffe sending their children to private schools, becoming more like the amateurs in how they lived their lives. Even in 1914, Albert seemed to belong to the past, as *The Times* pointed out in his obituary: 'The modern professional is very different – and in many ways superior – to his predecessor, but in older days there were many more of the class that may be called "characters", and Trott was essentially one of these.' This, coming less than four years after he had played his last game for Middlesex, showed how quickly times had changed and how he already belonged to the past, an old pro from a different epoch.

It may be tempting to apportion the blame for Albert's financial pressures to the hypocrisy of the amateur and professional divide, but, while W.G. Grace made a fortune from the game, there were amateurs who struggled to find the money to preserve their social status. Respectability in St John's Wood cost more than a working-class life in Willesden, as Andrew Stoddart found out, finding it difficult to live on his salary of £300 a year as secretary of Queen's Club. Stoddart, along with other Middlesex amateurs, had received direct payments from the club. After failing to pay his MCC subscriptions on three occasions, he was not reinstated as a member. Archie MacLaren, another former England captain, suffered a similar embarrassment. Both men were continually short of money, and in 1915 Stoddart, troubled by debt, shot himself. An ability to play the game well and an amateur status did not automatically bring financial rewards and a better standard of life. Unless you were born into wealth or had lucrative outside interests, you had to either make money directly from the game or hunt around its fringes. And Albert was incapable of doing that. As P.J. Moss of the *Daily Mirror* pointed out: 'Had he been gifted with a temperament capable of concentrating itself on cricket as a business, rather than a sport, he would have been even a greater genius.'

And this is the irony of Albert Trott: a man who spent his whole life as a professional cricketer played the game like a gilded amateur because he loved what he did. It was his kindly spirit that gave a boundary to a young player close to his century; it was his delight to please the crowd with an attacking display. He knew that people came to watch because they wanted to see the unexpected and he often provided it. The *Yorkshire Post*, after bemoaning the importing of colonial players, said the practice had some compensations: 'It served to introduce to us more than one distinctive personality, who came to give pleasure to thousands of spectators, and very possibly to teach a thing or two to some of our native players. Such a one was Albert Trott, a man with the perfect genius for performing the unexpected, who did much to colour the all too brief period during which he batted, bowled and fielded in a totally different way from any player before or since.' They had always appreciated his talents in Yorkshire.

And there it rests. There is no portrait of Albert Trott in the Long Room in the pavilion at Lord's, and neither should there be. His place is outside, in the professionals' pavilion, in the nets, experimenting with a new delivery, showing others how it should be done, on his way to meet someone. He can also be found further north as a Willesden man, in the pubs and clubs, the Australian pro who came over and found that he liked England and they liked him, so he stayed on. One September afternoon, he played for the Cross Arrows and hit the ball to square leg over the hotel. In a group photograph taken at the game, now long disappeared, he is holding a black cat and nursing it for luck. He must have known that he would need it.

Selected sources

BOOKS
Cricket Books
Beckles, H.M. and Stoddart, B. (eds), *Liberation Cricket: West Indies Cricket Culture* (Cambridge University Press, 1995).

Beldam, G.W. and Fry, C.B., *Great Batsmen: Their Methods at a Glance* (London: Macmillan, 1906).

Beldam, G.W. and Fry, C.B., *Great Bowlers and Fielders: Their Methods at a Glance* (London: Macmillan, 1906).

Birley, D., *A Social History of English Cricket* (London: Aurum Press, 2000).

Booth, K., *George Lohmann: Pioneer Professional* (Cheltenham: Sportsbooks, 2007).

Booth, K. and Richardson, T., *A Bowler Pure and Simple* (Cardiff: Association of Cricket Statisticians and Historians, 2012).

Cardus, N., *Autobiography* (London: Hamish Hamilton, 1984).

Clarke, A.E., *East Melbourne Cricket Club: Its History 1860–1910* (Melbourne: George Robertson & Co., 1910).

Coldham, J.P., *Lord Hawke: A Cricketing Legend* (London: Tauris Parke, 2003).

Fingleton, J., *The Immortal Victor Trumper* (London: Collins 1978)

Foley, C., *Autumnal Foliage* (London: Methuen, 1935).

Frith, D., *My Dear Victorious Stod* (Guildford: Lutterworth Press, 1977).

Frith, D., *Silence of the Heart: Cricket Suicides* (Edinburgh: Mainstream Publishing, 2001).

Giffen, G., *With Bat & Ball: Twenty-Five Years' Reminiscences of Australian and Anglo-Australian Cricket* (London: Ward, Lock, 1898).

Grace, W.G., MacLaren, A.C. and Trott, A.E., *Cricket: A Handbook of the Game* (London: Greening, 1907).

Grierson, H., *The Ramblings of a Rabbit* (London: Chapman & Hall, 1924).

Gilbank, P., *Frank Mitchell: East Yorkshire's Greatest Sportsman* (Unpublished typescript, 2008).

Haigh, G., *The Big Ship Warwick Armstrong and the Makings of Modern Cricket* (London: Aurum Press, 2002).

Hart-Davis, D., *Pavilions of Splendour: An Architectural History of Lord's* (London: Methuen, 2004).

Harte, C., *A History of Australian Cricket* (London: Andre Deutsch, 1993).

Hawke, Lord, *Recollections & Reminiscences* (London: Williams & Norgate, 1924).

Hearne, J.W., *Wheelwrights to Wickets: The Story of the Cricketing Hearnes* (Goostrey, Cheshire: Boundary Books 1996).

Hendren, P., *My Book of Cricket and Cricketers* (London: Link House, Athletic Publications, 1927).

Hutchinson, H.G., *Cricket* (London: Country Life, 1903): Chapter 14, 'Cricket in South Africa', by Pelham Warner.

Kynaston, D., *WG's Birthday Party* (London: Bloomsbury, 1990).

Lee, H.W., *Forty Years of English Cricket* (London: Clerke and Cockeran, 1948).

Lynch, S. (ed.), *Wisden on the Ashes* (London: John Wisden, 2011).

Malies, J., *Great Characters from Cricket's Golden Age* (London: Robson Books, 2000).

Marqusee, M., *Anyone but England: Cricket, Race and Class* (London: Bloomsbury, 1993).

McKinstry, L., *Jack Hobbs: England's Greatest Cricketer* (London: Yellow Jersey Press, 2012).

Murray, B. and Vahed, G. (eds), *Empire and Cricket: The South African Experience 1888–1915* (University of South Africa, 2009).

Pollard, J., *The Turbulent Years of Australian Cricket* (London: Angus and Robertson, 1987).

Rae, S., *W.G. Grace A Life* (London: Faber and Faber, 1998).

Smith, R., *Blighted Lives: The Story of Harry and Albert Trott* (Prospect, Tasmania: Apple Books, 2010).

Stoddart, B. and Sandiford, K.A., *The Imperial Game: Cricket, Culture and Society* (Manchester: Manchester University Press, 1998).

Tomlinson, R., *Amazing Grace: The Man Who Was W.G.* (London: Little, Brown, 2015).

Warner P.F., *The Book of Cricket* (London: Sporting Handbooks Ltd, 1945).

Warner P.F., *How We Recovered the Ashes* (London: Methuen, 2003).

Warner P.F., *Long Innings: The Autobiography of Sir Pelham Warner* (London: George G. Harrap, 1951).

Warner P.F., *My Cricketing Life* (London: Hodder and Stoughton, 1921).

Wilde, S.R., *The Strange Genius of Ranjitsinhji* (London: Aurum Press, 1999).

Williams, J., *Cricket and England: A Cultural and Social History of the Inter-War Years* (London: Routledge, 2004).

Wilton I., *C.B. Fry: King of Sport* (London Metro Publishing, 2002).

Wisden Cricketers' Almanack.

Woods, S.M.J., *My Reminiscences* (London: Chapman & Hall, 1925).

Wynne-Thomas, P., *Give Me Arthur* (London: Arthur Barker, 1985).

Wynne-Thomas, P., *The Complete History of Cricket Tours at Home and Abroad* (London: Hamlyn, 1989).

General and Other Books

Ackroyd, P., *London: The Biography* (London: Vintage, 2000).

Early Collingwood Memories – PDF document, Collingwood Historical Society.

Finkelstein, M., *The Newest Woman: The Destined Monarch of the World* (Melbourne: Sportswoman, 1895).

Gaspar, D.B. and Hine, D.C. (eds), *Beyond Bondage: Free Women of Color in the Americas* (Urbana and Chicago, Illinois: University of Illinois Press, 2004).

Harding, J., *George Robey and the Music Hall* (London: Hodder and Stoughton, 1990).

Inwood, S., *City of Cities* (London: Macmillan, 2005).

Lycett, A., *Conan Doyle: The Man Who Created Sherlock Holmes* (London: Weidenfeld and Nicolson, 2008).

Singleton, Dr J., *A Narrative of Incidents in the Eventful Life of a Physician* (Melbourne: M.L. Hutchinson, 1891).

NEWSPAPERS
UK

Athletic News (London)

Baily's Magazine (London)

Birmingham Gazette

Birmingham Mail

Bristol Mercury and Daily Post

Daily Express (London)

Daily Mail (London)

Daily Mirror (London)

Daily News (London)

Daily Telegraph (London)
Derby Mercury
Evening News (London)
The Graphic (London)
Hastings and St Leonards Observer
Illustrated Police News (London)
Illustrated Sporting and Dramatic News (London)
Lichfield Mercury
Lika Joko (London)
London Chat
Morning Post (London)
Nottinghamshire Guardian (Nottingham)
Nottingham Evening Post
Newcastle Journal
Pall Mall Gazette (London)
Penny Illustrated Newspaper (London)
Royal Cornwall Gazette (Falmouth)
The Scotsman (Edinburgh)
The Sketch (London)
Somerset County Gazette (Taunton)
Sporting Life (London)
Sporting Times (London)
Taunton Courier, and Western Advertiser (Taunton)
The Times (London)
Yorkshire Post (Leeds)
Yorkshire Telegraph and Star (Sheffield)
Western Daily Press (Bristol)

Australia
Adelaide Observer
The Age (Melbourne)
The Argus (Melbourne)
The Australasian (Melbourne)
Australian Star (Sydney)
Ballarat Star (Ballarat, Victoria)
Barrier Miner (Broken Hill, New South Wales)
Bendigo Advertiser (New South Wales)
Bird O'Freedom (Sydney)
The Bulletin (Sydney)
The Chronicle (Adelaide)

The Empire (Fremantle)
The Inquirer and Commercial News (Perth)
Evening Journal (Adelaide)
Express and Telegraph (Adelaide)
Kalgoorlie Miner (Western Australia)
Launceston Examiner (Tasmania)
The Leader (Melbourne)
Mercury and Weekly Courier (Victoria)
North Melbourne Advertiser
Punch (Melbourne)
The Referee (Sydney)
Singleton Argus (New South Wales)
South Australian Chronicle (Adelaide)
South Australian Register (Adelaide)
Sunday Times (Perth)
Sydney Mail and New South Wales Advertiser
Sydney Morning Herald
The Tasmanian (Launceston)
The Telegraph (Brisbane)
Truth (Perth)
The Week (Brisbane)
Weekly Times (Melbourne)
West Australian (Perth)
Yorke's Peninsula Advertiser and Miners' News (South Australia)

New Zealand
Auckland Star
Evening Post (Wellington)
Evening Star (Dunedin)
Free Lance (Wellington)
Hastings Standard (Hawke's Bay)
Hawera and Normanby Star (Taranaki)
Otago Daily Times (Dunedin)
Otago Witness (Dunedin)

South Africa
Cape Argus (Cape Town)

Magazines
Badminton Magazine of Sports and Pastimes (London)
Black and White (London)

Blackwood's Magazine (Edinburgh)
Cricket: A Weekly Record of the Game (London)
Cricket Lore (London)
The Cricketer (London)
The Field (London)
World of Cricket (London)

Websites
Ancestry – https://www.ancestry.co.uk
Cricket Archive – http://cricketarchive.com
Cricinfo – http://www.cricinfo.com
Legacies of British Slave Ownership – http://www.ucl.ac.uk/lbs/
Victorian Premier Cricket (VCA) – http://premier.cricketvictoria.
    com.au
Victorian Heritage Database – http://vhd.heritagecouncil.vic.gov.au

Archives
London Metropolitan Archive
MCC minutes 1896–1914, Lord's Library
Middlesex CC minutes 1896–1914, Lord's Library
Public Record Office, London

Other Sources
Hall, B. and Schulze, H., 'The Cricketing Brothers Tancred, Part 2', *Cricket Statistician* (Association of Cricket Statisticians and Historians), No. 112, 2000.
Lowes, S., 'They Couldn't Mash Ants: The Decline of the White and Non-White Elites in Antigua, 1834–1900', chapter in Olwig, K.F. (ed.), *Small Islands, Large Questions: Society, Culture and Resistance in the Post-Emancipation Caribbean* (London: Routledge, 1995).
Linwood, D., 'Albert Trott: Middlesex Cricketer and Willesden Resident' (*Willesden Local History Journal*, Summer 1997).
Neal, S., 'Over and Out', essay on Albert Trott in *The Nightwatchman*, Issue 6, June 2014.
Pearson, L., 'The Architecture of Cricket: Pavilions Home and Away', paper presented at the British Society of Sports History Conference (London, September 2011).
Williamson, L., 'Albert Trott, the Lord's Pavilion and £1,000', essay published in *Cricket Lore*, 1992.

Index